BEYOND SMOKE AND MIRRORS

BEYOND SMOKE AND MIRRORS

MEXICAN IMMIGRATION IN AN ERA OF ECONOMIC INTEGRATION

Douglas S. Massey, Jorge Durand, and
Nolan J. Malone

Russell Sage Foundation • New York

The Russell Sage Foundation

The Russell Sage Foundation, one of the oldest of America's general purpose foundations, was established in 1907 by Mrs. Margaret Olivia Sage for "the improvement of social and living conditions in the United States." The Foundation seeks to fulfill this mandate by fostering the development and dissemination of knowledge about the country's political, social, and economic problems. While the Foundation endeavors to assure the accuracy and objectivity of each book it publishes, the conclusions and interpretations in Russell Sage Foundation publications are those of the authors and not of the Foundation, its Trustees, or its staff. Publication by Russell Sage, therefore, does not imply Foundation endorsement.

Library of Congress Cataloging-in-Publication Data

Massey, Douglas S.
Beyond smoke and mirrors : Mexican immigration in an era of economic integration / Douglas S. Massey, Jorge Durand, Nolan J. Malone.
p. cm.
Includes bibliographical references and index.
ISBN 0-87154-589-6 (cloth) ISBN 0-87154-590-X (paper)
1. United States—Emigration and immigration—Government policy.
2. Mexico—Emigration and immigration—Government policy.
3. Mexicans—United States. 4. United States—Foreign relations—Mexico. 5. Mexico—Foreign relations—United States. 6. Emigration and immigration law—United States. I. Durand, Jorge. II. Malone, Nolan J. III. Title.

JV6483 .M33 2002
325'.272073—dc21

2001055712

The paper used in this publication meets the minimum requirements of American National Standard for Information Sciences—Permanence of Paper for Printed Library Materials. ANSI Z39.48–1992.

Text design by Suzanne Nichols

RUSSELL SAGE FOUNDATION
112 East 64th Street, New York, New York 10021
10 9 8 7 6 5 4 3 2 1

Contents

About the Authors

Douglas S. Massey is professor of sociology and public policy at Princeton University.

Jorge Durand is professor-investigator in the Department for the Study of Social Movements at the University of Guadalajara and a fellow of Mexico's National System of Investigators.

Nolan J. Malone is a doctoral candidate in sociology and demography at the University of Pennsylvania and research scientist at the Kamehameha Schools in Honolulu, Hawaii.

Acknowledgments

THIS BOOK is a product of the Mexican Migration Project (MMP) and thus rests upon the combined efforts of many people who have worked on it as staff members, students, and postdoctoral fellows. Although it is not possible to individually name all those who have contributed to the MMP's success, special thanks go to those who have served as project managers (Kristin Espinosa and Emilio Parrado), fieldwork coordinator (Emma Peña), data entry specialists (Verónica Lozano and Raquel Carvajal), and web master (Elisa Muñoz Franco). Their attention to quality made it possible for us to conduct the analyses necessary for this book. Particular gratitude goes to the National Institute of Child and Human Development and the William and Flora Hewlett Foundation, whose long-term grant support has enabled the work of the MMP to continue. We also thank the Fogarty International Center of the National Institutes of Health, the Andrew W. Mellon Foundation, and the Social Science Research Council for their support of individual students and postdoctoral fellows who have worked on the project. Finally, the authors thank their respective friends and families for their ongoing support and unflagging encouragement.

Chapter 1

Ghost in the Machine: Interventions in the Mexico-U.S. Immigration System

If one does not understand how a complicated piece of machinery works, one should not try to fix it. Without a clear picture of how a mechanical system functions, what its basic principles are, and how its various parts interconnect to influence one another, one is unlikely to be able to restore the machinery to health if it is not working well, or to modify it effectively if a different outcome is desired. Without a clear conception of how the various moving parts of the machine fit together to function as an integrated whole, one cannot readily predict how a change introduced into one part of the system will influence other parts to alter operations and affect outcomes. Blindly tinkering with a gear here or a cog there, or adding new levers and springs simply because they "look good," is to invite a host of unintended consequences, and perhaps to cause a calamity that no one expected or desired.

Gumming up the Works

In a very real way, the Mexico-U.S. migration system functioned as a complicated piece of machinery in the years from 1965 through 1986. It was composed of a set of delicately balanced social and economic processes that had emerged gradually over many years in response to specific changes in the political economies of Mexico and the United States. Cross-border population movements had a characteristic form, and over time they acquired a relatively stable structure and a well-defined geographic organization. Migration between Mexico and the United States followed predictable paths in accordance with well-established scientific principles.

Once one appreciates the workings of a complicated piece of socioeconomic machinery, then it is theoretically possible to intervene at various points to influence outcomes and improve results. However, if one intervenes in arbitrary ways and for reasons that are largely disconnected from the system's actual operation, then one should not expect much of an improvement. Just as it is not advisable to take a wrench to a precision clock if one is not a qualified clockmaker, it is not wise to pull policy levers if one has no real conception of how the underlying system functions. Yet this is exactly what happened beginning in 1986, when the U.S. Congress and successive presidents presided over a series of legislative and bureaucratic changes that fundamentally changed the rules under which the Mexico-U.S. migration system operated.

These changes were enacted largely for symbolic political purposes in the United States, with little concern for the underlying realities of migration and North American economic integration. The 1986 Immigration Reform and Control Act (IRCA) ushered in a new era of restrictive immigration policies and repressive border controls that transformed what had been a well-functioning, predictable system into a noisy, clunking, dysfunctional machine that generated a host of unanticipated outcomes that were in neither country's interests. These errors were compounded by additional legislation passed in 1990 and 1996 that reduced Mexican access to legal visas, militarized key sectors of the Mexico-U.S. border, and penalized legal but noncitizen immigrants.

The arbitrary intervention of U.S. policymakers into one of North America's crucial socioeconomic systems would have been bad enough by itself, but at the same time, in another policy arena, U.S. officials were moving in a diametrically opposed direction. Even as they sought to restrict the movement of workers across the Mexico-U.S. border, U.S. authorities were constructing a framework to integrate North American markets to facilitate the cross-border movement of goods, capital, commodities, and information, a vision that became reality with the implementation of the North American Free Trade Agreement (NAFTA) in 1994. The apparent contradiction of simultaneously promoting integration while insisting on separation does not seem to have troubled either Congress or Presidents George Bush and Bill Clinton.

These contradictory policies did not succeed in slowing down either documented or undocumented migration from Mexico; if anything, they encouraged more of both. They did, however, create a black labor market for Mexican labor, lower the wages of *legal* U.S. residents, increase U.S. income inequality, and worsen conditions in

U.S. labor markets. At the same time they pushed migrants decisively away from seasonal, circular migration toward permanent settlement and transformed Mexican immigration from a regional phenomenon affecting a handful of U.S. states into a broad social movement touching every region of the country. The hapless intervention of U.S. authorities into the complicated machinery of North American migration offers a textbook example of how ill-conceived policies cannot only fail to achieve their manifest goals but unleash a host of unintended consequences and amplify them to the fullest.

Laying out the Blueprint

Politicians and the media are wont to frame immigration as a disorderly, chaotic process that somehow must be brought "under control." Immigrants are portrayed as desperate people fleeing endemic violence and poverty in the Third World, where stagnant economies, growing populations, and decaying infrastructures leave inhabitants little choice but to seek refuge abroad. Two kinds of metaphors are customarily employed to dramatize the resulting population movements.

A series of hydraulic tropes depicts immigration as a "rising tide" that pounds against U.S. shores in endless "waves," threatening to wash away a shaky "dike" as it sprouts numerous "leaks" that threaten the country with massive "flooding" by an immense "sea" of foreigners. A second set of metaphors is martial in nature. Immigration is visualized as a "war" in which outgunned Border Patrol officers heroically "hold the line," "defending" America against "hordes" of alien "invaders" who "attack" the "fortress," occasionally resorting to "banzai charges." Foreigners already inside the United States are seen as a "fifth column" of potential spies and terrorists.

Rather than basing policies on metaphors that are, at best, dubiously connected to underlying social and economic realities, we seek to provide policymakers and citizens with a more accurate blueprint of the nuts and bolts of the Mexico-U.S. migration system. We offer a kind of "owner's manual" to explain how the system works theoretically, how it was built historically, and how it functions substantively, or at least how it did function until the 1986 Immigration Reform and Control Act threw it out of synch. We then describe how IRCA and successive policies disrupted the system's smooth operation to bring about a variety of negative, and largely unforeseen, consequences. We conclude by offering a blueprint for immigration reform to guide policymakers in fixing the now-broken machinery of Mexico-U.S. migration.

Mexico-U.S. migration is neither a flood nor a war, but a piece of well-ordered machinery that operates in a predictable fashion according to a patterned logic that has been intensively studied and well described by social scientists. Chapter 2, entitled "Principles of Operation," draws on recent theory and research to describe the natural laws governing the evolution and behavior of modern international migration systems. We offer logical explanations for why immigration begins, why immigrant flows expand over time, and why they develop a stable structure across time and space.

Understanding a system in theory is all well and good, but if one really wants to know how a complicated piece of machinery works, there is no substitute for taking the device apart and putting it back together again. This is the project we undertake in chapter 3, "System Assembly," where we describe in detail how the machinery of Mexico-U.S. migration was built historically and how it functioned for decades as an important system within the political economies of both Mexico and the United States. We demonstrate how, with the acceleration of binational economic integration after 1982 and its concrete realization under NAFTA, Mexico-U.S. migration became an integral part of the broader social and economic machinery operating within North America.

Having laid out the operating principles, design, and operation of the machinery of Mexico-U.S. migration, we then seek to calibrate its performance. In chapter 4, "System Specifications," we draw upon high-quality empirical data from the Mexican Migration Project (see appendix A) to describe the moving parts of the system and document their efficient operation. Rather than being out of control, Mexico-U.S. migration functioned during the period 1965 to 1985 according to measurable parameters that were stable over time and produced regular, structured patterns of movement within the system. We divide the process of international migration into a series of discrete stages corresponding to key decision points in the migratory career and show how behavior at each point was not only patterned and predictable but broadly consistent with theoretical expectations.

In chapter 5, "A Wrench in the Works," we describe the flawed understandings that underlay U.S. attempts to modify the machinery of Mexico-U.S. migration from 1986 onward. We highlight the fundamental contradictions of U.S. policy toward Mexico: on the one hand, that policy seeks to integrate North American markets for goods, commodities, capital, and information, but on the other hand, it somehow wishes to prevent the integration of labor markets. Immigration and border policies after 1986 were not grounded in any real understanding of Mexico-U.S. migration or its role in North American integration, but in cold war ideology, anti-drug hysteria, and crude ethnic scapegoating, all of which were deliberately packaged and served up for domestic political consumption by cynical politicians. Although the symbolic politics of border enforcement may have produced short-term gains for a few enterprising politicians, it did serious, long-term damage to the social and economic fabric of Mexico and the United States. Over the course of the 1980s and 1990s the machinery of Mexico-U.S. migration increasingly grew out of synch with the larger engine of North American integration.

In chapter 6, "Breakdown," we catalog the damage done as a result of misguided U.S. immigration and border policies. Reliable data indicate that U.S. enforcement actions did not deter undocumented Mexican migrants from heading northward, crossing the border, or getting U.S. jobs. They did, however, discourage migrants from returning home, encourage their long-term settlement north of the border, and increase the prevalence of dependents over workers, all while wasting billions of dollars of taxpayers' money and destroying hundreds of lives. U.S. policies were also instrumental in transforming Mexican migration from a regional into a national phenomenon while pushing immigrants decisively toward naturalization to ensure the future immigration of millions more. In the end, U.S. policies transformed what had been a relatively open and benign labor process with few negative consequences into an exploitative underground system of labor coercion that put downward pressure on the wages and working conditions not only of undocumented migrants but of legal immigrants and citizens alike.

In chapter 7, we offer a "repair manual" based on our earlier understanding of the design, principles, and operation of international migration in the context of North American economic integration. We offer specific proposals to undo the damage caused over the past two decades and to restore the engine of North American integration to its maximum efficiency. Our approach requires policymakers to bring North American labor migration aboveboard and accept it as a normal part of the emerging transnational political economy. Rather than denying the reality of labor migration, we recommend regularizing it and working to manage it so as to promote economic development in Mexico, minimize costs and disruptions for the United States, and maximize its benefits for all concerned.

Some may argue that the United States should abandon its project of North American integration entirely and seek to harden the border and make it impervious not only to flows of immigrants but also to capital, goods, ideas, and information. Unfortunately, the creation of such a "Fortress America" is neither practical nor desirable, and some observers have labeled the dream of a controlled border as an illusion of "smoke and mirrors" (Baum 1997). Politicians lack the skills of a good magician, however, and the trick has flopped. The issue is not *whether* North America will integrate, but *how* it will happen.

Like it or not, the United States is inextricably bound to Mexico by geography, history, demography, and economics. Given a sixty-year history of continuous movement back and forth across the border, the flowering of binational trade and investment, the continent-wide expansion of transportation and communication networks, and the blending of cultures and peoples in both directions, the two nations are already substantially integrated. What remains is for Mexican and American policymakers to face up to the reality of North American integration and bring labor migration into the broader structure and organization of the North American Free Trade Agreement, helping Mexico to grow economically and ultimately to assume its rightful place as an equal partner in the global system of investment and trade that will be the foundation of prosperity and stability in the twenty-first century.

Chapter 2

Principles of Operation: Theories of International Migration

MOST CITIZENS and public officials *think* they understand the mechanics of international migration, of course, or they would not advocate such bold proposals or act with such assured abandon. In the North American case particularly, the reasons for Mexican immigration seem obvious. The prevailing wisdom begins with the commonsense observation that the United States is a rich country and Mexico, by comparison, is not. Although Mexico's 1997 GNP per capita of $3,700 places it in the upper tier of developing nations, it pales in comparison to the U.S. figure of $29,000, and nowhere else on earth is there such a sharp contrast along a land border, much less one that is two thousand miles long.

As a result of this stark income differential, the standard of living is much higher north than south of the border. In per capita terms, Mexican private consumption is only 10 percent of that enjoyed in the United States. Obviously, simply by heading northward, crossing the border, and finding a job in the United States, the average Mexican can raise, often quite dramatically, his or her standard of living. Even at the current U.S. minimum wage, a migrant working full-time for a year would earn roughly three times the Mexican average income. Under these circumstances, what rational, self-interested Mexican would *not* want to emigrate to the United States? Simply by crossing a line, he or she would not only earn more income but gain access to better schooling, a richer infrastructure, improved social services, superior medical care, and a fuller array of consumer alternatives.

As far as most people are concerned, Mexican immigrants *choose* to come to the United States, making just such cost-benefit calculations. They believe that Mexicans rationally understand that the costs of migrating to the United States are more than offset by a variety of benefits. Even discounting for the costs of moving, crossing the border, looking for work, and adapting to a foreign culture, the material well-being of most Mexicans is substantially improved by relocating to the United States and pursuing work there, and each year hundreds of thousands of Mexicans seem to make precisely this decision. As long as the wage differential between Mexico and the United States is great, most people believe, workers south of the border have a strong incentive to move northward.

Although migration between Mexico and the United States goes back to the nineteenth century and has ebbed and flowed for more than a century, U.S. citizens and politicians have never been entirely comfortable with immigrants in general or Mexicans in particular (see Higham 1955; Espenshade and Calhoun 1993; Espenshade and Hempstead 1996). Public sentiment against immigrants has generally oscillated in tandem with expansionary and recessionary times and in conjunction with broader ideological currents (Meyers 1995). U.S. immigration policies have consequently swung back and forth between recruitment and restriction, acceptance and exclusion (Timmer and Williamson 1998).

For a variety of reasons, the late 1980s and early 1990s were a time of restrictive sentiment. The most obvious way to accomplish the assumed goal of reducing Mexican immigration, based on the understanding outlined earlier, was to lower the incentives by raising the costs and reducing the benefits of entry from Mexico. Unfortunately, the principal benefit—higher income—is not easily manipulable through policy mechanisms. No politician could ever vote to lower U.S. income as a means of reducing the incentives for immigration, and while U.S. political leaders might support efforts to raise incomes in Mexico, its economy is not under their direct control.

Given these constraints, U.S. policymakers focused on other, more malleable, costs and benefits. On the benefit side, the United States sought to reduce access to employment by criminalizing the hiring of undocumented workers and barring immigrants, undocumented and sometimes even documented, from receiving public services. On the cost side, the government hired more Border Patrol officers, increased their resources, and granted them new powers to detain, prosecute, and deport unauthorized aliens. By increasing the costs and lowering the benefits of undocumented migration, authorities hoped to deter Mexicans from entering and staying in the United States.

That something is seriously wrong with these policies and their underlying premises is suggested by the fact that they have not worked very well. As we document later, American attempts to raise the costs and lower the benefits of living and working in the United States have had little effect on the likelihood of undocumented migration, on increasing the odds of migrants returning home, on decreasing the odds of unauthorized employment, or on reducing the probability that migrants will undertake a successful border crossing. Other, more perverse consequences, however, have followed from these policies. The fundamental problem is that current policies are based on a rather narrow conceptualization of migration. The reality of contemporary immigration is considerably more complex than a simple calculus of costs and benefits.

A full understanding of international migration requires facing up to four basic questions: What are the forces in sending societies that promote out-migration, and how do they operate? What are the forces in receiving societies that create a demand for immigrant workers, and how do they function? What are the motivations, goals, and aspirations of the people who respond to these forces by migrating internationally? And what are the social and economic structures that arise in the course of migration to connect sending and receiving societies? The commonsense understanding of migration as a simple cost-benefit decision deals only with the third question, and it offers only one of several possible motivations for movement. In this chapter, we seek to develop a comprehensive explanation for international migration that addresses all four questions.

Why People Migrate

The conceptualization of Mexican immigration widely shared by legislators and the public as a cost-benefit decision corresponds to the theoretical apparatus of *neoclassical economics.* According to this theory and its extensions, international migration stems from geographic differences in the supply of and demand for labor (Ranis and Fei 1961). Countries with large endowments of labor relative to capital have low wages, while those with limited endowments of labor relative to capital have high wages. The resulting international differential causes workers from low-wage countries to move to high-wage countries. As a result of this movement, the supply of labor falls and wages rise in the former while they do the opposite in the latter, leading, at equilibrium, to an international wage differential reflecting the costs of international movement, pecuniary and psychic.

Associated with this macro theory is an accompanying microeconomic model of decisionmaking. Rational actors choose to migrate through a cost-benefit calculation that leads them to expect positive net returns, usually monetary, from international movement. Migration is analogous to investment in human capital (Sjaastad 1962), where human capital consists of personal traits and characteristics that increase a worker's productivity. Early in their lives, people invest in education to make themselves more productive and later reap benefits in the form of higher earnings.

Where one lives can be viewed as an individual trait that rational actors change by investing in a move. Migrants seek to go to places where, given their skills, they can be more productive and earn more money. Before they can reap this benefit, however, they must undertake certain investments: the material costs of traveling, the costs of sustenance while moving and looking for work, the effort involved in learning a new language and culture, the difficulty experienced in adapting to a new labor market, and the psychological burden of cutting old ties and forging new ones (Todaro and Maruszko 1987). According to neoclassical theory, migrants estimate the costs and benefits of moving to various international locations and then go to wherever the expected net returns are greatest (Borjas 1989, 1990).

In stylized terms, actors estimate expected net returns by taking the earnings anticipated in the destination country and multiplying them by the probability of obtaining and holding a job there, thus deriving an estimate of "expected destination earnings." These are then subtracted mentally from those projected for the community of origin (observed earnings multiplied by the probability of getting and holding a job there), and the difference is summed year by year over the individual's expected working life (with future years being discounted because money earned now carries more utility than money earned later). From this integrated difference the estimated costs of the move are subtracted to yield the total expected net return to international migration, and migrants go to wherever they expect that total return to be greatest (Todaro and Maruszko 1987; Massey and García España 1987).

A variety of anomalous observations suggest, however, that motivations for migration go beyond such cost-benefit calculations. Under neoclassical theory, migration should not occur in the absence of a wage differential, yet such flows are frequently observed. Moreover, if there are no legal barriers to movement, migration should continue until the wage differential between two areas is eliminated, yet migration streams commonly end well before wage gaps disappear. Widely observed patterns of circular migration are also difficult to explain from a strict neoclassical viewpoint; each year thousands of undocumented migrants and even many legal immigrants decide to return to Mexico (Warren and Kraly 1985; Jasso and Rosenzweig 1982, 1990; Lindstrom 1996; Reyes 2001). If the world really worked according to neoclassical principles, why would anyone migrate abroad *temporarily* to remit money back home in anticipation of an eventual *return?* A rational utility-maximizing actor logically should want to stay abroad permanently to enjoy forever the higher wages and consumption available in the United States, yet each year billions of dollars are remitted back to Mexico by migrants to improve their lives at home (Massey and Parrado 1994; Lozano Ascencio 1993, 1998).

These anomalies occur because the lifetime maximization of expected income is only one of several potential economic motivations for international migration, and not necessarily the most important. Neoclassical economics *begins* with the assumption that markets for goods and services exist, that they are complete and function well, that information and competition are perfect, and that rational individuals enter the market with exogenous tastes and preferences in order to maximize their utility (that is, they look out for number one). Given these assumptions, deductive logic is employed to discover what the world would look like if it indeed functioned according to neoclassical principles.

Yet reality is considerably more complex than the enabling assumptions of neoclassical economics. Markets for goods and services may not exist, they may be imperfect, and sometimes they may fail entirely, especially during the early phases of economic development. In addition, information is usually scarce and constrained by an individual's position in the social structure, and competition is far from perfect. Finally, even if individuals are rational and self-interested, they do not enter markets as atomized individuals but as members of families, households, and sometimes larger communities, social groupings that allow for *collective* strategies, which at times may dovetail with those of individuals and at other times be at odds with them.

If we imagine a world where families and households face the prospect of poorly functioning, missing, or failed markets, we come to a very different line of theoretical reasoning known as the *new economics of labor migration* (Stark and Bloom 1985). Unlike the neoclassical model, it does not assume that migration decisions are made by isolated actors, but that they are taken within larger units of interrelated people, typically families or households but sometimes entire communities. Within these units, people not only act individually to maximize expected income but also work collectively to overcome failures in capital, credit, and insurance markets (Taylor 1986, 1987; Stark 1991).

In most developed countries the risks to a household's material well-being are managed through private markets and government programs. Crop insurance and futures markets give farmers a means of protecting themselves against natural disasters and price fluctuations, and unemployment insurance and welfare programs protect workers against the vagaries of the business cycle and the dislocations of structural change. Private and government-sponsored pension systems allow citizens to minimize the risk of poverty in old age.

In relatively poor countries like Mexico, markets for futures and insurance are not well developed, and the Mexican government is in no position to fill the gap by offering substitutes. As a result, Mexicans are not only poorer than other North Americans; they are also exposed to substantially greater *risk*. If society were indeed made up of atomized individuals acting solely in their immediate self-interest, then Mexicans probably would just have to suffer the risks quietly. However, most Mexicans do not live as solitary individuals but within households united by powerful family ties that precede the market (Vélez-Ibañez 1983; Lomnitz 1977; Adler-Lomnitz and Pérez Lizaur 1987; Camp 1989). Unlike atomized individuals, households can manage risk by diversifying their allocation of productive resources, one of which is labor.

Just as investors diversify risks by purchasing stocks across a range of firms, households diversify risks by sending out members to work in different labor markets. While some members (say, the wife and younger children) remain behind to work in the local economy, others (say, older sons and daughters) move to work elsewhere in Mexico, and still others (perhaps the household head and oldest son) migrate to work in the United States. As long as conditions in the various labor markets are negatively or weakly correlated, a household can manage risk through diversification. In the event that conditions at home deteriorate through rising unemployment, falling wages, failing crops, sagging prices, or high inflation, households can rely on migrant remittances as an alternative source of income.

In developing countries such as Mexico, markets for capital and credit are also weak or absent, preventing families from borrowing to smooth consumption or undertake productive activities (Taylor et al. 1996a, 1996b). In the absence of an efficient banking system, international migration becomes a reasonable strategy that poor families can use to accumulate cash in lieu of formal borrowing for consumption or investment. Households simply send one or more workers abroad to take advantage of higher wages to build up savings over a short time horizon.

Contexts of Decisionmaking

Individuals and households are almost always embedded within broader social systems that have their own organization and values, such as kinship networks, class hierarchies, ethnic and racial groupings, occupational sectors, and industrial or bureaucratic organizations. As social scientists have repeatedly shown, an individual's position within the social structure determines the context in which decisions are made. A person's structural position strongly influences his or her tastes, preferences, values, information, learning, resources, and, ultimately, the relative costs and benefits of any action being considered. By altering the context within which microlevel decisions are made, structural change in society can have rather pronounced effects in raising or lowering the probability of international migration.

Social and economic structures are commonly transformed through powerful macrolevel forces that are *exogenous* to actors within any particular family or community, and social scientists have thus developed *structural theories* of international migration to acknowledge this fact. Building on the work of Immanuel Wallerstein (1974), a variety of theorists (Portes and Walton 1981; Petras 1981; Castells 1989; Sassen 1988, 1991; Morawska 1990) have linked the origins of international migration not so much to the decisions of individuals or households as to the changing scope and structure of global markets, a line of reasoning that is generally known as *world systems theory*. In this scheme, the expansion of markets into peripheral, nonmarket or premarket societies creates mobile populations that are prone to migrate.

Driven by a desire for higher profits and greater wealth, owners and managers of large firms in developed nations enter poor countries on the periphery of the world economy in search of land, raw materials, labor, and markets. Migration is a natural outgrowth of the disruptions and dislocations that occur in this process of market expansion and penetration. As land, raw materials, and labor come under the control of markets, flows of migrants are generated. For example, when farmers shift from cultivating for subsistence to cultivation for markets, competition pushes them to consolidate land holdings, mechanize production, introduce cash crops, and apply industrially produced inputs. Land consolidation destroys traditional tenure systems based on common usufruct. Mechanization decreases the need for labor and makes unskilled agrarian workers redundant to production. The substitution of cash crops for staples undermines traditional social and economic relations, and the use of modern inputs, by producing high crop yields at low unit prices, drives out peasant farmers. All of these forces contribute to the creation of a mobile labor force: agricultural workers, displaced from the land, experience a weakened attachment to the community and become more prone to migrate internationally (Massey 1988; Hatton and Williamson 1998).

The extraction of raw materials for use in developed economies likewise requires new industrial methods reliant on paid labor. Offering wages to former peasants also serves to undermine traditional forms of social organization based on systems of reciprocity and fixed role relations, creating instead incipient labor markets based on new conceptions of individualism, private gain, change, and adaptation. Multinational firms enter poor nations to establish assembly plants and take advantage of their relatively low wages, often within special export-processing zones created by modernizing governments. The demand for factory workers strengthens local labor markets and further weakens traditional productive relations.

The insertion of foreign factories into peripheral regions undermines traditional economies in other ways: by producing goods that compete with those made locally; by feminizing the workforce without providing sufficient factory-based employment for men; and by socializing women for industrial work and modern consumption without providing a lifetime career capable of meeting these needs. The result once again is the creation of a population that is socially and economically uprooted and prone to migration, typically with international spillovers.

feminizing the workforce causes men to migrate

The same economic processes that operate globally to create migrants in peripheral areas simultaneously make it easier for them to migrate to the developed world (Sassen 1991). To ship goods, deliver machinery, extract and export raw materials, coordinate business operations, and manage foreign assembly plants, firms in core nations build and expand transportation and communication links to the peripheral countries where they have invested. These links not only facilitate the movement of goods, commodities, information, and capital but promote an opposing flow of people by reducing the costs of movement along reverse paths. Because global investment is inevitably accompanied by the creation of transportation and communication infrastructures, the international migration of labor generally parallels the international movement of goods and capital, only in reverse.

Economic globalization also creates cultural links between developed and developing nations. Sometimes the cultural links are longstanding, reflecting prior colonial relationships. Yet even in the absence of a colonial history, the cultural consequences of economic penetration can be profound. Although Mexico was colonized by Spain, Mexicans increasingly study at U.S. universities, speak English, and follow U.S. consumer styles, reflecting America's global economic hegemony. These cultural links naturally dispose them to migrate to the United States rather than other places, including Spain.

true

The world economy is managed from a relatively small number of urban centers in which banking, finance, administration, professional services, and research are concentrated (Castells 1989; Sassen 1991). In the United States these global cities include New York, Chicago, Los Angeles, and Miami; in Europe they include London, Paris, Frankfurt, and Milan; and qualifying for this status on the Pacific Rim are Tokyo, Singapore, and Sydney (Friedman 1986). Within these cities a wealth is concentrated to generate a strong demand for services from unskilled laborers (busboys, gardeners, waiters, hotel workers, domestic servants). At the same time the shifting of heavy industry overseas, the growth of high-tech manufacturing in electronics, computers, and telecommunications, and the expansion of services such as health and education all work to create a bifurcated labor market with strong demand for workers at both the top and the bottom of the occupational hierarchy, but with relatively weak demand in between.

The Demand for Immigrants

The bifurcation of labor markets in global cities predicted by world systems theory dovetails with a larger line of theorizing known as *segmented labor market theory,* which grew out of institutional economics. Michael Piore (1979) has argued that international migration stems from a relatively permanent demand for unskilled labor that is built into the economic structure of developed nations. In his view, immigration is not caused by push factors in sending countries (such as low wages or high unemployment), but by pull factors in receiving societies (a chronic and unavoidable need for low-wage workers). The intrinsic demand for inexpensive labor stems from four fundamental problems faced by advanced industrial economies.

The first problem is *structural inflation.* Wages not only reflect conditions of supply and demand but confer status and prestige, social qualities inherent to specific jobs. In general, people believe that wages should reflect social status, and they have rather rigid notions about the correlation between occupational status and pay. As a result, wages offered by employers are not free to respond to changes in the supply of workers. A variety of informal social expectations and formal institutional mechanisms (such as union contracts, civil service rules, bureaucratic regulations, and human resource classifications) ensure that wages correspond to the hierarchies of prestige and status that people perceive.

If employers seek to attract workers for unskilled jobs at the bottom of an occupational hierarchy, they cannot simply raise wages for those jobs. Doing so would upset socially defined relationships between status and remuneration. If wages are increased at the bottom, employers will encounter strong pressure to raise wages at other levels of the job hierarchy. If the wages of busboys are raised in response to a labor shortage, for example, their wages may overlap with those of waitresses, thereby threatening the status of waitresses and prompting them to demand a corresponding wage increase, which threatens the position of cooks, who also pressure employers for a raise, and so on. As a result, the cost of raising wages to attract entry-level workers is typically more than the cost of those workers' wages alone. Thus, the prospect of structural inflation—the need to raise wages proportionately throughout the job hierarchy to maintain consistency with social expectations—provides employers with a strong incentive to seek easier and cheaper solutions, such as the importation of immigrants.

The demand for cheap, flexible labor is also augmented by the *social constraints on motivation* that are inherent to job hierarchies. Most people work not only to generate income but to accumulate social status. Acute motivational problems arise at the bottom of the job hierarchy because there is no status to be maintained and there are few avenues for upward mobility. The problem is inescapable because the bottom can never be eliminated from labor markets. Mechanization to eliminate the lowest and least desirable classes of jobs simply creates a new bottom tier composed of jobs that used to be just above the bottom rung. Since there always has to be a bottom of any hierarchy, motivational problems are inevitable. What employers need are workers who view bottom-level jobs simply as a means to the end of earning money and for whom employment is reduced solely to a matter of income, with no implications for status or prestige.

Immigrants satisfy this need on a variety of counts, at least at the beginning of their migratory careers. Migrants generally begin foreign labor as target earners: they are seeking to make money for a specific goal that will solve a problem or improve their status at home (such as building a new house, buying land, or acquiring consumer goods). Moreover, the disjuncture in living standards between developed and developing societies makes low wages abroad appear generous by the standards of the sending country. Finally, even though a migrant may realize that a foreign job carries low status, he does not view himself as a part of that society but as embedded within the status system of his home community, where hard-currency remittances buy considerable social status.

The demand for immigrant labor also stems from the *duality of labor and capital*. Capital is a fixed factor of production that can be idled by lower demand but not laid off; owners of capital bear the costs of its unemployment. Labor, in contrast, is a variable factor of production that can be released when demand falls, so that workers bear the costs of their own unemployment. Whenever possible, therefore, industrialists seek out the stable, permanent portion of demand and reserve it for the deployment of capital, leaving the variable portion of demand to be met by the addition and subtraction of labor, a dualism that creates distinctions among workers and leads to segmentation of the labor force.

Workers in the capital-intensive primary sector get stable, skilled jobs working with good tools and equipment. Employers are forced to invest in their human capital through training and education. Primary-sector jobs are complicated and require considerable knowledge and experience to perform, leading to the accumulation of firm- and job-specific knowledge. Primary-sector workers also tend to be unionized or highly professionalized, with contracts that require employers to bear a substantial share of the costs of layoffs (in the form of severance pay and unemployment benefits). Because of these costs and continuing obligations, workers in the primary sector become expensive to let go; they become more like capital.

The labor-intensive secondary sector, in contrast, is composed of poorly paid, unstable jobs from which workers may be laid off at any time with little or no cost to the employer. During down cycles an employer's first act is to shed such workers to cut the payroll. The resulting dualism thus yields a segmented labor market structure. Low wages, unstable conditions, and the lack of reasonable mobility prospects make it difficult to attract native workers into the secondary sector. They are instead drawn into the primary, capital-intensive sector, where wages are higher, jobs are more secure, and there is a possibility of occupational advancement. To fill the shortfall in demand within the secondary sector, employers turn to immigrants.

Taken together, motivation problems, structural inflation, and economic dualism create a demand for a particular kind of worker: one who is willing to labor under unpleasant conditions, at low wages, in jobs with great instability and little chance for advancement. In the past this demand was met by women, teenagers, and rural-to-urban migrants. Historically women tended to participate in the labor force up to the time of their first birth, and to a lesser extent after their children had grown. They were not primary breadwinners, and their principal social identity was that of a daughter, wife, or mother. They were willing to put up with the low wages and instability because they viewed the work as transient and the earnings as supplemental; the positions they held were not threatening to their main social status, which was grounded in the family.

Likewise, teenagers historically moved into and out of the labor force with great frequency to earn extra money, gain experience, and try out different occupational roles. They did not view "dead-end" jobs as a problem because they expected to get better jobs in the future, after completing school, gaining experience, and settling down. Moreover, teenagers derive their primary social status from their parents, not their jobs. They view work instrumentally as a means of earning spending money, which they use to enhance their status among their peers by buying clothes, cars, and music; the job is just a means to an end.

Finally, rural areas of developed nations for many years provided industrial cities with a steady supply of low-wage workers. Movement from social and economic backwaters to dynamic cities created a sense of upward mobility regardless of the modesty of the circumstances at the place of destination. Even menial jobs in cities provided access to housing, food, and consumer goods that represented a step up in the world for impoverished migrants from the countryside.

In advanced industrial societies, however, these three sources of entry-level workers have drastically shrunk over time because of four fundamental demographic trends: the rise in female labor force participation, which has transformed women's work into a career pursued for social status as well as income; the rise in divorce rates, which has transformed women's employment into a source of primary support; the decline in birthrates and the extension of formal education, which have produced small cohorts of teenagers entering the labor force; and the urbanization of society, which has eliminated farms and rural communities as potential sources for new migrants to the city. The imbalance between the structural demand for entry-level workers and the limited domestic supply of such workers has generated an underlying, long-run demand for immigrants in developed countries.

Why People Continue to Migrate

Immigration may begin for a variety of reasons, but the forces that initiate international movement are quite different from those that perpetuate it. Although wage differentials, market failures, and structural change may motivate people to move in the first place, new conditions arise in the course of migration to make additional movement more likely, leading to the perpetuation of international migration across time and space. There has been a great deal of work on the perpetuation of international migration under the rubric of *social capital theory.* According to Pierre Bourdieu and Loic Wacquant (1992, 119), "social capital is the sum of the resources, actual or virtual, that accrue to an individual or a group by virtue of possessing a durable network of more or less institutionalized relationships of mutual acquaintance and recognition." The key characteristic of social capital is its convertibility: it can be translated into other social and economic benefits (Harker, Mahar, and Wilkes 1990).

People gain access to social capital through membership in interpersonal networks and social institutions and then convert it into other forms of capital to improve or maintain their position in society (Bourdieu 1986; Coleman 1990). Migrant networks are an important source of social capital for people contemplating a move abroad. They are sets of interpersonal ties that connect migrants, former migrants, and nonmigrants at places of origin and destination through reciprocal ties of kinship, friendship, and shared community origin. They increase the likelihood of international movement because they lower the costs and risks of movement and increase the expected net returns to migration.

In keeping with the dictum that "social capital . . . is created when the relations among persons change in ways that facilitate action" (Coleman 1990, 304), migration itself serves as the catalyst for change. Everyday ties of friendship and kinship provide few advantages, in and of themselves, to people seeking to migrate abroad. Once someone in a person's network has migrated, however, the ties are transformed into a resource that can be drawn upon to gain access to foreign employment and all that it brings. Each act of migration creates social capital among people to whom the migrant is related, thereby raising the odds of their migration (Massey, Goldring, and Durand 1994).

The first migrants who leave for a new destination have no social ties to draw upon, and for them migration is costly, particularly if it involves entering another country without documents. After the first migrants have left, however, the potential costs of migration are substantially lowered for the friends and relatives left behind. Because of the nature of kinship and friendship structures, each new migrant expands the set of people with social ties to the destination area. Migrants are inevitably linked to nonmigrants, and the latter draw upon the obligations implicit in relationships such as kinship, friendship, and even community to gain access to employment and assistance at the point of destination.

Once international migration has begun, private institutions and voluntary organizations also arise to satisfy the demand created by the growing imbalance between the large number of people who seek entry into capital-rich countries and the limited supply of visas they typically offer. This imbalance and the barriers that developed countries erect to keep people out create a lucrative niche for entrepreneurs dedicated to promoting international movement for profit, yielding a black market in migration services. As this underground market creates conditions conducive to exploitation and victimization, humanitarian organizations also arise to enforce the rights and improve the treatment of both legal and undocumented migrants (Hagan and Gonzalez Baker 1993; Christiansen 1996). Such organizations offer migrants another source of social capital (Goss and Lindquist 1995) by providing a range of services, such as border smuggling, clandestine transport, labor contracting, counterfeit documents, information and advice, and lodging, credit, and shelter at the points of destination (Prothero 1990).

The way in which social capital accumulates over time to perpetuate international migration represents a specific manifestation of a broader process that has been described as the *cumulative causation of migration* (first identified by Myrdal 1957). The causation of migration becomes cumulative because each act of migration alters the social context within which subsequent migration decisions are made, thus increasing the likelihood of additional movement. Once the number of network connections in a community reaches a critical threshold, migration becomes self-perpetuating because each act of migration creates the social structure needed to sustain it (Hugo 1981; Taylor 1986; Massey 1990; Massey, Goldring, and Durand 1994; Massey and Zenteno 1999).

In any bounded population, of course, processes of cumulative causation cannot continue ad infinitum. If migration continues long enough, networks eventually reach a point of saturation within any particular community. More and more community members reside in branch settlements overseas, and virtually all of those at home are connected to someone who lives abroad or has substantial foreign experience. When networks reach such a high level of elaboration, the costs of migration do not fall as sharply with each new migrant, and migration loses its dynamic momentum for growth. The prevalence of migration in the community approaches an upper limit, and migratory experience becomes so diffused that the stock of potential new migrants becomes very small and is increasingly composed of women, children, and the elderly.

If migration continues long enough, labor shortages and rising wages in the home community may further dampen the pressures for emigration (Gregory 1986), causing the rate of entry into the international migrant workforce to trail off (Hatton and Williamson 1994). When observed at the national level, this trend may be difficult to detect as new communities are continuously incorporated into the migratory stream. As the rate of out-migration decelerates in places with longer histories of migration, new areas are drawn into transnational circuits and their rates of migration begin to accelerate. As a result, the total outflow from the nation as a whole may continue to grow as migration spreads from place to place.

A Schematic Diagram

Because the theories discussed in this chapter posit causal mechanisms operating at multiple levels of aggregation, the various explanations are not logically contradictory. It is entirely possible for individuals to engage in cost-benefit calculations; for households to seek to minimize risk and overcome barriers to capital and credit; for both individuals and households to draw upon social capital to facilitate international movement; and for the socioeconomic context within which migration decisions are made to be determined by structural forces operating at the national and international levels, often influenced by migration itself. Thus, a synthetic approach to theory construction is in order.

As we see it, international migration originates in the social, economic, and political transformations that accompany the expansion of markets. The entry of markets and capital-intensive production into nonmarket or premarket societies disrupts existing social and economic arrangements and brings about a displacement of people from customary livelihoods, thus creating a mobile population of workers who actively search for new means of sustenance. One means by which people displaced from traditional jobs seek to ensure their economic well-being is by selling their services overseas. However, higher foreign wages are not the only factor motivating people to emigrate. Households struggling to cope with the jarring transformations of economic development also use international migration as a means of overcoming frequent failures in markets for labor, insurance, capital, and credit.

The absence of unemployment insurance in developing nations creates an incentive for families to self-insure by sending one or more members overseas for work. By allocating workers to different geographic regions—rural, urban, and foreign—households diversify their labor portfolios to reduce risks to income. Moreover, as households plunge into the risky and unknown world of capitalist production, the absence of crop insurance and futures markets leaves them vulnerable to economic disaster, providing yet another incentive to self-insure through international migration. Families seeking to increase agricultural production or establish new business enterprises need capital, and the shift to a market economy creates new demands for expensive consumer items. The financing of both requires cash, and the inability of poorly developed banking systems to meet the demand for loans and credit gives households one final motivation for international movement. By sending a family member temporarily abroad for work, households can accumulate savings quickly to self-finance production or consumption.

While the early phases of economic development in poor nations create migrants, later phases of economic growth in wealthy nations yield segmented labor markets that attract them. Primary-sector jobs provide steady work and high pay for native workers, while jobs in the secondary sector offer low pay, little stability, and few opportunities for advancement, repelling natives and generating a strong demand for immigrant workers. The process of labor market segmentation is most acute in global cities, where a concentration of managerial, administrative, and technical expertise leads to a concentration of wealth and a strong ancillary demand for low-wage services. Unable to attract native workers, employers turn to immigrants and often initiate immigrant flows directly through formal recruitment.

Although often instrumental in initiating immigration, recruitment becomes less important over time because the same market processes that create flows of immigrants also create links of transportation and communication, as well as of politics and culture, to make international movement easier and cheaper. Immigration also stems from the actions that developed nations undertake to maintain international security, protect foreign investments, and guarantee access to raw materials overseas. Foreign entanglements create links and obligations that generate ancillary flows of refugees, asylum seekers, and military dependents.

Eventually labor recruitment becomes superfluous: once begun, immigration displays a strong tendency to continue through the growth and elaboration of migrant networks. Over time the process of network expansion becomes self-perpetuating because each act of migration creates social infrastructure to promote additional movement. As receiving countries implement restrictive policies to counter rising tides of immigrants, moreover, they only create a lucrative niche into which enterprising agents move to create migrant-supporting institutions, providing even more social capital for international migration.

During the initial phases of emigration from any sending country, the effects of capitalist penetration, market failure, network formation, and cumulative causation dominate in explaining the flows, but as the level of out-migration reaches high levels, the costs and risks of international movement drop and movement is increasingly determined by international wage differentials and labor demand. As developing nations grow economically, international wage gaps diminish and well-functioning markets for capital, credit, insurance, and futures come into existence, reducing the incentives for emigration. If these trends continue, the country ultimately becomes integrated into the global economy as a developed, capitalist society, whereupon it undergoes a migration transition: net out-migration ceases, and the nation becomes an importer of labor. Historically, this process of development, emigration, and transition took European nations eight or nine decades, but by the late twentieth century the process seemed to have been compressed into just thirty or forty years.

Chapter 3

System Assembly: A History of Mexico-U.S. Migration

IN THE history of international migration, that between Mexico and the United States is unique in several ways. First and foremost is the fact that it involves not just any pair of countries, but two with widely disparate standards of living that share a two-thousand-mile land border. Although the United States also shares a long border with Canada, the latter's level of economic development is roughly comparable to the U.S. level and its average income is only fractionally lower. In addition, its population is less than one-third of Mexico's. As a result, legal Canadian immigration to the United States averages only around 21,000 persons per year—just 8 percent of the number arriving from Mexico—and it is offset by a roughly equal number of U.S. citizens moving northward, yielding a net flow that fluctuates around zero (Massey et al. 1998). Moreover, Canada's relationship to its southern neighbor has generally been cordial, and the two nations have long cooperated as allies. Canada has never been invaded by the United States, and despite a series of historical threats, it has never been forced to cede territory to its more powerful neighbor to the south.

A second unique feature of Mexico-U.S. migration is its age. Its origins can be traced to the Treaty of Guadalupe Hidalgo, which in 1848 officially ended the Mexican-American War. In exchange for the cessation of hostilities, the end of U.S. occupation, and a payment of $18.3 million, Mexico surrendered the present-day states of California, Arizona, New Mexico, and Texas, along with parts of Colorado, Nevada, and Utah. Although the border was adjusted once more in 1853 (when for another $10 million the United States purchased the southern portions of present-day Arizona and New Mexico to secure a rail route into southern California), since that date the border has remained essentially fixed except for minor adjustments.

The number of Mexicans who "entered" the United States by virtue of the Treaty of Guadalupe Hidalgo was quite small, probably no more than about 50,000 (Jaffe, Cullen, and Boswell 1980). Nearly all of today's 15 million Mexican Americans trace their origins to people who migrated to the United States *after* 1848. During the nineteenth century movement between the two countries was mostly local, involving short trips back and forth between places that had earlier been single, undivided communities. The border was relatively unpopulated and, once it left the Rio Grande River, poorly demarcated and only sporadically policed. As a result, one cannot properly speak of "international migration" between Mexico and the United States until the twentieth century. True international migration required separation and self-definition, an ideological process that assumed different forms at different locations along the Mexico-U.S. border.

In El Paso del Norte, for example, the historical name of the community remained on the U.S. side (albeit in shortened form) while inhabitants of the southern side languished nameless until 1888, when Ciudad Juárez was finally incorporated (Durand and Arias 2000). Elsewhere, Mexican settlements continued to use their original name but preceded it with the adjective "new" to distinguish it from its northern counterpart. After 1848, for example, the southern portion of Laredo became known as Nuevo Laredo, even though the two settlements continued to celebrate common holidays and public events (Ceballos 1999). The town of Nogales, for its part, adopted neither of these options: on both sides of the border the settlement continued to use the original name, a solution that was probably facilitated by the fact that no river divided the northern and southern halves.

In general, only those communities that arose entirely *after* the border was fixed made explicit in their naming the country to which they belonged—hence the mirror images of Mexicali, Mexico, and Calexico, California. Tijuana, which ultimately became the largest and most dynamic city on the border, was just a small *rancho* of 242 people in 1900, connected to the rest of Mexico by neither road nor rail. Its early growth and development were more closely tied to events north than south of the border, and for many years it functioned more as an extension of Los Angeles and San Diego than as a Mexican town (Zenteno 1995).

In sum, the Mexico-U.S. border has not always existed as a practical reality. On the contrary, it was defined slowly but steadily through a process of *social construction*. The process of reification began with the smuggling of contraband, the first human endeavor that marked the Mexico-U.S. frontier as a significant dividing line. During the U.S.

Civil War, in particular, the border between the states of Tamaulipas and Texas provided a route around the Union's naval blockade of the Confederacy, giving life and importance to the twin communities of Brownsville and Matamoros (Hart 1987). After the war the solidification of the border continued when it prevented both U.S. and Mexican authorities from pursuing Indians, criminals, and deserters fleeing in both directions (Durand 1994). The advent of prohibition in the United States gave the border additional substance, transforming Mexican communities into staging areas for bootlegging and diversion. The expansion of bars, prostitution, and black markets gave many border cities a reputation for "sinfulness" they have yet to live down.

The Mexican Revolution (1910 to 1917) also heightened the importance of the border by converting U.S. communities into locations of political refuge as well as points of assembly and debarkation for soldiers, arms, and war matériel. After the Revolution, the new Mexican government (led not coincidentally by generals from the north) increased the nation's investment in the infrastructure of the border states. These investments provided a foundation for the high rates of economic and population growth during the 1960s and 1970s.

The social construction of the border probably received its most important impetus with the formation of the U.S. Border Patrol in 1924. For the first time the U.S. government itself assumed direct responsibility for defending the border against unauthorized intrusions using physical, not just administrative, means. Even this systematic enforcement, however, was more symbolic than real: the Border Patrol originally consisted of just 450 officers, who were expected to guard not only the two-thousand-mile border with Mexico but also the long frontier with Canada.

Although one cannot say with precision exactly when the border became something more than a mental construction, its reification as a socially, economically, and politically meaningful dividing line is mostly a product of the twentieth century. Hence, we begin our account of Mexican migration in 1900, dividing subsequent years into five periods corresponding to different alignments of social, economic, and political forces. Our review suggests that international movement within the Mexico-U.S. system has never operated solely according to the laws of neoclassical economics. Rather, the circulation of migrants has been driven by a complex set of social and economic forces understandable only by drawing on *all* of the theoretical paradigms discussed in chapter 2.

The Era of the Enganche: 1900 to 1929

Just as railroads were crucial to the development and settlement of Mexico's northern frontier, they were likewise instrumental in enabling and promoting mass migration to the United States (Cardoso 1980). With the opening of the Mexican Central Railroad from Mexico City to the border community of Ciudad Juárez in 1884, Mexico was definitively connected to the United States through four rail lines that met across the border in El Paso: the Atchison, Topeka, and Santa Fe, the Southern Pacific, the Texas & Pacific, and the Galveston, Harrisburg, and San Antonio. By 1888 service had been established between Mexico City and two other border cities, Piedras Negras and Nuevo Laredo, and by 1890 virtually all of Mexico's principal population and production centers were connected to markets in all forty-eight contiguous U.S. states and territories. (For a map of the border states and cities, see figure 3.1.) It was this linkage by rail that made mass migration between Mexico and the United States possible, if not inevitable.

The arrival of the railroads initiated a sustained boom in the American Southwest by connecting its fertile valleys and natural resources to lucrative markets and burgeoning industries back east. Just as the boom took off, however, restrictive policies enacted in Washington, D.C., closed off immigration from traditional sources in Asia. The Chinese Exclusion Act of 1882 and the 1907 Gentlemen's Agreement with Japan brought Asian immigration to an abrupt halt, creating serious labor shortages in key sectors of the western economy, particularly railroads, mining, agriculture, and construction. Desperate for workers, U.S. employers turned to private labor contractors, who employed a variety of coercive measures to recruit Mexican laborers and deliver them to jobs north of the border.

Being paid for each worker they provided, U.S. recruiters sought to obtain as many as possible by any means necessary short of actual enslavement (Durand and Arias 2000). The coercive policies they employed became known collectively as *el enganche,* which translates literally as "the hook" but might be translated more politely as "indentured." The people who employed these techniques were called *enganchadores.* Following the rail lines southward from the United States, enganchadores crossed through the empty borderlands and first encountered sizable population centers in Mexico's west-central states—Guanajuato, Jalisco, Michoacán, San Luis Potosí, and Zacatecas. Recruiters arrived in towns and villages throughout this region with tales of high wages and untold riches to be had by working in the north.

The enganchadores typically offered to advance naive peasants

Figure 3.1 The Mexico-U.S. Borderlands

Source: Mexican Migration Project.

whatever money they needed to travel northward and get a U.S. job. The loan, plus interest, would then be deducted from their wages upon arrival. Once in the United States, however, recruits usually discovered that wages were lower than promised, working conditions worse than expected, and interest rates higher than anticipated. Since they were required to work until they paid off their "debt" to the recruiter and/or employer, they considered themselves "hooked," at least for a time (Cardoso 1980).

The outbreak of World War I halted European immigration in late 1914, just when the war was inducing an enormous expansion in U.S. industries. Facing a tightening labor market, industrialists in Chicago, Kansas City, Los Angeles, and other cities relied even more on the enganchadores. Eventually the U.S. government itself got into the act.

When Congress sought to restrict immigration in 1917 by imposing a head tax and literacy test on all new arrivals, the attorney general immediately exempted Mexicans from these provisions. Once the United States entered the war, the government assumed a direct role in labor recruitment by creating its own worker recruitment program (Reisler 1976; Morales 1982).

When the war ended, so did the labor program, but the United States nonetheless continued to pursue a lax immigration policy toward Mexico throughout the boom years of the 1920s. Even as Congress moved to close off European immigration by implementing strict quotas that restricted immigration from southern and eastern Europe, it remained silent on the issue of immigration from the countries of the Western Hemisphere. Although the total number of immigrants was capped at 357,000 in 1921, then lowered to 164,000 in 1924 and 154,000 in 1929, these numerical limitations were never applied to Mexico, whose nationals were free to enter without quantitative restriction and did so in large numbers.

Within Mexico conditions in the early twentieth century also evolved in ways that encouraged massive out-migration. The decade 1900 to 1910 was the high tide of the Porfiriato, a long period of stable rule under President Porfirio Díaz, who came to power in 1876 with significant backing by U.S. industrialists (Hart 1987). As president, he promoted the development of Mexico along liberal economic lines, offering generous incentives to investors in the United States, Britain, and France to finance the development of railroads, mining, petroleum, and manufacturing. In the countryside the power of the Mexican state was used to privatize lands that for centuries had been held in common by independent towns and Indian villages. Through the consolidation of land and the mechanization of farming, property owners drastically increased production (and profits), and they switched from the cultivation of basic foodstuffs (corn and beans) to the production of cash crops (sugar, cotton, hemp, wheat) for sale on international markets.

Over the course of the Porfiriato, Mexico began to shift from an agrarian to an industrial footing. From 1876 to 1910 the total length of railroad track went from a mere 380 miles to more than 12,000, the production of gold and silver quadrupled, sugar production more than doubled, and exports increased tenfold (Meyer and Sherman 1991). This remarkable spurt of economic development came at a price, however. Through privatization, enclosure, and land consolidation, more than 95 percent of rural households had become landless by 1910 (Cardoso 1980). At the same time the mechanization of agriculture and the switch to cash crops drastically reduced rural work opportunities; the marked decline in rural wages that resulted was cruelly accompanied by an increase in food prices. Meanwhile, rural artisans who had traditionally handcrafted products for local consumption found themselves undercut by cheap, industrially produced products imported by rail from manufacturing cities in Mexico and the United States (Massey et al. 1987).

In this new rural landscape some families eked out a living as sharecroppers on large haciendas, while many others migrated to Mexico's swelling cities in search of factory or service work. Although urban jobs were being created and city wages rose early in the Porfiriato, by 1900 the small domestic market for Mexican manufactures had been saturated and industrialization had stalled (Haber 1989). As displaced rural families continued to arrive in the cities looking for work, urban wages fell and conditions deteriorated, prompting a wave of violent strikes between 1905 and 1910 (Hart 1987).

By 1910 the structural limitations of the Porfirian political economy had reached a breaking point, and revolt spread throughout the country. Until 1912 the Mexican Revolution was relatively peaceful and socioeconomic relations did not change radically. From 1913 to 1917, however, the Revolution entered a violent phase during which various factions fought for military supremacy; this bloody and protracted struggle brought the Mexican economy to its knees and led to a "demographic catastrophe." Over the course of the revolutionary decade from 1910 to 1920, Mexico experienced 1.4 million excess deaths, 500,000 lost births, and 200,000 net emigrants to the United States (McCaa 2001), the first and only instance of significant refugee migration from Mexico. (U.S. authorities built Fort Bliss in the border city of El Paso to manage the situation.)

The political consolidation of the Revolution after 1917 led to a resumption of economic growth in the 1920s, but along new lines. In the new political economy, wealthy Creole landowners and foreign bankers no longer dominated the state for their own ends. Rather, the state was controlled by a dynamic, forward-looking mestizo class that sought to expand its power by arbitrating relations between labor and capital, peasants and landowners. Rather than serving the interests of a narrow, landed, Creole elite, the new state would balance the interests of an expanded mestizo-Creole elite against those of peasants and workers to promote the welfare of the nation as a whole.

Within urban Mexico, the coalition of old Creole families and foreign investors gave way to a new alliance of mestizo politicians and industrialists willing to cooperate with the state in fomenting economic growth. In the countryside, hacienda owners were eliminated as a cohesive social class, and the foundations were set for a massive land redistribution (not fully realized until the 1930s). The transformation of Mexico from agrarian to industrial society, launched during the Porfiriato, would thus continue after the Revolution. Markets would continue to be the main mechanism for producing growth and economic expansion, but now they would be managed for the benefit of society by a powerful and independent state.

Obviously, the forces responsible for instigating Mexican migration during the first decades of the twentieth century are a far cry from the simple aggregate of cost-benefit decisions made by atomized individuals acting in isolation. In a very real sense, the cost-benefit calculations hypothesized under neoclassical economics were foisted upon Mexicans by the massive transformations going on around them, first under the Porfiriato, then under ten years of revolution, and finally when a new state-dominated political economy was created. Even with these massive transformations, however, Mexican migration probably would not have begun had it not been for parallel structural transformations in the United States that created a demand for labor so intense that U.S. employers, and later the federal government itself, turned to private firms to undertake direct, purposive recruitment of Mexican labor.

The motivations of the earliest Mexican migrants were generally not to relocate permanently north of the border for a lifetime of U.S. work and earnings. Rather, they sought to move northward temporarily to solve economic problems their families faced at home, problems associated with the market failures of the Porfirian economy and later on of the Revolution. What the first migrants sought were ways to manage the risks associated with the structural transformations at home, to buffer the vicissitudes of civil war, and to acquire the capital they could not otherwise hope to gain so as to be able to buy land, construct homes, purchase equipment, and generally enter the emerging market economy as producers and consumers. Embedded within these strategies of migration were expectations of return.

The end result of this alignment of forces north and south of the border was a dramatic explosion in migration to the United States after 1900. Whereas only 13,000 Mexicans had emigrated to the United States in the entire five decades from 1850 to 1900 (with only 971 recorded entries during the 1890s), over the next three decades the outflow totaled 728,000. Figure 3.2 shows trends in the rate of outmigration between Mexico and the United States from 1900 to 1939. The term "legal immigrants" refers to Mexicans admitted for permanent residence (taken from U.S. Immigration and Naturalization Service 1998); "contract laborers" are those admitted for temporary wage labor (compiled from Cornelius 1978; Cardoso 1980; Calavita 1992);

Figure 3.2 Mexican Emigration to the United States, 1900 to 1939

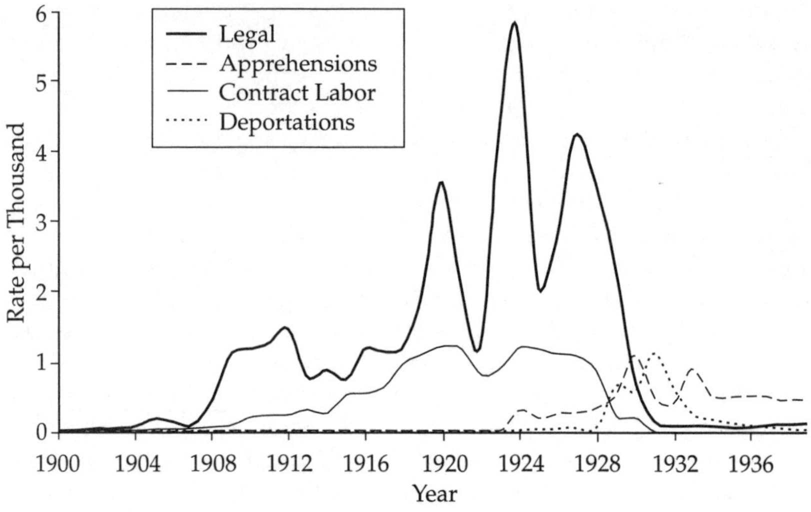

Source: U.S. Immigration and Naturalization Service.

and the number of undocumented migrants is proxied by the total number of apprehensions reported by the U.S. Border Patrol (taken from Cornelius 1978; Cardoso 1980). Rates were derived by dividing these counts by the population of Mexico during the year in question, then multiplying by 1,000.

At the turn of the century the rate of legal out-migration to the United States was essentially zero, and it fluctuated at relatively low levels until 1907, the year when immigration from Japan was finally curtailed, effectively eliminating Asia as a labor source. Legal Mexican immigration then began a rapid rise and peaked at about 1.5 per 1,000 during 1912, but fell once again during the period 1913 to 1916 as the Mexican Revolution degenerated into violent civil war (Hart 1987).

Following U.S. entry into World War I in 1917, the rate of out-migration tripled to peak at 3.5 per 1,000 in 1920 before falling back again to about 1.2 per 1,000 in 1922, when demobilization and the transition to a civilian economy created a brief recession that reduced demand for immigrant workers and triggered the first significant repatriation campaign directed at Mexicans (Durand 1994). By 1924, however, the economy had recovered, and legal immigration once again surged to a rate of nearly 6.0 per 1,000, a level not equaled again until the unusual circumstances of the early 1990s. Beginning in 1914, the recruitment of contract laborers also surged, rising to a rate of 1.2 per 1,000 in 1921 before dipping temporarily in 1922, then returning to this high level in 1924.

The 1920s were a period of intense nativism in the United States (Higham 1955), and immigrants came to be viewed as a threat to American well-being. Over the course of the decade Congress passed a series of increasingly restrictive quota laws to check immigration from southern and eastern Europe, whose immigrants were widely thought to be "unassimilable." To confront the rising volume of immigration from Mexico, however, Congress chose a different mechanism: the U.S. Border Patrol. Founded in 1924, the new force organized the first systematic, federally directed deportation campaign in U.S. history. Apprehensions began, and the rate of legal out-migration dropped to around 2.0 per 1,000 in 1925.

Despite the nativism of U.S. citizens, the imposition of quotas, and the formation of the Border Patrol, the booming U.S. economy of the "Roaring Twenties" continued to generate a high demand for unskilled workers, and given the restrictions on European and Asian immigration, U.S. employers continued to look southward for workers. After 1925 the rate of legal out-migration from Mexico once again doubled, reaching 4.1 per 1,000 in 1928, and the rate of contract labor migration remained steady at just above 1.0 per 1,000. It would take something more powerful than nativism, quotas, and the creation of the Border Patrol to end Mexican immigration.

The Era of Deportations: 1929 to 1941

Despite the increase in apprehensions and deportations during 1924 and 1925, immigration from Mexico revived and continued apace until the onset of the Great Depression. The stock market crash in October 1929 ushered in a new era in the history of Mexico-U.S. migration, one characterized by massive expatriation and limited international movement. With the deepening of the depression in the early 1930s, the attitudes of U.S. citizens toward Mexican immigrants hardened and grew quite hostile. As unemployment rose to record levels in the United States, Mexican immigrants became convenient scapegoats for widespread joblessness and budget shortfalls. Paradoxically, they were blamed simultaneously for "taking away jobs from Americans" and "living off public relief" (Hoffman 1974).

Although U.S. politicians were at a loss as to how the faltering economy might be revived, there was one decisive action they could take that would address, if only symbolically, the concerns of frightened U.S. workers: a massive roundup and deportation of Mexican immigrants. In Mexican population centers and agrarian zones throughout the United States, federal authorities, in cooperation with state and local officials, mounted a coordinated series of deportation campaigns that, over the course of the 1930s, succeeded in reducing the size of the Mexican population of the United States by 41 percent (Jaffe et al. 1980).

Whereas during the 1920s the annual flow of legal immigrants had averaged around 46,000, throughout the 1930s it never exceeded 2,700 (Cornelius 1978). On the contrary, during the period 1929 to 1937 some 458,000 Mexicans were arrested and forcibly expelled from the United States, and thousands more, facing a political climate of great hostility and poor economic prospects, decided to return home "voluntarily," a decision that was encouraged by the intensification of land redistribution in Mexico under President Lázaro Cárdenas. During his administration (1934 to 1940) some 45 million acres of land were confiscated from hacienda owners and given to local communities for allocation to agrarian families, creating a new class of small farmers that ultimately came to control half of Mexico's arable land. As a result of these events, the number of Mexicans enumerated by the U.S. census fell from 639,000 in 1930 to just 377,400 in 1940 (Jaffe et al. 1980).

Figure 3.2 shows the effect of these events on the rate of out-migration to the United States. After 1930 the rate of legal out-migration plummeted to 0.1 per 1,000, compared with rates that had never fallen below 2.4 per 1,000 during the period 1923 to 1929. Contract labor disappeared entirely as agricultural growers ended their reliance on Mexican laborers and hired "Oakies" and other internally displaced Americans. The rates of apprehension and deportation, meanwhile, rose to new heights, with notable peaks in 1929–30 and 1932–33. Through the massive use of repressive force and police powers, the U.S. government sought to undo in the 1930s what it had actively encouraged over the preceding two decades. Owing to a lack of political opposition to this massive violation of civil rights and the absence of an effective demand for Mexican labor, it proved to be a remarkably successful strategy.

The Bracero Era: 1942 to 1964

In the wake of the Great Depression, the U.S. political economy was significantly restructured by President Franklin Roosevelt's New Deal. As in Mexico, the government came to assume a more central role in the management and organization of economic life, enacting new laws to govern the banking and securities industries, regulate trade, and mediate labor relations. The earlier laissez-faire program of limited government and balanced budgets gave way to a new, Keynesian project of deficit spending and direct investment in key sectors of the economy, such as transportation, communication, utilities, housing, the military, and science. With the entry of the United States into World War II in December 1941, the stage was set for a sustained economic boom that would last for decades.

The mobilization of American industry for the war effort and the enactment of military conscription created the prospect of serious labor shortages in American agriculture. The Oakies and other displaced native workers disappeared from the countryside as quickly as they had arrived. Whereas in the 1930s displaced farmers had been grateful to perform agricultural labor under difficult conditions at near-subsistence wages, they now shunned such poorly paid and demeaning work. Those who were not drafted streamed into cities such as Los Angeles, San Francisco, Seattle, Dallas, and Houston to take high-paying, unionized jobs in shipyards, docks, defense plants, and other factories.

Agricultural growers grew alarmed at the prospect of a labor shortage and turned to Congress and the president for help. Federal authorities, for their part, wanted no disruption of the food supply during war mobilization, and once again they approached Mexico to recruit the necessary workers. In early 1942 the Roosevelt administration negotiated a binational treaty for the temporary importation of Mexican farmworkers, who became known as *braceros.* (Derived from the Spanish word *brazo,* or "arm," the word can be translated loosely as "farmhand.") The bracero program was originally operated jointly by the U.S. Departments of State, Labor, and Justice; the key agency was Justice's Immigration and Naturalization Service (INS), which was given authority to regulate entries and departures and enforce the terms of temporary visas. On September 29, 1942, the first batch of five hundred braceros was delivered by federal authorities to growers outside of Stockton, California (Calavita 1992). The bracero era had begun.

The resurrection of labor recruitment came at an opportune time in Mexican economic history. The 1930s presidency of Lázaro Cárdenas was a time of great structural transformation and social change in Mexico (Hansen 1971; González 1981). The institutionalization of political stability, the acceleration of state-led development, and the creation of internal markets through a policy of import substitution industrialization (ISI) sparked a sustained economic boom that lasted for three decades. From 1940 through 1970 the real rate of economic growth averaged around 6 percent per year, and the period came to be known as the "Mexican economic miracle."

Despite this impressive growth, the rate of job creation in urban areas was no match for Mexico's burgeoning rural population. Moreover, although the agrarian reform program enacted by President Lázaro Cárdenas had given millions of peasants access to land, it had not granted them access to the financial resources necessary to make their new plots productive. The need to buy equipment, seeds, insecticides, and infrastructure created a great surge in demand for capital and credit throughout rural Mexico that the country's rudimentary banking system was ill prepared to meet. For rural families suddenly in possession of land and searching vainly for a way of financing production, the arrival of the bracero program truly seemed a godsend (Massey et al. 1987).

In all, some 168,000 braceros were recruited to the United States during the war years (1942 to 1945). Although originally envisioned as a temporary wartime measure, the booming postwar economy perpetuated growers' fears of a labor shortage, and under considerable pressure from the Texas and California delegations, Congress extended the bracero program on a year-to-year basis through the late 1940s. Despite these extensions, the number of braceros remained insufficient to meet the demand emanating from the fields, and during the late 1940s agricultural growers increasingly took matters into their own hands by recruiting undocumented workers.

In doing so, they incurred no liability under U.S. immigration law: the well-known "Texas Proviso" (named for the congressional delegation that originally wrote it) had explicitly prohibited the prosecution of employers for hiring undocumented workers (Teitelbaum 1986). Being handed this gaping loophole, growers simply spread the word among braceros that jobs would be waiting for any friends or relatives who chose to come. Once these new workers arrived, employers either filed papers to have them legalized ex post facto as braceros or just let them continue working illegally. Although the number of bracero visas issued annually by the INS expanded to around 100,000 in 1949 (partly because of ex post facto legalization), the size of the program still was insufficient to meet demand, particularly after 1950 as the cold war turned hot in Korea, resulting in a reinstatement of the draft and a dramatic increase in industrial production. As a result, the number of undocumented migrants grew very rapidly, with apprehensions rising from 69,000 in 1945 to 883,000 in 1950.

In response to continued pressure from growers, Congress in 1951 passed Public Law 78 to give the bracero program a permanent statutory basis. Passed at the height of the Korean War with little discussion and virtually no opposition, the program remained in place for thirteen years (Calavita 1992). Given the program's new statutory authority, the INS immediately doubled the number of bracero visas to around 200,000. Despite the program's growth, undocumented migration continued to rise as well, and the recession that followed the end of the Korean War combined with the paranoia of the McCarthy era to make illegal migration a hot political issue in 1953 and 1954.

At this time a mobilized citizenry clamored for federal authorities to "do something" to "control the border," even as agricultural growers continued to press for more workers. As the bureaucratic agency in charge, the INS found itself between a rock and a hard place, facing intense but contradictory pressures from equally powerful, highly mobilized constituents. The agency's response was a bureaucratic tour de force. In 1954 the INS launched a well-publicized, two-pronged attack known as "Operation Wetback" (Calavita 1992) that brilliantly managed to satisfy all sides, putting the INS simultaneously in good stead with growers, the public, nativists, and members of Congress.

In cooperation with state and local authorities, the INS took the lead in militarizing the border and organizing a mass roundup of undocumented migrants. During 1954 the number of migrants apprehended by the INS swelled to over 1 million for the first time in U.S. history. At the same time, however, the INS more than doubled the number of bracero visas, an expansion that finally met growers' demand for agricultural workers. From 1955 to 1960 annual bracero migration fluctuated between 400,000 and 450,000 workers. At one point the INS was raiding agricultural fields in the southwestern United States, arresting undocumented workers, transporting them back to the border, and deporting them into the waiting arms of officials from the U.S. Department of Labor, who promptly processed them as braceros and retransported them back to the very fields where they had been arrested in the first place! (Calavita 1992.) Operation Wetback was applied with particular force in Texas, where U.S. authorities deliberately sought to break growers of their traditional habit of illegal hiring and to steer them toward the new, preferred mode of bracero employment (McBride 1963).

This two-pronged strategy was a resounding success for the INS (Calavita 1992). The expansion of bracero migration satisfied growers, while the militarization of the border and the massive number of apprehensions reassured voters and assuaged their nativist fears, creating the widespread perception that the border was under control. After peaking in 1954, the annual number of apprehensions plummeted, and from 1955 through 1964 it never again exceeded 100,000. Illegal

Figure 3.3 Mexican Emigration to the United States, 1940 to 1964

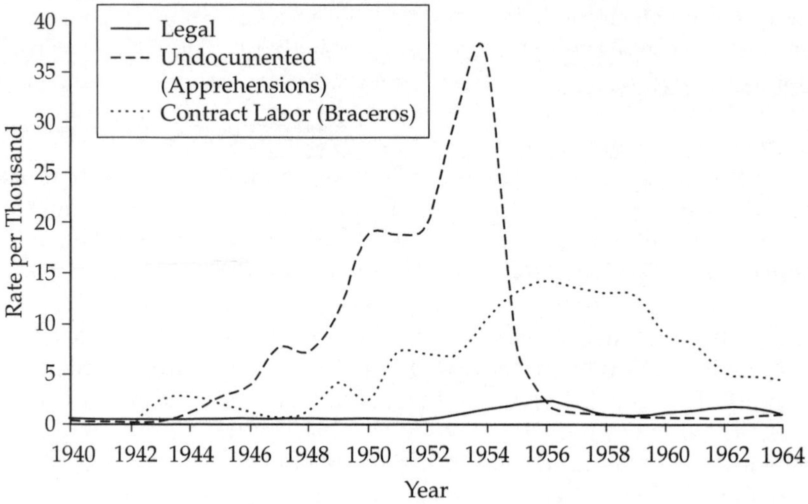

Source: U.S. Immigration and Naturalization Service.

migration effectively disappeared from public consciousness. Everyone, it seemed, was happy with the bracero compromise: growers got a plentiful supply of workers on favorable terms, while the public got the perception of a controlled border. As the federal agency orchestrating this legerdemain, the INS acquired new respect, prestige, and resources.

The direct trade-off between bracero and undocumented migration is illustrated in figure 3.3, which shows fluctuations in the rate of out-migration from Mexico between 1940 and 1964. During the first two years of the 1940s there was virtually no migration of any kind across the Mexico-U.S. border. Bracero recruitment started in late 1942, and the rate of contract labor migration began to rise. By 1944 undocumented migration, stimulated by the recruitment of braceros, also began to increase; when the number of bracero visas was temporarily reduced after the war, undocumented migration surged.

The subsequent expansion of bracero recruitment in 1948 and 1949 once again brought a dip in the rate of apprehension in 1948, but the curtailment of bracero recruitment in 1950 led to another surge in the rate of apprehension. The definitive expansion of the rate of bracero migration from 1955 to 1960, along with the incipient growth of legal immigration, combined to reduce the flow of undocumented migrants to a trickle. Whereas the rate of apprehension stood at about 37 per

1,000 in 1954, within two years it had fallen to around 1 per 1,000 (about the same rate as legal immigration), where it remained until the early 1960s.

The relative peace of the bracero era rested on a delicate compromise between competing interests: a nativist citizenry demanding that the border be controlled, and a well-organized lobby of growers who sought free access to Mexican labor. For a time the bracero program allowed the United States to have its cake and eat it too. Growers were plentifully supplied with farm labor in the form of contract workers, and the public was satisfied with the appearance of a controlled border. Nearly 5 million Mexicans entered the United States during the program's twenty-two-year history—a figure that dwarfs the combined total of legal and contract labor between 1900 and 1929—but this massive movement remained out of the public eye. With government assistance, braceros were whisked across the border and taken directly to the fields, bypassing large urban population centers and largely escaping the attention of the media.

By the early 1960s, however, political conditions in the United States were changing in ways that boded ill for the future of the bracero program. By then the nativist fears of the McCarthy era had waned, the economy was again booming, and Americans were becoming increasingly self-confident. Given the explosive growth in income and rising standards of living, U.S. citizens were able to turn their attention to moral contradictions at home. Even as the United States took the lead in a cold war against Communist dictatorships abroad, it tolerated an ugly, racialized tyranny at home in the form of legal segregation. In the affluent and forward-looking society of the early 1960s, this contradiction proved to be unsustainable.

Legalized discrimination against African Americans in the southern states and informal discrimination against them elsewhere in the country came to be seen as an embarrassment by most Americans, and during the 1960s a powerful civil rights movement gathered force. A broad coalition of labor unions, church groups, northern liberals, and civil rights activists pushed hard for federal legislation to combat racial discrimination in American life. With strong support from President Lyndon Johnson, himself a master of legislative politics, the movement achieved a remarkable string of successes in Congress, notably the 1964 Civil Rights Act, the 1965 Voting Rights Act, and the 1968 Fair Housing Act.

In an era of expanding civil rights, immigration policies that systematically blocked the entry of Asians, Africans, southern Europeans, and eastern Europeans came to be seen as intolerably racist. As part of the broader move to end racism in federal law, the civil rights coalition also sought to modify U.S. immigration law by repealing the national-origins quotas and the Asian exclusion acts and replacing them with a neutral system that allocated visas among countries in a fair and objective manner. Prodded by legislators who were often themselves descendants of southern and eastern Europeans still smarting from the sting of Anglo exclusion (men like Peter Rodino and Dan Rostenkowski), Congress in 1965 passed landmark amendments to the Immigration and Nationality Act, finally extirpating overt racism from U.S. immigration policy. At the time the bill was seen as more of a piece of civil rights legislation than a fundamental change in U.S. immigration policy, and no one foresaw its far-reaching consequences (Glazer 1980).

The 1965 amendments created a new visa allocation system for the Eastern Hemisphere—Europe, Africa, the Middle East, Asia, and the Pacific. Henceforth, each country from these regions would be granted a quota of up to 20,000 visas annually to be allocated on the basis of family ties to U.S. residents, U.S. occupational needs, and humanitarian considerations. A new "preference system" was created to rank-order the various claims on entry. At the top were unmarried sons and daughters of U.S. citizens (first preference), followed by spouses and unmarried sons and daughters of legal resident aliens (second preference); artists, scientists, and professionals of unusual ability (third preference); married sons and daughters of U.S. citizens (fourth preference); brothers and sisters of U.S. citizens (fifth preference); skilled and unskilled workers in short supply (sixth preference); and refugees (seventh preference). Spouses, parents, and unmarried children of U.S. citizens were exempt from the preference system and not subject to numerical limitation; they entered outside the quotas entirely.

In addition to the 20,000-per-country limit, immigrants from the Eastern Hemisphere were subject to a hemispheric cap of 170,000 visas annually. Although neither the per-country limit nor the preference system was applied to nations in the Western Hemisphere (Latin America, the Caribbean, and Canada), the region was given an overall quota of 120,000 visas, to be applied beginning in 1968. This hemispheric ceiling represents the first attempt ever made by U.S. authorities to limit numerically the number of Latin American (and hence Mexican) immigrants to the United States.

At the time these legal reforms were not expected to have a marked effect on either the size or composition of immigration to the United States (Glazer 1980). What Congress generally expected was a modest increase in immigration from eastern and southern Europe and a clearing of the backlog from Asia. Little new migration was anticipated from either Asia or Africa, and with one exception, the entry of Latin Americans was given little thought. The one exception was the bracero program, which constituted a second front of attack on what were seen as prejudicial immigration policies.

As the civil rights era progressed, the bracero program came to be seen as an exploitative and discriminatory system detrimental to the socioeconomic well-being of Mexican Americans, who had emerged as loyal allies of African Americans in the campaign for civil rights. In a 1960 television documentary aired at Thanksgiving entitled *Harvest of Shame,* Edward R. Murrow exposed the deplorable working conditions of migrant farmworkers (Andreas 2000), and beginning in that year a coalition of unions, religious organizations, and civil rights groups began to whittle down the annual number of bracero visas, which fell from 438,000 in 1959 to 178,000 in 1964. By the early 1960s, moreover, growers had grown dissatisfied with the program, which had become increasingly corrupt in allocating worker contracts. Ranchers found it easier to hire undocumented workers without having to submit to costly bureaucratic procedures. With growers giving up resistance, in early 1965 the civil rights coalition succeeded in killing the program entirely. The bracero era was finally over.

The Era of Undocumented Migration: 1965 to 1985

Along with the sharp break in U.S. immigration policy that occurred in 1965, a variety of other conditions had also changed by the mid-1960s. First, growers had become heavily dependent on Mexican labor. In theory, growers could always have drawn native workers back into the agricultural workforce by raising wages and improving working conditions, but in practice they were reluctant to take these steps, which would have increased prices, induced structural inflation, and put them at a competitive disadvantage in the highly competitive food industry. Second, even if growers could raise wages, another problem loomed: after twenty-two years of a near-monopoly by Mexican labor, agricultural work within the United States had come to be defined socially as "foreign" and thus unacceptable to citizens. The social organization of U.S. labor markets had been changed permanently so as to create a built-in, *structural* demand for immigrant workers (see Böhning 1972; Piore 1979).

By the mid-1960s, not only had the nature of U.S. labor demand changed, but so had Mexican migrants themselves. Whereas in the 1940s and 1950s they had generally been target earners, seeking to earn as much money as possible, as quickly as possible, to recoup their costs of moving, attain a predetermined income goal, and return home, by the 1960s their perceptions and motivations had changed. Sustained access to high U.S. wages had created new standards of material well-being and instilled new ambitions for upward mobility that involved additional trips and longer stays. As households containing braceros altered their consumption patterns and displayed the fruits of their U.S. labor, nonmigrant families came to feel relatively deprived and themselves sought to migrate (Reichert 1981).

The bracero program also generated a significant stock of migration-related human capital in Mexico. Between 1942 and 1965 hundreds of thousands of braceros were able to familiarize themselves with U.S. employment practices, become comfortable with U.S. job routines, master American ways of life, and learn English. As a result of this new knowledge—this new human capital—the costs and risks of taking additional trips dropped and the potential benefits rose. In addition to generating new human capital, moreover, the bracero program created significant social capital in hundreds of Mexican communities. Each time a bracero departed, social capital was created among his circle of friends and relatives, and that social capital in turn reduced the costs and risks of their own international movement and increased their access to U.S. employment.

In practical terms, therefore, the bracero program functioned as a government-sponsored initiative that set in motion the self-perpetuating forces of cumulative causation. In Mexico, meanwhile, the vaunted economic miracle began to unravel during the mid-1960s. A massacre of student demonstrators in downtown Mexico City in late 1968 shook the political establishment and threatened the stability upon which economic growth had depended (Poniatowska 1971). A massive increase in the size of the state and a surge in deficit spending during the presidency of Luis Echeverría led to capital flight, political unrest, and a devaluation of the peso in 1976 (Centeno 1994). Although the discovery of new petroleum reserves bought Mexico a few years of additional time, by 1982 world oil prices had fallen, and the Mexican economy finally collapsed once and for all.

Despite the end of the economic miracle, undocumented migration would probably *not* have grown after the demise of the bracero program had it not been followed immediately by the imposition of new limits on the legal immigration of Mexicans. If pre-1965 policies had remained in force, it is likely that the flow of Mexicans would simply have shifted from bracero to resident alien visas and Mexican immigration would have continued apace under a different name. Indeed, as it became clear to growers that the days of the bracero program were numbered, many began petitioning for an "adjustment of status" of their former braceros (Reichert and Massey 1979; Massey and Liang 1989). Whereas annual legal immigration from Mexico stood at 23,000 persons in 1959, by 1963 it had doubled to more than 55,000, and during the short window of time from 1960 through 1968 when Mexicans were able to enter the United States without numerical restriction, some 386,000 Mexicans received permanent resident visas, a 43 percent increase over the period 1950 to 1958.

Beginning in 1968, Mexican immigration became subject to increasing numerical restriction. In that year the hemispheric cap of 120,000 was applied, forcing Mexicans, for the first time, to compete for a limited supply of visas with immigrants from other countries in Latin America and the Caribbean. As the exodus of refugees from Cuba grew, the competition for visas grew so intense that Mexican plaintiffs ultimately sued the INS, claiming that they were being unfairly denied access to hemispheric visas by political decisions taken in Washington. The courts agreed, and in 1977 the INS was ordered to set aside for Mexicans 144,946 visas originally used to admit Cuban refugees and to provide them *in addition to* the hemispheric ceiling. The resulting Silva program (named for the lead plaintiff in the lawsuit) ran from 1977 to 1981 and temporarily expanded Mexican access to U.S. visas.

High inflation, rising unemployment, and sagging wages in the United States during the 1970s made Mexican immigration increasingly salient as a political issue, and in 1976 Congress responded once again. In new amendments to the Immigration and Nationality Act, it prevented young U.S.-born children from sponsoring their parents' immigration by stipulating that only U.S. citizens age twenty-one and over could petition for the legal entry of their parents. More important, it extended the 20,000-per-country limit to the Western Hemisphere and placed it under the dictates of the preference system.

Legal Mexican immigration immediately fell by 40 percent, reaching just 45,000 in 1977, the lowest level since the end of the bracero program in 1964. In 1978 Mexican access to visas was further limited by amendments that eliminated the separate hemispheric ceilings and created a single 290,000 worldwide cap, which was subsequently reduced to 270,000 in 1980. Between 1968 and 1980, therefore, the number of visas accessible to Mexicans dropped from an unlimited supply to just 20,000 per year (excluding immediate relatives of U.S. citizens), and even these were allocated in competition with immigrants from other nations against a fixed worldwide cap. Although Mexican immigration temporarily swelled to a record 101,000 in 1981, the final year of the Silva program, Mexican entries once again dropped sharply when that program ended, hovering between 55,000 and

Figure 3.4 Mexican Emigration to the United States, 1965 to 1998

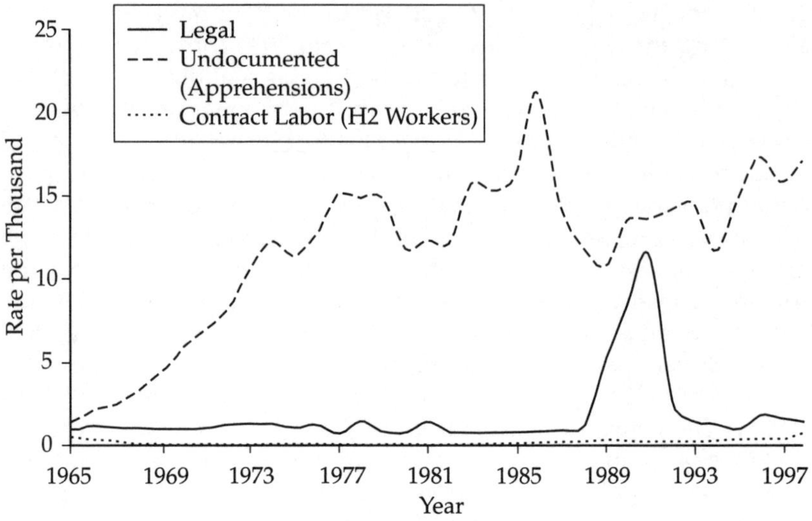

Source: U.S. Immigration and Naturalization Service.

60,000 through 1985, a level well below that observed in the mid-1920s, when Mexican immigration had peaked at 88,000 per year. Compared with the 450,000 work visas made available *annually* to Mexicans during the height of the bracero era, moreover, the number of Mexican immigrant visas granted during the 1970s was small indeed.

The sharp reduction in the accessibility of legal visas coincided with a time of rapid population growth and declining economic fortunes in Mexico. Given this pairing and the accumulation of so much migration-related human and social capital during the bracero era, only one outcome was possible: an explosion of undocumented migration. Figure 3.4 shows the rate of out-migration to the United States from 1965 through 1997. With a few minor and one notable exception, the rate of *legal* immigration has been essentially fixed at around 1.0 per 1,000 since 1965. The rate dipped a little in 1977 with the inclusion of Mexico in the country quotas, and it went to 1.4 per 1,000 during 1978 and 1981 because of the additional Silva visas, but these represented minor blips in a fairly flat trend line that persisted through the late 1980s. U.S. policy clearly succeeded in reducing and limiting Mexican access to legal visas.

With contract labor migration limited to trivial levels throughout the period, undocumented migration was the only possible outlet for the powerful migration-promoting forces set in motion by the bracero program and ongoing structural changes in Mexico and the United States. From a rate slightly above 1.0 per 1,000 in 1965, the relative number of Mexicans apprehended rose to 21.0 per 1,000 in 1986. Although this rate is high, it still does not come close to the rate of 37.0 per 1,000 achieved during the height of Operation Wetback in 1954, owing mainly to the larger size of the Mexican population.

Nonetheless, undocumented migration steadily came to dominate the flow of migrants to the United States during the period 1965 to 1986. According to estimates by Douglas Massey and Audrey Singer (1995), roughly 28.0 million Mexicans entered the United States as undocumented migrants during this period, compared with just 1.3 million legal immigrants and a mere 46,000 contract workers. For the most part, this massive movement was circular. Massey and Singer also found that the 28.0 million entries were offset by 23.4 million departures, yielding a net increase of only 4.6 million. Since around 200,000 legal Mexican immigrants also returned to Mexico during the same period (Warren and Kraly 1985; U.S. Immigration and Naturalization Service 1997), total net Mexican immigration from 1965 through 1986 was probably on the order of 5.7 million, of whom 81 percent were undocumented.

During the twenty-one-year history of mass undocumented migration, the United States, in effect, operated a de facto guest-worker program. Just enough resources and personnel were allocated to border enforcement to reassure the public that the border was under control. The costs of border crossing were raised to the point where some selection was achieved, but they were never raised high enough to hamper seriously the flow of Mexican workers to U.S. jobs. During the late 1970s and early 1980s the odds that an undocumented Mexican would be apprehended while trying to enter the country averaged around one in three (Espenshade 1990, 1994; Massey and Singer 1995).

Although border enforcement served an important symbolic purpose by signaling that the nation was being defended, it did not really deter Mexicans from attempting an undocumented border crossing. Even if they were unlucky enough to be caught and returned to Mexico, they simply tried again until they got in, a process that Thomas Espenshade (1990) has called the "repeated trials model." If the odds of capture are only 33 percent on any given attempt, the likelihood that a migrant will successfully enter the United States over the course of four attempts is 80 percent. In short, most migrants who made it to the border eventually got in (Singer and Massey 1998).

Even though they did not seriously hinder the ultimate arrival of undocumented migrants, the rigors of clandestine crossing, together with the possibility of arrest and deportation, did have the advantage of skewing the flow toward those most motivated and able to work—young men just before or in the early stages of family formation (Massey et al. 1987). Such people had little incentive to work in the United States for very long, since most were target earners who had left friends and family at home; they also knew that they could always return to the United States whenever the need arose. Hence, the odds of return migration were high.

Once again, in seeking to reconcile the conflicting interests surrounding immigration, the INS had evolved a strategy in which the United States could have its cake and eat it too. U.S. employers continued to enjoy ready access to Mexican workers, while the American public was reassured that the border was under control. For more than two decades the system worked well to select highly motivated workers at little cost to the government, ensure their arrival at U.S. work sites at their own expense, and then encourage their relatively prompt return, once again at their own expense.

In addition to reassuring the public, the steady increase in border apprehensions served another important bureaucratic purpose: each arrest at the border justified the need for additional resources for the U.S. Border Patrol, yielding a self-fulfilling cycle that worked strongly to the agency's advantage. From 1965 to 1986 the Border Patrol steadily increased in size, from about 1,500 officers to 3,700, and the number of apprehensions rose from 55,000 to 1.7 million. From the Border Patrol's point of view, the only drawback of the increasing number of apprehensions was the bureaucratic load it put on agents. There was no particular problem in the late 1960s when fewer than 60,000 undocumented migrants were apprehended each year. As the annual number of arrests rose toward the 1 million mark, however, logistical problems became substantial, leading to the evolution of a bureaucratic coping strategy that Josiah Heyman (1995) has called the "voluntary departure complex." Other researchers have labeled it "a game of cat-and-mouse" (Chavez 1992; Koussoudji 1992) and a "revolving door" (Durand 1994).

During the migration regime that prevailed from 1965 through 1986, the career interests of Border Patrol officers were best served by making a large number of arrests and processing them quickly. The interests of the migrants, naturally, were to avoid apprehension if possible, but when arrested, to return to Mexico quickly to try crossing again. The bureaucratic form that evolved to institutionalize these complementary interests was called the "voluntary departure order."

Technically, each undocumented Mexican arrested while entering the United States had the right to a hearing before an immigration judge, but neither the migrant nor the Border Patrol officer was really interested in pursuing this course of action. Upon arrest, therefore, 97 percent of Mexican migrants signed a "voluntary departure order" waiving their right to a hearing and authorizing the Border Patrol to transport them "voluntarily" back to Mexico.

All parties understood that, once repatriated, the migrant would simply try to cross the border again and that on the next or subsequent attempt he or she would probably get in. After two decades of undocumented migration and millions of apprehensions, the social encounter between Border Patrol officers and Mexican migrants became highly ritualized (Heyman 1995). As the comptroller general of the United States explained in a 1976 report: "Presently the border is a revolving door. . . . We repatriate undocumented workers on a massive scale . . . [and] the illegals cooperate by agreeing to voluntarily depart, and significant numbers promptly re-enter" (quoted in Andreas 2000, 37).

The Great Divide: 1986 to 2000

As the absolute number of apprehensions continued to climb year after year, the voluntary departure strategy began to unravel. In the eyes of lawmakers and the public, the upward spiral of apprehensions ultimately served less to justify the need for more enforcement resources than to prove that past expenditures had been ineffective and that the border was again spiraling out of control. In addition, even though Mexican migration remained highly circular, growing numbers were inevitably settling permanently in the United States. The ratio of settlers to migrants remained small, but as the volume of undocumented migration rose, so did the absolute number of settlers, leading to the formation of large, growing, and highly visible Mexican communities in some of the nation's most important urban centers—Los Angeles, San Diego, San Francisco, Chicago, Dallas, Houston, and New York.

As undocumented Mexicans grew more visible, the United States underwent a period of substantial economic and political turmoil that left citizens feeling insecure, unconfident, and apprehensive about their own well-being. This combination of rising undocumented migration and deep social and economic anxiety made it imperative for lawmakers to find a "solution" to the "problem" of undocumented migration, and during the first half of the 1980s a variety of bills were introduced to tighten border enforcement. Most, however, were bottled up in committee by the conflicts inherent to the immigration debate (see Fuchs 1990).

Suddenly, in late 1986, a historic compromise orchestrated by Senator Alan Simpson (R-Wyo.) and Representative Peter Rodino (D-N.J.) miraculously balanced the interests of growers, immigrants, Latinos, restrictionists, free traders, nativists, and employers to secure the passage of the Immigration Reform and Control Act (IRCA). Although the speed with which the legislation cleared both houses of Congress surprised many observers, IRCA was promptly signed into law by President Reagan and took effect on January 1, 1987, ushering in a new era of Mexico-U.S. migration.

U.S. concerns about Mexico and Mexican immigration did not stop at the border, nor were they all addressed by IRCA. The collapse of the Mexican peso during the summer of 1982 brought another round of hyperinflation, national insolvency, and looming default on international loans. The lion's share of the foreign debt was owed to U.S. banks, and faced with a potential financial catastrophe, the U.S. government pressured Mexico to deregulate its economy, undertake monetary and fiscal reforms, downsize the state, and liberalize trade.

In Mexico, meanwhile, the economic crisis brought to power a new group of U.S.-trained technocrats who were well schooled in market economics and committed to dismantling the political economy of import substitution industrialization that had prevailed since the 1930s (Centeno 1994; Camp 1996). During the late 1980s and early 1990s these technocrats, led by President Carlos Salinas de Gortari, worked assiduously to dismantle trade barriers, eliminate controls on ownership and investment, reduce tariffs, dismantle subsidies, deregulate markets, and generally privatize the economy.

These changes were looked upon with great favor and strongly supported by free-marketeers of the Reagan and Bush administrations, and when President Salinas sought to institutionalize the reforms and make them permanent, U.S. officials eagerly embraced the vehicle he chose: the North American Free Trade Agreement. By tying trade liberalization, privatization, and market economics to a treaty with the United States, Salinas would make it difficult, if not impossible, for a successor to dismantle the political economy he had put in place. Despite opposition from unions, workers, environmentalists, and isolationists in the United States, a bipartisan coalition of congressional Democrats and Republicans succeeded in ratifying NAFTA early in the administration of President Bill Clinton, and on January 1, 1994, the North American Free Trade Agreement went into effect.

Even as it moved progressively toward more restrictive immigration policies, therefore, the United States simultaneously committed itself to a broader process of economic integration with Mexico, ensuring that the new age of Mexico-U.S. migration would be one of profound ambivalence. Despite the obvious fact that NAFTA would inevitably create more elaborate and efficient transportation and communication links between the two nations, and even though the treaty would obviously forge a broader network of professional contacts and social ties through expanding business, tourism, scientific interchanges, and cultural exchanges, U.S. officials somehow wished to believe that this new integration would not lead to the transnational movement of labor. Indeed, a common refrain was that NAFTA would enable Mexico "to export goods and not people."

Once again, the United States sought to have its cake and eat it too. This time, however, the fundamental contradictions were more difficult to finesse than during the bracero or undocumented eras, and federal officials found themselves relying on increasingly harsh and repressive policies to create the impression that the border was still a meaningful dividing line during an era of rampant, government-sponsored transnational integration (Andreas 1998). To increase the costs of entry, IRCA authorized an immediate 50 percent increase in the INS enforcement budget (Bean, Vernez, and Keely 1989; Goodis 1986). To lower benefits, IRCA imposed sanctions against employers who knowingly hired undocumented migrants and increased the Labor Department's budget to carry out work-site inspections. These restrictions, however, came at a political price. To secure support from civil rights organizations, immigrant advocacy groups, and Latino lobbies, IRCA also authorized an amnesty for long-term undocumented residents, and to placate agricultural growers it included a special legalization program for undocumented farmworkers.

Thus, IRCA contained both deeply restrictive and wildly expansive provisions. Despite the increase in border enforcement and the imposition of employer sanctions, it ended up legalizing some 2.3 million formerly undocumented Mexicans (U.S. Immigration and Naturalization Service 1992). As figure 3.4 shows, this legalization hugely increased the rate of legal immigration. The legalizations processed from 1988 through 1992 raised the rate of legal entry to around 11.0 per 1,000 in 1991, exceeding even the high rates registered during the 1920s.

As in the earlier bracero era, the figure suggests a trade-off between legal and undocumented migration. Once the legalization programs were announced in late 1986, millions of undocumented migrants chose to remain in the United States and begin the process of applying for a visa. As a result, the rate of apprehension dropped immediately from about 22.0 per 1,000 in 1986 to just 11.0 per 1,000 in

1988. As the legalization program wound down, however, undocumented migration rose once again, with the rate of apprehension going back up to 17.0 per 1,000 by 1996.

Practical Mechanics of Mexico-U.S. Migration

As the foregoing review indicates, migration between Mexico and the United States has never been a result of simple cost-benefit decisions taken by individuals, nor have migrants been motivated solely by a desire to relocate permanently north of the border to maximize lifetime earnings. Although Mexicans have clearly made decisions to enhance their well-being, income maximization is only one of several potential motivations, and their decisions have never been taken in isolation but within larger social and economic structures that have been transformed over time in ways that have strongly influenced the motivations for and the likelihood of international migration.

Since the late nineteenth century, the Mexican political economy has undergone three wrenching structural transformations. The first was the *liberal revolution* of Porfirio Díaz (1876 to 1910), who attracted massive foreign investment to build an incipient industrial base, create a national market, and link Mexico, via new ports and railroads, to the global trading system. The second was the *Mexican Revolution,* which created a powerful corporatist state that assumed a central role in planning, organizing, and financing economic growth. The third was the *neoliberal revolution* of the 1980s that privatized state-owned industries, dramatically downsized government, limited subsidies, and opened Mexico to global trade and foreign investment.

At each historical juncture, the structural transformations wrought by these three revolutions influenced the circumstances faced by everyday Mexicans, causing them to see international migration as a potential solution to their problems. Usually the motivation for migration was not simple income maximization. Equally important were the goals of minimizing risk and overcoming barriers to the acquisition of money for consumption and investment. Even given such incentives to emigrate, however, migratory flows generally had to be instigated by recruitment, first during the period 1910 to 1920 and then again from 1942 to 1964. In the course of state-sponsored labor migration, social networks evolved to support international movement and make recruitment increasingly irrelevant. At the same time migration transformed social and economic structures on both sides of the border in ways that encouraged additional migration.

The current migratory system has thus been a century in the making. With the exception of a brief hiatus during the 1930s, migration between Mexico and the United States has gone on continuously since the dawn of the twentieth century. During this time all of the theoretical forces reviewed in chapter 2 came into play, although different combinations prevailed in different historical epochs. Considering the entire historical panorama of Mexico-U.S. migration, what has changed over time is not so much the *fact* or *rate* of immigration as the *auspices* under which it has occurred. From 1900 to 1929 Mexicans entered as legal immigrants, from 1942 to 1964 as braceros, and from 1965 to 1985 as undocumented migrants. The rate of legal immigration during the 1920s was higher than at any time up to 1991, and the rate of undocumented migration (measured by the apprehension rate) during the early 1980s was roughly comparable to the rate of bracero migration in the late 1950s. By the 1970s Mexico-U.S. migration had evolved into a well-regulated, highly predictable, and largely self-sustaining system based on the circular movement of undocumented male workers.

Chapter 4

System Specifications: Empirical Parameters and Constants in the U.S.-Mexican Immigration System, 1965 to 1985

THE DEMISE of the bracero program and increasing restrictions on legal immigration after 1965 transformed a de jure system of circular migration based on the movement of legal guest workers into a de facto machinery of seasonal migration based on the recurrent movement of undocumented laborers. Rather than being "out of control," however, Mexico-U.S. migration by the early 1980s had evolved into a stable system with an identifiable structure. In this chapter, we describe the practical operation of this system from 1965 to 1985, focusing on seven key junctures in the migratory career: leaving, crossing, arriving, working, remitting, returning, and departing again. We show that at each step, Mexicans behaved in logical, consistent ways to produce a stable migratory system that yielded a well-defined population of transnational migrants.

Steps in the Migratory Career, 1965 to 1985

Our empirical characterization of Mexico-U.S. migration is based on data from the Mexican Migration Project (MMP), a large, binational data set for which detailed information has been compiled over the past two decades on documented and undocumented migrants from a diverse set of seventy-one binational communities created through the continuous movement of inhabitants back and forth across the border. At the time of this writing, the MMP database included 12,322 households and 83,527 subjects, of whom 17,602 had taken at least one trip to the United States. The MMP and its data files are described in appendix A, and complete documentation and all data from the project are available from the MMP website (*www.pop.upenn.edu/mexmig/*). Systematic evaluations of these data have shown them to be reliable and accurate. Although the MMP database is not strictly representative of either Mexico or Mexican migrants, in practical terms the characteristics of migrants included in the MMP sample closely match those identified in a representative national survey (Zenteno and Massey 1999). Unlike the representative surveys, however, the MMP data provide a wealth of detailed information about the migrant experience itself and generally do a better job of capturing household members who are temporarily absent for work abroad (Massey and Zenteno 2000).

Leaving

The starting point in any migratory process is the decision to leave on a first trip. We use MMP data on date of first trip to compute the probability that Mexican men and women undertook an initial trip to the United States in the years from 1965 through 1985 (see figure 4.1). Following the procedures of Douglas Massey and Marcela Cerrutti (2001), we take all person-years observed in our sample during this period and follow individuals through life beginning at age fifteen. The denominator of our ratio is the number of men or women alive in a particular year who have *never* been to the United States, and the numerator is the number of those people who left on their first U.S. trip during the year in question. Probabilities are estimated separately for men and women and for those with and without documents. To smooth out irregularities stemming from sampling error and to clarify long-term trends, we follow Timothy Hatton and Jeffrey Williamson (1998) and express the yearly probabilities as three-year moving averages. The resulting figures are graphed in figure 4.1.

Consistent with the data presented earlier, we see an escalation in the probability of undocumented migration among Mexican men after 1965. In this year the annual probability that a male age fifteen or older would leave on a first undocumented trip was just .007, but by 1975 it had reached .021, a threefold increase in only ten years. Although an annual probability of .021 may not seem like much, if sustained year after year it yields a rather significant cumulative probability of out-migration. For example, if one thousand men, starting at age fifteen, go through life subject to this annual risk of out-migration, roughly one-third of them will have left for the United States by age thirty-five.

Figure 4.1 Probability of a Mexican Taking a First U.S. Trip, 1965 to 1985

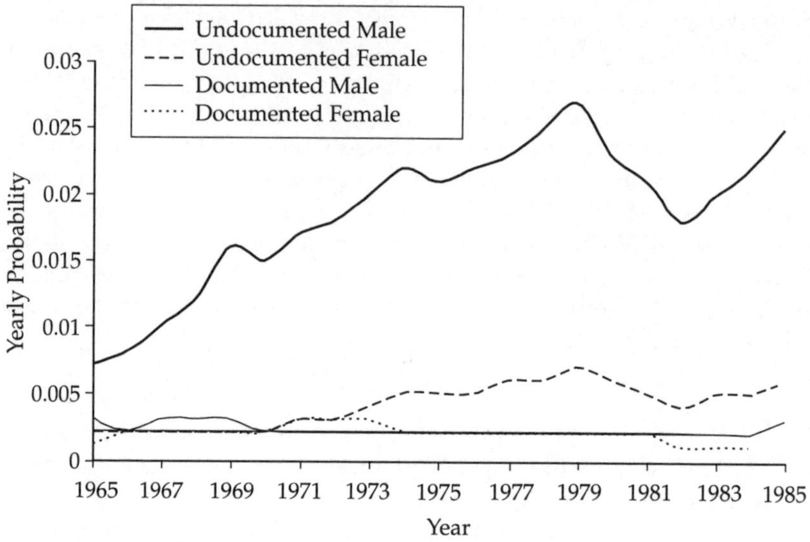

Source: Mexican Migration Project.

Of course, the figure of .021 is an average across all ages above fifteen, including many older men who are relatively unlikely to take a first U.S. trip. In reality, first migration probabilities vary by age in a characteristic way: they start low at age fifteen and rise rapidly to a peak in the twenties before declining gradually. In their analysis, for example, Douglas Massey and René Zenteno (2000) found that the overall probability of out-migration from Mexico to the United States was .004 among males age ten to fourteen, but rose to .071 among those age twenty to twenty-four, then fell to .059 in the age interval twenty-five to twenty-nine, to .042 in the interval thirty to thirty-four, and to .028 in the interval thirty-five to thirty-nine. As a result, the actual likelihood of taking a first trip between ages fifteen and thirty-five is much higher than the average of .021 would suggest, with cumulative likelihoods more in the range of 55 to 65 percent (see Massey 1985; Massey et al. 1987; Phillips and Massey 2000).

The purpose of the present exercise is not to study how migration probabilities vary over the life cycle, however, but to see how they change over time. As figure 4.1 indicates, after steep increases following the end of the bracero program, there was a pause in the mid-1970s and then a renewed increase that peaked in 1979. The probability of undocumented male migration fell sharply during the heyday of the Mexican oil boom (1979 to 1982), but once the peso devaluation had triggered economic collapse in late 1982, undocumented migration by men resumed its secular rise, reaching .025 in 1985.

In contrast to the changing probabilities of male undocumented migration, there were few shifts over time in the likelihood of male documented migration. Among both males and females with documents, annual probabilities of out-migration never exceeded .004 throughout the period. There was a small surge in the probability of legal migration among men in the late 1960s, probably reflecting the legalization of sons of former braceros (who were themselves legalized by their employers in the late 1950s and early 1960s). There is also a flatter and more modest increase in the probability of legal migration among women between 1965 and 1975 (probably the wives and daughters of former braceros), but by the mid-1970s these two minor waves of legalization had run their course, and the odds of taking a first trip with documents remained at very low levels through the rest of the 1970s and early 1980s.

During the 1970s, however, there was a modest but sustained increase in the likelihood of *undocumented* migration by women, with annual probabilities reaching levels of around .007 by the end of the decade. As undocumented men made additional trips and stayed longer north of the border, they increasingly brought along their dependents, and as men spent longer periods of time away from the community, the wives themselves began to pressure their husbands to let them come along, yielding the observed increase in undocumented migration by females (see Cerrutti and Massey 2001).

Despite this increase, and irrespective of the relatively high likelihood of male undocumented migration, we find little evidence that the migratory system was spinning "out of control" in the 1980s. On the contrary, figure 4.1 suggests that relative stability had been achieved by the late 1970s and that during the short economic boom that preceded 1982, probabilities of undocumented migration actually declined among men. The acceleration after 1982 was more of a return to the status quo ante of the 1970s than a dramatic new upsurge in undocumented movement.

Crossing

For undocumented migrants, deciding to depart for the United States is only the first step in a longer and more involved social process. The next hurdle is crossing the border. With the breakdown of the bracero

Figure 4.2 Linewatch-Hours and Apprehensions at the Mexico-U.S. Border, 1965 to 1985

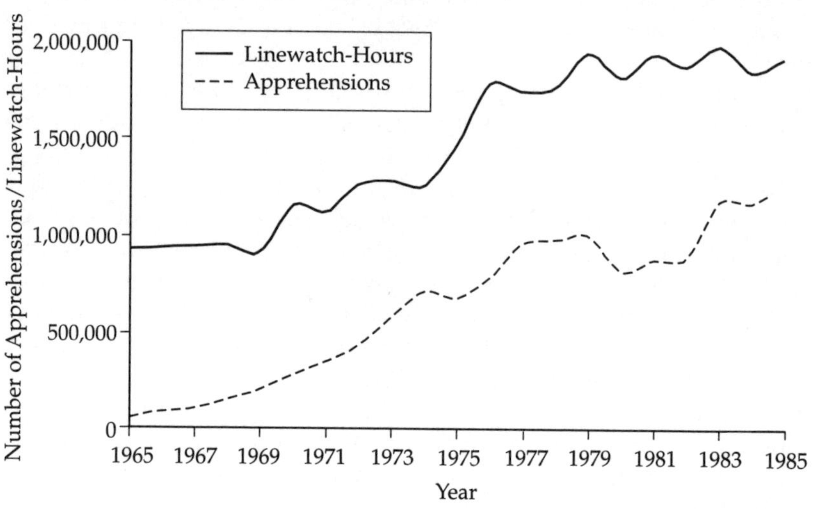

Source: U.S. Immigration and Naturalization Service.

regime in the early 1960s, the INS shifted to a strategy of frontline deterrence that involved a ritualized cat-and-mouse game between Border Patrol officers and undocumented migrants along the border; this strategy became institutionalized as the "voluntary departure complex." After 1965 the INS began to request and receive new resources to hire Border Patrol officers. The additional enforcement resources yielded a growing number of apprehensions, and the increase in apprehensions, in turn, justified the need for more enforcement resources, which yielded still more apprehensions to create a self-feeding cycle of escalation (see Heyman 1995; Andreas 2000).

Figure 4.2 depicts this concomitant rise in enforcement and apprehensions from 1965 through 1985. In the mid-1960s Border Patrol officers fielded just under 1 million "linewatch-hours" per year (1 million person-hours spent patrolling the border). Starting around 1969, however, the number of linewatch-hours began to move significantly upward as more Border Patrol agents were added, with a particularly dramatic increase around 1975. By the early 1980s the annual number of linewatch-hours was fluctuating at just under 2 million.

Although apprehensions and linewatch-hours both increased rapidly from 1965 to 1980, it does not necessarily follow that migrants experienced a higher risk of arrest and deportation over this period.

Figure 4.3 Probability of Apprehension on an Undocumented Border Crossing, 1965 to 1985

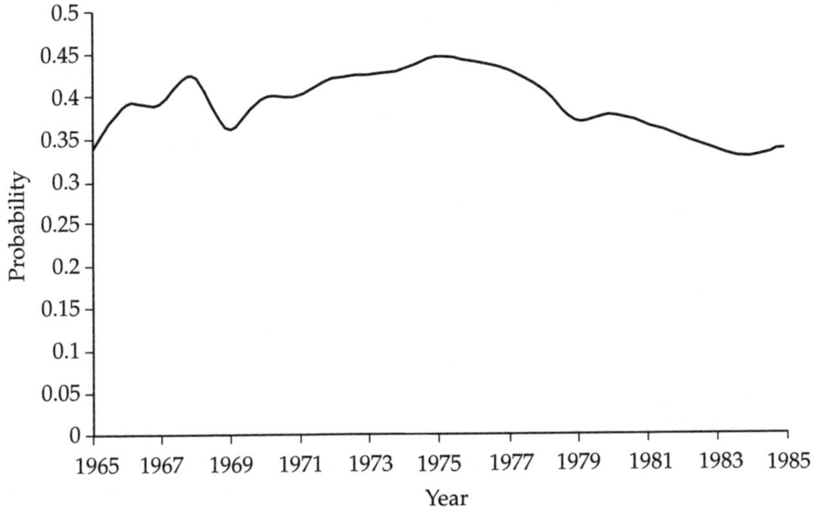

Source: Mexican Migration Project.

Indeed, our data suggest that the rising enforcement effort kept pace with the growing volume of undocumented migration, yielding a relatively constant probability of apprehension. The MMP data include complete histories of border crossing for all undocumented household heads. These histories provide counts of the number of apprehensions experienced while crossing the border on each undocumented trip. They allow us to compute annual probabilities of apprehension, following the approach of Massey and Singer (1995). The resulting probabilities of apprehension are shown in figure 4.3 for the period 1965 to 1985.

During the first fifteen years after 1965, when apprehensions and linewatch-hours were both increasing, there was no clear trend in the odds of getting caught while attempting to cross the border. The probability of apprehension fluctuated between .35 and .45 and averaged around .40. After 1981 the likelihood of apprehension fell somewhat, reflecting the stabilization of linewatch-hours as the likelihood of undocumented migration continued to increase, but by 1985 the probability of apprehension had once again stabilized in the range of .33. In other words, during the early 1980s Mexican migrants crossing the border surreptitiously could expect to evade detection and slip through successfully on roughly two of every three attempts. These figures provide little evidence of a border out of control. U.S. enforcement efforts kept pace with the volume of undocumented migration from 1965 through 1980, yielding a relatively constant probability of apprehension.

One reason U.S. enforcement efforts never increased the odds of capture much above 40 percent is that undocumented Mexicans are able to marshal significant social resources to facilitate clandestine entry and avoid detection. As time progressed, more and more Mexicans could draw upon the prior experience of family members to help them get across. Singer and Massey (1998) have shown that having a relative who has already undertaken a border crossing increases the likelihood of using a formal crossing guide, which in turn decreases the likelihood of getting caught. As figure 4.4 shows, the percentage of migrants who reported having a U.S. migrant sibling rose steadily over the period, as did the percentage using the services of a *coyote*, or paid border smuggler.

The percentage of first-time migrants with siblings who had already been to the United States rose from 38 percent in 1965 to 48 percent in 1985, while the percentage using a *coyote* went from 40 percent in 1965 to values in excess of 70 percent after 1975. In other words, the increasing devotion of INS person-hours to border enforcement was countered by the greater use of paid guides, and to a lesser extent of experienced family members. As the U.S. government withdrew its sponsorship of documented border crossing by terminating the bracero program and tightening legal immigration, private entrepreneurs (coyotes) rushed in to fill the gap, creating an informal border-crossing industry and an extensive social infrastructure to support and sustain undocumented migration.

Arriving

Among all the U.S. states, Texas shares the longest border with Mexico and is closest to Mexico's interior population centers. During the first half of the twentieth century, Texas served as the principal point of entry for most Mexican migrants to the United States. It was here that the earliest transnational rail lines crossed the border and private recruitment firms located. Prior to the 1940s, migrants to other U.S. states generally went through Texas. Given their long-standing and direct access to Mexican labor, growers in Texas at first had little interest in the bracero program and initially did not participate in bracero recruitment; their lack of involvement was fine with Mexican authorities, since Texas had a well-deserved reputation for prejudice

Figure 4.4 Access to Border-Crossing Guides and Migrant Siblings on First U.S. Trip, 1965 to 1985

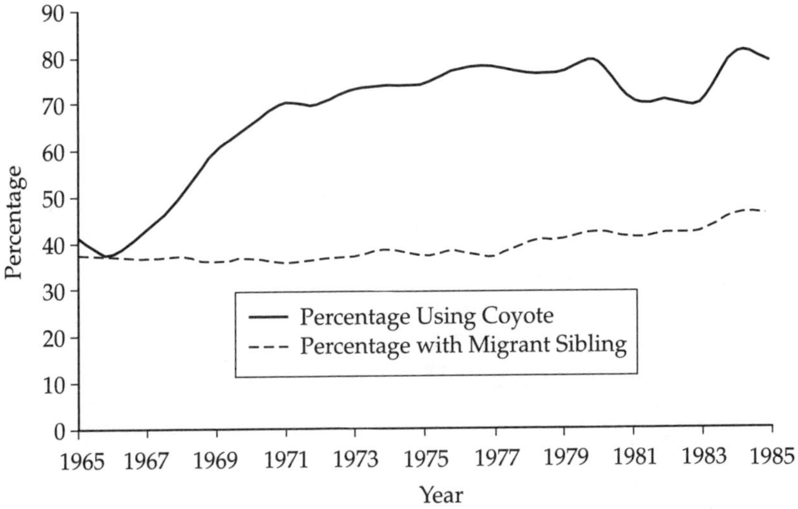

Source: Mexican Migration Project.

and discrimination toward Mexicans. It was not until 1954–55, in the wake of Operation Wetback, which simultaneously cracked down on undocumented migration and expanded bracero migration as the only permissible way to gain access to Mexican workers, that growers in Texas began to participate. The bracero program was thus instrumental in channeling the movement of Mexican workers away from Texas and toward California. According to U.S. census data, only 22 percent of all Mexican immigrants resided in California during 1920, and by 1940 the figure was only 36 percent. After two decades of bracero migration, however, the percentage had risen to 53 percent in 1970, and among those Mexican immigrants who arrived between 1965 and 1970, 60 percent went to California (Durand, Massey, and Charvet 2000).

The dominance of California as an immigrant destination is reflected in the MMP data. As figure 4.5 shows, throughout the period 1965 to 1985 the percentage of migrants going to California fluctuated closely around 70 percent, with about 40 percent going to southern California alone, and 30 percent going to Los Angeles. With the institutionalization of California as a leading destination and Los Angeles as the premier urban magnet, the percentage of Mexican immigrants crossing at Tijuana increased steadily from about 28 percent in 1965 to

Figure 4.5 The Geography of Border Crossing, 1965 to 1985

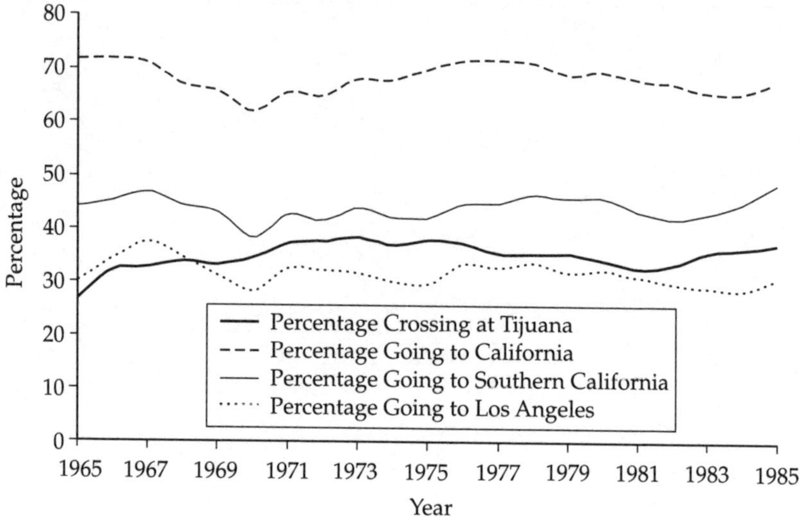

Source: Mexican Migration Project.

around 38 percent in 1985. The de facto guest-worker system of undocumented migration was thus anchored in California, and with the exception of Chicago, nearly all the rest went to other southwestern locations. The effects of Mexican migration were thus limited to a handful of border states: Arizona, California, New Mexico, and Texas, plus Illinois, the exception that proves the rule. Although massive in scale, Mexican immigration during the undocumented era was relatively restricted geographically.

Working

Although the bracero program recruited migrants almost exclusively for work in agriculture (there was for a time a small program of railroad recruitment), by 1965 most Mexican immigrants were working in other sectors. What the bracero program did was provide an opening to 4.5 million Mexican men, giving them initial experience, contacts, and an opportunity to familiarize themselves with English, U.S. employment practices, and other aspects of U.S. society. As more Mexicans acquired these resources, increasingly they used them to qualify for more stable, better-paying jobs, often in urban areas. Studies have shown that as migrants accrue education, U.S. experience, and English-language skills, they are increasingly likely to shift

Figure 4.6 Occupation on First U.S. Trip, 1965 to 1985

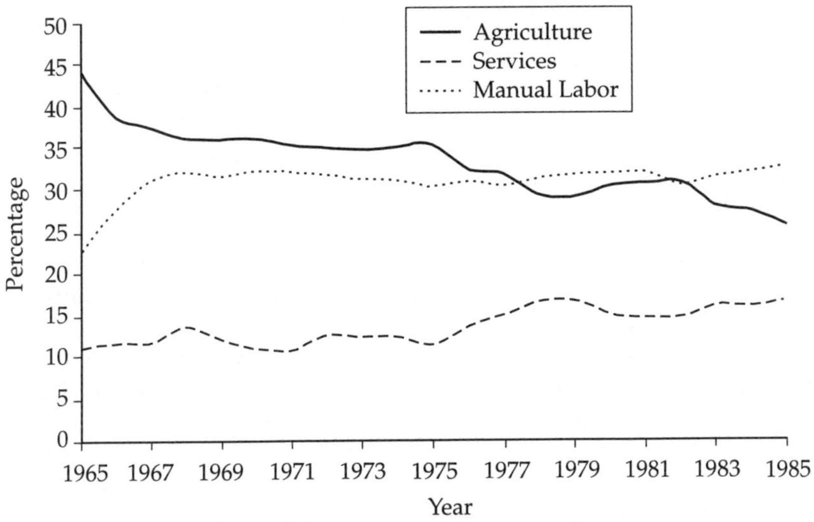

Source: Mexican Migration Project.

from agricultural to industrial work and from rural to urban areas (Massey et al. 1987). The net result has been a steady movement of both documented and undocumented migrants away from agriculture.

The evolving occupational composition of Mexican migrants is shown in figure 4.6, which depicts the percentage of migrants working in agriculture, services, and manual labor on their first U.S. trip. The main trend is one of slow decline in the prevalence of agricultural work, from around 45 percent of all migrants leaving in 1965 to about 25 percent of those leaving in 1985. This shift reflects the growing mechanization of agriculture as well as the expansion of urban employment opportunities. It is accompanied by modest gains in other occupational categories. There was a dip in the relative number of manual workers during the oil boom of 1980 to 1982, but it rebounded quickly with the onset of the economic crisis.

Wages were also fairly stable throughout the period, at least in nominal terms, hovering at around $4.00 per hour (data not shown). The percentage of workers earning below the legal minimum wage fell initially, then rose and stabilized. Whereas 13 percent of migrants reported wages below the legal minimum in 1965, the percentage bottomed out at around 10 percent during the first half of the 1970s, then rose rapidly to reach 20 percent in 1980, where it remained. Prior research shows that there was little wage discrimination on the basis of legal status prior to 1986: documented and undocumented workers earned the same hourly wage once relevant background characteristics (such as education and experience) were controlled (Massey 1987a; Phillips and Massey 1999).

Remitting

The massive movement of migrants to the United States for work does not imply a lack of connection to families and communities in Mexico. When they first leave for the United States, most migrants are not interested in relocating north of the border permanently. This assertion is backed up by the very high rates at which money is remitted back to families at home and the extensive repatriation of U.S. savings. The primary motivation for most new migrants is to deal with economic problems in Mexico through short-term work in the United States.

As shown in figure 4.7, throughout the undocumented era the vast majority of migrants sent regular remittances back to Mexico and most also returned with savings. The percentage remitting fluctuated over time but generally rose from 60 percent or less in the early 1960s to over 70 percent in the early 1980s. Over the same period the percentage who returned with savings went from 45 to 50 percent in the late 1960s to around 65 percent in the early 1980s. By 1985 the total volume of money repatriated to Mexico by migrants working in the United States exceeded $2 billion per year, and in some communities the flow of "migradollars" equaled or exceeded the value of all locally earned income (Massey and Parrado 1994). Although most migradollars were spent on consumption, households also invested in productive enterprises when personal circumstances and community conditions warranted (Durand, Parrado, and Massey 1996). For a majority of Mexicans leaving on their first U.S. trip, foreign labor was not a strategy for lifetime income maximization through permanent settlement abroad, but a means of solving short-term problems at home and improving their lives in Mexico.

Returning

The high rates of remitting reported by Mexican migrants in the undocumented era suggest that most of them saw migration as a temporary strategy and that they anticipated returning to Mexico. As figure 4.8 indicates, the likelihood of returning to Mexico within two years of departure was indeed quite high among undocumented males,

Figure 4.7 Migrants Who Remitted and Returned with Savings, 1965 to 1985

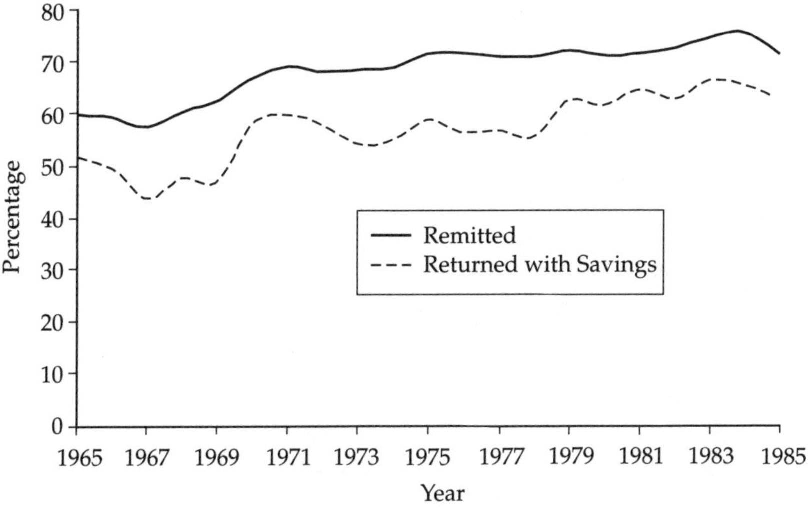

Source: Mexican Migration Project.

with the probability generally ranging from .55 to .60. Undocumented women were less likely than men to return once they had begun migrating, owing to the greater risks faced by women in clandestine border crossing. (In addition to robbery and the usual risks of injury, thirst, or drowning, they also face the threat of sexual assault.) Except for the years 1973 to 1977, the likelihood that an undocumented woman would return to Mexico within two years was in the .30 to .40 range throughout the undocumented era. Several studies indicate that once women begin migrating, the odds of a family's permanent settlement increase substantially (Massey et al. 1987; Kanaiaupuni 2000; Espinosa 1998; Cerrutti and Massey 2001). Nonetheless, a return probability of .40 to .50 within two years is still quite high.

Documented migrants display a clearer tendency to remain in the United States. For documented men, the likelihood of return migration fell from .50 in 1965 to values fluctuating around .20 to .30 in the late 1970s and early 1980s. The odds of return migration among documented women also seemed to stabilize in the same range during this period. Thus, even among documented migrants the odds of return migration were still significant—about 20 to 30 percent during the early 1980s, an estimate roughly in line with those developed by other

Figure 4.8 Probability of Returning Within Two Years of Entering the United States on First Trip, 1965 to 1985

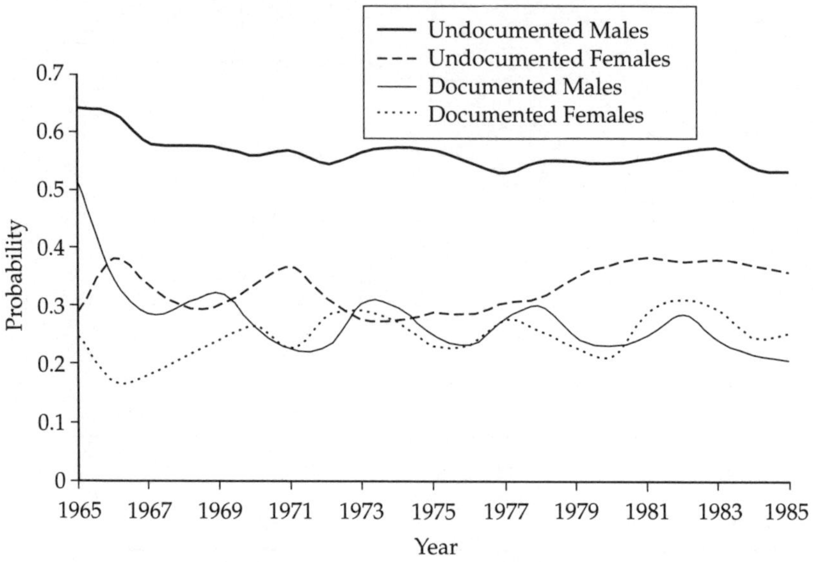

Source: Mexican Migration Project.

researchers using different data sources (Jasso and Rosenzweig 1982; Warren and Kraly 1985). Given these propensities for return migration, the net inflow of undocumented migrants was rather modest during the undocumented era, despite the size of the gross inflow. Massey and Singer (1995) estimate that 26.7 million undocumented migrants entered the United States from 1965 to 1985, but that these entries were offset by 21.8 million departures, yielding a net increase of just 4.9 million over a twenty-year period.

Going Again

Returning to Mexico to rejoin family and friends, reincorporate into the community, and make use of migradollars for consumption or investment is not the end of the story, however, for return only sets the stage for another round of migration. Once a migrant has left and returned, he or she is very likely to make another U.S. trip, setting off another cycle of crossing, arriving, working, remitting, and returning. Studies consistently show that once someone has migrated, the odds of going again are quite high (Massey 1985; Massey 1987b; Massey et

Figure 4.9 Probability of Taking a Second U.S. Trip for Male Household Heads, 1965 to 1985

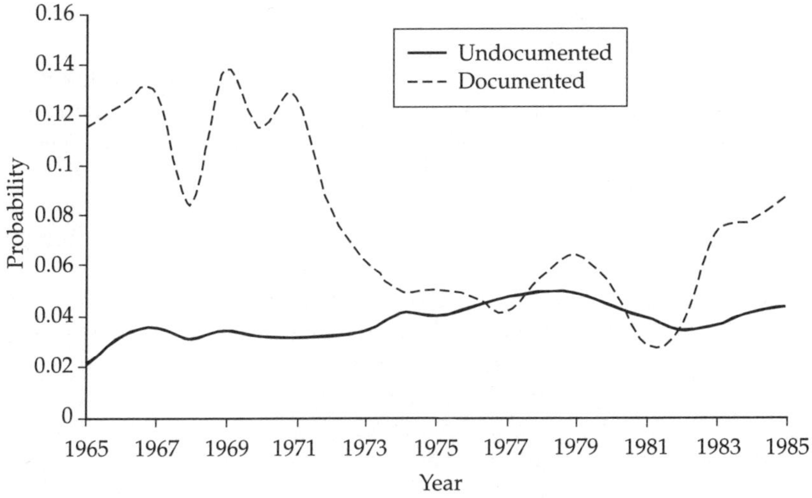

Source: Mexican Migration Project.

al. 1987; Donato 1998). Because the initial trip affords an opportunity to acquire valuable human capital (English-language ability and U.S. work experience) as well as new tastes and motivations, the odds of taking another trip grow with each trip already taken.

The MMP data do not allow us to compute annual probabilities of taking a second trip for all migrants, only for male household heads. Figure 4.9 thus shows the odds of taking a second U.S. trip for male heads with and without documents. These figures demonstrate the higher risk of migration once someone has been to the United States. Whereas the annual probability of taking a first undocumented trip starts at .007 in 1965 and peaks at .027 around 1980, the likelihood of taking a second trip begins at .020 and slowly rises to a high of .050 in 1979, a value that is nearly twice as high. Since 1980 the likelihood of taking a second trip without documents has fluctuated around a value of .040, with little change in spite of the onset of the economic crisis in 1982.

Although migrants with documents are much less likely to return to Mexico than those who lack the legal right to live and work in the United States, every year a significant fraction of legal U.S. residents do in fact go back to Mexico. As figure 4.8 shows, in the period 1965 to 1973 these legal immigrants displayed a significantly higher likelihood of returning to the United States than their undocumented counterparts. Starting around 1974, however, the probability of repeat migration fell substantially for documented migrants and fluctuated around .04 until the onset of the economic crisis in 1982, when the odds of remigration rose once again.

In sum, from 1973 through 1983 the annual probability of taking a second U.S. trip stabilized at around .04 for both documented and undocumented migrants, roughly twice the probability that a Mexican male would undertake a first undocumented trip. Thus, the simple fact that a migrant had already been to the United States dramatically increased the odds that he or she would go again. Although an annual probability of .04 may not seem very high, once again, over a prolonged period, it yields very high cumulative rates of out-migration. If 1,000 Mexicans were to return from their first U.S. trip and experience an annual probability of remigration of .04, then after ten years 330 would have made a second trip, and after twenty years 55 percent would have gone again. As with first migration, the odds of going again vary by age: the very high levels for those in their twenties fall for those in their thirties, then reach low levels for migrants in their forties and fifties.

The Migrants

The foregoing results suggest that the termination of the bracero program and the imposition of new restrictions on legal entry after 1965 combined with a steady increase in border enforcement to generate a relatively stable, predictable, and routinized system of labor migration by the late 1970s, yielding a population of international migrants readily identifiable in terms of demographic, socioeconomic, and migratory characteristics. Table 4.1 draws on MMP data compiled for all migrants about their most recent U.S. trip to profile the binational population of Mexican migrants prevailing in the undocumented era, dividing the era into two cohorts: those who left on their latest trip from 1965 to 1974 and those who left between 1975 and 1985.

As the table reveals, the profile of a Mexican migrant remained remarkably constant over the course of the undocumented era. Roughly two-thirds were men, and most of them were married. The vast majority came from midsize towns and cities. Just under one-fifth were from rural villages (2,500 or fewer inhabitants). The average age was twenty-one to twenty-three. Reflecting Mexico's relatively low level of educational development, migrants averaged about five years of schooling, but the typical migrant had considerable work experience, averaging eighteen years. Only a little more than one-

Table 4.1 Characteristics of Mexican Migrants on Last U.S. Trip, 1965 to 1985

Category and Characteristic	Migrated 1965 to 1974	Migrated 1975 to 1985	Total
Demographic			
Male	65.2%	67.6%	67.0%
Married[a]	97.4%	98.6%	98.2%
Rural	18.5%	19.1%	19.0%
Average age	21.1%	22.7%	22.3%
Socioeconomic[b]			
Average years of education	5.0	5.5	5.4
Years of work experience	17.9	17.6	17.7
Agrarian	28.0%	25.7%	26.3%
Unskilled	22.2%	24.0%	23.6%
Services	12.0%	15.8%	14.9%
Skilled	10.8%	8.5%	9.1%
Social capital			
Migrant parent[c]	42.6%	37.4%	38.7%
Migrant sibling[c]	16.6%	18.2%	17.8%
Adults with U.S. experience	27.8%	33.3%	31.9%
Migratory			
Documented	44.9%	33.0%	36.1%
Average number of trips	1.9	2.0	2.0
Average years of U.S. experience	14.1	7.7	9.4
Strategy of migration			
Temporary	30.6%	37.7%	35.6%
Recurrent	4.5%	5.2%	5.0%
Settled but returned	13.5%	13.2%	13.3%
Settled and stayed	51.5%	38.5%	41.8%

Source: Mexican Migration Project.
a. Male household heads only.
b. Migrants age sixteen or older.
c. Sample of parents and children only.

quarter of the migrants came from an agrarian occupational background, nearly another one-quarter were unskilled manual workers, about 16 percent were service workers, and just under 10 percent reported a skilled occupation.

A typical migrant thinking about making a trip to El Norte had access to considerable social resources. Around 40 percent had a parent with U.S. experience, around 18 percent had a migrant sibling, and the typical person came from a community where one-third of the townspeople had been to the United States. The typical migrant also had considerable personal resources to facilitate international movement, having made two U.S. trips already on average. Those who traveled between 1965 and 1974 boasted nearly fourteen years of total U.S. experience, whereas those who left from 1975 to 1985 had about eight years of total experience. Reflecting the increasingly scarce avenues for legal migration, the percentage of documented migrants dropped from 45 percent in the period 1965 to 1974 to 33 percent from 1975 to 1985. Reflecting the fact that two-thirds of the most recent cohort were undocumented, a distinct minority had adopted a strategy of permanent settlement in the United States: 38 percent had undertaken only temporary sporadic moves, 6 percent were moving back and forth recurrently, and 13 percent had settled (stayed for more than three years) but then returned. Only 37 percent had adopted a strategy of permanent settlement, the vast majority of them documented.

The foregoing profile was based on data for all persons with U.S. experience identified in the MMP database. More detailed information about migrants' last trip is available from a battery of questions asked only of household heads with U.S. experience, and these data are summarized in table 4.2. The vast majority of household heads migrating in the period 1965 to 1985 were *not* accompanied by a spouse. In general, less than one-fifth of the migrants reported having a spouse in the United States, and even fewer (16 percent) were accompanied by children. Those children who did accompany the household head northward were generally older sons joining their father for work.

While in the United States, migrants generally worked hard, putting in an average of forty-five to forty-six hours of work per week for around eight months per year. The employment rate was 96 percent, and most worked in formal jobs that were paid by check with federal taxes deducted. Only some 18 percent reported being paid in cash, which is generally a sign of informal employment, and only 36 percent indicated that no federal taxes were withheld from their pay. In keeping with the high rate of labor force participation, the vast majority of migrants had never drawn upon U.S. social services on any of their U.S. trips. Despite their generally low incomes, on average only 13 percent had ever received unemployment benefits, only 5 percent reported ever receiving food stamps, only 3 percent had ever received welfare, and only 1 percent left unpaid medical bills. (Recall that about one-third of the migrants were documented and thus *entitled* to these benefits.) Only 19 percent had ever had a child enrolled

Table 4.2 Situation of Migrant Household Heads on Last U.S. Trip, 1965 to 1985

Category and Characteristic	Migrated 1965 to 1974	Migrated 1975 to 1985	Total
Social situation			
With spouse in United States	21.1%	16.5%	18.0%
With children in United States	17.9%	15.0%	16.0%
Average number of immediate family in United States	1.2	1.4	1.3
Economic situation			
Employed	95.2%	96.3%	96.0%
Average hours worked per week	46.2	45.6	45.8
Average months worked per year	7.9	8.1	8.0
Paid in cash	18.8%	17.0%	17.5%
Paying federal taxes	63.1%	64.6%	64.1%
Use of social services			
With child in U.S. schools	22.1%	17.4%	18.8%
Ever received unemployment	16.4%	11.0%	12.6%
Ever received food stamps	5.3%	4.7%	4.9%
Ever received welfare	3.6%	3.3%	3.4%
Reporting unpaid medical bills	0.4%	1.5%	1.2%

Source: Mexican Migration Project.

in a U.S. school, although the figure was higher (22 percent) among those in the earlier cohort.

Parameters of a Stable System

During the late 1960s and early 1970s a new migratory regime arose in North America to replace the bracero system, which had ended in 1964. Given the increasing restrictions on access to legal resident visas, the new regime was based largely on the movement of undocumented migrants. From 1965 to 1970 the odds of male undocumented migration rose substantially, and by the mid-1980s that rate had reached a steady state roughly on a par with that of the bracero era. The likelihood of undocumented migration by women, or of documented migration by either men or women, changed little between 1965 and 1985 and remained at fairly low levels throughout the period. As in the earlier era, movement during the undocumented era was highly circular, and crossing the border was not difficult. While working in the United States, Mexican migrants maintained strong contact with their home communities and regularly sent back monthly remittances, and most returned with savings. Given these ongoing investments in Mexico, a majority of undocumented men returned within two years of arriving in the United States, although the odds of remigration were significant.

All of these processes came to be characterized by stable, measurable empirical parameters. By 1985 the yearly probability of first migration for undocumented men stood at around 2.5 percent; the likelihood that they would return home within two years was around 55 percent; and the probability that they would go again was about 4 percent. The odds of being apprehended on any given attempt at clandestine border crossing were about one in three, and nearly everyone got in after a few tries. Two-thirds went to California, and around 40 percent crossed the border near Tijuana. Roughly two-thirds of all migrants regularly sent home remittances, and about the same fraction returned with savings. The yearly probabilities of first migration for undocumented women were generally under 0.7 percent, as was the probability of first migration with documents for both men and women.

Over the course of the undocumented migrant era, these parameters produced a stable, well-defined population of international migrants who were young (the average age was in the early twenties), largely undocumented (two-thirds lacked legal visas), heavily male (two-thirds were men), and drawn mostly from Mexican small towns and cities (nearly three-quarters came from communities with populations between 2,500 and 100,000). These migrants went to a handful of states. Although their educational levels were modest by U.S. standards, they were typical for those prevailing in Mexico, and the vast majority of migrants (nearly 80 percent) were from a non-agricultural background.

Drawing upon substantial stocks of social capital accumulated during the years of the bracero program, migrants easily entered the United States and found employment. Most pursued a temporary or recurrent migration strategy, and relatively few settled north of the border permanently. The typical trip lasted around nine months, and the average migrant had accumulated two prior trips and nine years of U.S. experience. According to our classification scheme, only around 39 percent pursued a settled migration strategy, whereas 43 percent were pursuing a temporary or recurrent strategy; another 13 percent had returned to Mexico after spending at least three years abroad. In keeping with the transient nature of their stay in the United States, 80 percent of migrants were not accompanied by their spouse, and an even larger share had no children with them. Life in El Norte was dedicated mainly to work, with the typical migrant working forty-five hours a week for eight months. The vast majority (more than 80 percent) worked in formal jobs for which wages were paid by check and federal taxes were generally deducted. In the course of their serial trips, migrants were relatively unlikely to have made use of U.S. social services such as welfare, food stamps, unemployment insurance, and schools.

The evidence is thus consistent in showing that a relatively stable, smoothly functioning migration system was functioning in the mid-1980s. In general, it was a system that minimized the negative consequences and maximized the gain for both countries. The United States got a steady supply of workers for jobs that natives were loath to take, and by slowly increasing the enforcement effort in tandem with the volume of undocumented migration, it maintained a level of deterrence that selected workers who were both the ablest and the least likely to carry serious social costs: young men of prime productive age traveling without dependents. Illegal status had the added benefit of encouraging migrants to return home. Given the relatively porous border, however, migrants knew that they could return to the United States for additional labor whenever the need arose, thus encouraging a pattern of circular rather than settled migration. Moreover, since the hiring of undocumented workers was completely legal, employers had no incentive to discriminate on the basis of legal status, limiting downward pressure on wages. Finally, for historical reasons, the direct effects on the United States of Mexican migration—both positive and negative—were regionally isolated and confined to a very small number of states.

For its part, Mexico got an "escape valve" that reduced employment pressures as it went through a series of crises leading to a massive structural transformation, yet the circularity of the movement meant that the migrants were not permanently lost for productive purposes. Mexico also acquired an important source of foreign exchange in the form of migrant remittances and savings. By the late 1980s migradollars totaled around $2 billion per year, making labor one of Mexico's leading exports: its revenues constituted 90 percent of Mexico's earnings from agricultural exports, 78 percent of its direct foreign investment, 59 percent of its earnings from tourism, and 56 percent of its earnings from the *maquila* industry (Massey and Parrado 1994). Because this money was quickly spent, moreover, it had important multiplier effects within the Mexican economy. Jorge Durand, Emilio Parrado, and Douglas Massey (1996) have estimated that the annual arrival of 2 billion migradollars generated $6.5 billion worth of additional production in Mexico, with particularly strong multiplier effects in the manufacturing and service sectors.

In 1986, however, this stable system came to an end as politicians in the United States manufactured an immigration "crisis" and created the false impression that the border was out of control. These constructions represented a form of symbolic politics that served domestic political purposes but had little to do with the real circumstances of Mexico-U.S. migration. Nonetheless, they led to a variety of legislative actions and policy shifts that had profound consequences for Mexico-U.S. migration. After 1986 the United States unilaterally embarked on a series of repressive policies, police actions, and political campaigns that dramatically changed the rules of system operation, ushering in a new era in Mexico-U.S. migration and guaranteeing that in the future its consequences would be neither benign nor limited.

Chapter 5

A Wrench in the Works: U.S. Immigration Policies After 1986

THE YEAR 1986 was pivotal for the political economy of North America. In that year, two events signaled the end of one era and the beginning of another: Mexico's entry into the General Agreement on Tariffs and Trade (GATT) and passage by the U.S. Congress of the Immigration Reform and Control Act (IRCA). In Mexico a new political elite had succeeded in overcoming historical opposition within the ruling party and orchestrated the country's entry into GATT. Then they boldly approached the United States to forge a new alliance that would ultimately create a free trade zone stretching from Central America to the North Pole. Even as U.S. officials worked closely with Mexican authorities to integrate the North American economy, however, they simultaneously acted to prevent the integration of its labor markets. Rather than incorporating the movement of workers into the new trade agreement, the United States insisted on the right to control its borders, and to underscore its resolve Congress passed IRCA.

Thereafter the United States would pursue a politics of contradiction—simultaneously moving toward integration while insisting on separation. In time-honored fashion, the United States sought to have its cake and eat it too—to move headlong toward a consolidation of markets for capital, goods, commodities, and information, but simultaneously to pretend that North American labor markets would remain separate and distinct. In the ensuing years the United States would spend increasing financial and human resources to demonstrate to the American public that the border was under control and *not* porous with respect to migrants or drugs, even as it was becoming increasingly permeable with respect to numerous other flows. Admitting Mexican workers while pretending not to do so was nothing new. But whereas this sort of hypocrisy could be maintained at a relatively low cost during the bracero and undocumented eras, after 1986 the illusion became increasingly expensive to sustain, not only for the migrants themselves but for citizens and taxpayers on both sides of the border.

The Roots of North American Integration

In the decades leading up to the 1980s, Mexico's political economy of import substitution industrialization (ISI) moved steadily toward its demise. As early as 1968, the limitations of ISI had become apparent. In that year what began as a small, localized movement of university students turned into a mass mobilization against the Mexican state. Demonstrators questioned the legitimacy of the political elite that had governed Mexico since the 1910 Revolution and challenged its commitment to social justice and democracy. Although Mexico's state-centered program of economic growth had succeeded in building an industrial infrastructure and creating an urban middle class, it had also brought about rising inequality, a stagnant agrarian economy, a growing concentration of urban poverty, widening regional imbalances, and a self-serving bureaucracy that showed little interest in relinquishing power or allowing reform.

The political mobilization of the late 1960s was ultimately put down by a bloody massacre of student demonstrators in Mexico City (Poniatowska 1971). Although the massacre quelled the uprising for the moment, it severely undermined the government's standing among its citizens and thoroughly compromised its legitimacy. In 1970 a new president, Luis Echeverría, assumed power and sought to restore the state's lost stature. Having been minister of the Interior at the time of the student massacre, and therefore at least formally responsible for the slaughter, he no doubt felt a special need to make amends.

Echeverría sought to refurbish Mexico's revolutionary credentials at home and abroad. Internationally he espoused an ideology of Third World liberation, cultivated relations with Cuba and other leftist governments, and made a point of voting against the United States in public forums such as the United Nations and the Organization of American States (OAS). Domestically he launched a massive expansion of the Mexican state, characterized by a sharp increase in social spending, a growing nationalization of private industry, and a rapid expansion of the federal bureaucracy. Over the course of his presidency the number of state-owned enterprises doubled, from 491 in

1970 to 845 in 1976; over the same period total government employment grew from 616,000 to 2.1 million (Centeno 1994). To protect the inefficient industries he had acquired for the Mexican state, Echeverría tightened barriers to trade by raising tariffs, imposing new quotas, and enacting regulations.

Prior to 1970 Mexican presidents had relied largely on domestic capital to promote national economic development, but domestic sources were insufficient to support Echeverría's ambitious plans. His grandiose spending habits also found little sympathy in the Ministry of the Treasury or among the nation's bankers. He therefore turned to foreign banks and international lending institutions, which happily provided the funds. Rather than channeling the money through the Ministry of the Treasury (Secretaría de Hacienda), however, Echeverría absorbed it directly into the Office of the Presidency, bypassing a traditional check on presidential power (Centeno 1994). The Office of the Presidency also assumed direct control over the distribution of these funds, thereby usurping the patronage functions traditionally managed by the Ministry of the Interior (Secretaría de Gobernación) and further centralizing the president's power and control over the Mexican state.

By 1976 Echeverría's nationalizations, spending, and populist rhetoric had deeply alienated Mexico's private sector. Mexico would have had a difficult time paying its foreign debt under any circumstances, but a loss of faith by entrepreneurs and foreign bankers sparked a massive flight of capital that turned a liquidity problem into a full-blown economic crisis. During his last year in office Echeverría was forced to devalue the peso, which caused inflation to soar to 27 percent per annum. The state's fiscal problems, in turn, compelled him to scale back social spending; to compensate for these humiliating retreats, in his final months he rashly expropriated millions of hectares of private land for ostensible redistribution to peasants. (It was mostly returned by his successor.) In the end Echeverría managed to antagonize virtually all sectors of society without restoring the luster of the Mexican miracle, thus deepening the crisis of the state.

As the date of the presidential succession approached (December 1, 1976), Mexico swirled with rumors of military plots, impending coups, guerrilla uprisings, and assassinations. When the new president, José López Portillo, finally assumed office, Mexico seemed on the brink of economic and political collapse. The private sector was worried about the huge foreign debt and the state's recent interventions in the economy, while international lenders doubted Mexico's ability to repay its ballooning foreign debt. López Portillo needed to reassure both audiences, and he quickly worked to demonstrate his commitment to moderation and reform. In a symbolic gesture, he sent former President Echeverría to the South Pacific as ambassador to Fiji, and in early speeches he promised fiscal reforms and restrained spending. Meanwhile, he discarded the populist poses and leftist rhetoric in favor of a more businesslike approach to national government.

Within a few months these gestures became superfluous, however, for shortly after assuming office López Portillo learned from the state oil company that vast new petroleum deposits had been discovered in the Mexican waters of the Gulf of Campeche. With oil prices spiraling upward, Mexico suddenly emerged as a major oil producer, at least potentially. With visions of petrodollars dancing in their heads, lenders backed off their demands for structural reform and reopened the spigots of capital.

Thanks to the miraculous and unanticipated discovery of oil, López Portillo was literally able to buy his way out of trouble. Rather than addressing the serious economic problems responsible for the problems of 1968 and 1976, he was able to put off the day of reckoning. Assuming that oil prices would remain at astronomic levels, he accelerated social spending and continued Echeverría's expansion of state employment. At the same time he borrowed heavily to cover the huge capital costs of extracting undersea oil and bringing it to market. In the heady days of the late 1970s, López Portillo was not the only leader of an oil-rich country to feel that his nation was somehow immune from the constraints and exigencies of the market. Awash in petrodollars, he believed he did not have to make difficult choices between consumption and investment.

By the dawn of the 1980s, however, new petroleum producers had entered the market, and the oil cartel began to lose its grip on supplies. After years of borrowing to undertake capital investments, oil prices began to fall just as Mexican oil really began to flow. López Portillo was suddenly denied the revenue stream he had counted on to pay off the massive foreign debt, and in the summer of 1982 he was forced to break his promise to defend the Mexican peso "like a dog." The currency was floated and promptly lost half its value. Faced with billions of dollar-denominated loans, Mexico was forced to suspend payments on its foreign debt, which were eating up 43 percent of the national budget (Wilkie 1990).

This time there were no miraculous discoveries to save the situation: the day of reckoning had finally arrived. Over the next year inflation soared to an annual rate of 100 percent, GDP fell by 8 percent, real wages dropped by 21 percent, and the gulf between rich and poor widened markedly (Sheahan 1991; Cortés and Rubalcava

1992). Unable to accept responsibility for the disaster, López Portillo blamed entrepreneurs and bankers for disloyalty and berated them for sending their assets abroad (a course of action that he and his ministers were also pursuing). Against the counsel of his advisers, and with just three months left in office, he suddenly nationalized Mexican banks in a fit of pique that represented the largest single expropriation of private property since the 1930s.

The private sector was stunned, and the move only deepened Mexico's financial problems, which grew into a prolonged economic crisis known as the "lost decade." From 1980 to 1989 Mexican GDP per capita fell by 9 percent, real minimum wages plummeted by 47 percent, and the percentage of families in poverty increased from 45 to 60 percent (Sheahan 1991). López Portillo's bank nationalization proved, however, to be the high-water mark of the old political economy. With a total of 1,155 state-owned entities and one out of every five workers employed either directly or indirectly by the Mexican state, ISI in 1982 had finally reached its limit. Thereafter the tide of state ownership would recede: the neoliberal revolution had begun.

The massive expansion of the state under Echeverría and López Portillo brought to power a new class of forward-looking technocrats who would be instrumental in imposing a new order—neoliberalism—on the Mexican political economy. Effective management of the huge state bureaucracy and its far-flung empire of para-state enterprises required centralized control and planning. To coordinate the growing state apparatus, late in his term Echeverría had instituted a national planning council headed by López Portillo, and when the latter assumed office, he formalized the planning process by creating the Ministry of Planning and Budget (Secretaría de Planificación y Presupuesto), better known by its initials SPP.

All other governmental departments and ministries were required to submit plans to the SPP, and it alone developed the global plan to which all agencies had to conform. It had the final say on policies and priorities, taxing and spending, program creation and elimination. The SPP functioned as a super-ministry with the power to approve or deny ventures throughout the state. Henceforth, whoever was in charge of the SPP would have de facto control of the state itself (Centeno 1994), and the minister of SPP thus became the most powerful person in Mexico after the president himself. It is no coincidence that the next two Mexican presidents were former SPP ministers.

The tasks of planning and budgeting, of course, rely heavily on quantitative data, rational analysis, and technical skills. Those advancing in the new ministry were young (in their thirties and forties) and U.S-educated, with graduate degrees in economics, public administration, or some technical specialty, usually from a prestigious private university. (The next three presidents would hold advanced degrees from either Harvard or Yale.) Growing up in and around Mexico City during the relative prosperity of the economic miracle, and coming from a homogenous class background, the new technocrats had great faith in the soundness of their analyses and their ability to foresee and solve Mexico's problems. With their advanced training, elite educations, and powerful positions in government, they came to believe they had a special mandate to modernize the nation and lead it forward into the next century.

In their view, Mexico's difficulties stemmed from its inward-looking, state-centered economy. They believed that growth, prosperity, and stability could be had only by creating a new, more liberal political economy connected to the global regime of trade and investment. Unlike earlier generations of Mexican politicians, they were neither suspicious nor resentful of the United States. Having been educated there, they understood it well and sought to capitalize on Mexico's privileged geographic position adjacent to the world's largest market to catapult it to the ranks of the First World.

The 1968 student massacre and the crises of 1976 and 1982 had thoroughly discredited the old regime, leaving it with little popular support. After 1982 modernizing neoliberals in the SPP took advantage of this opening and used their powerful positions to impose their technocratic vision on an often reluctant country, frequently running roughshod over the ruling party's older politicos, whom they derisively called "dinosaurs." President Miguel de la Madrid laid the foundations for the neoliberal revolution by lowering tariffs, abandoning quotas, easing state regulations, improving tax collections, rescheduling the foreign debt, privatizing enterprises, limiting wage increases, cutting social spending, balancing the budget, and attacking (at least symbolically) the corruption of the López Portillo era. In the fourth year of his term he decisively broke from the past by securing Mexico's entry into GATT, which in both real and symbolic terms inaugurated the neoliberal era in Mexican society.

Rather than seeking to create closed internal markets, de la Madrid and the neoliberals sought to attract foreign investment to produce goods for sale on international markets, following the model of export industrialization used so effectively by the "Asian Tigers" of the 1970s. Despite de la Madrid's reforms and his relative success in restructuring the country economically, however, the crisis was hardly over. As oil prices experienced a new round of deflation, economic conditions deteriorated and domestic inflation reached new heights, soaring to 106 percent in 1986 and 159 percent in 1987. Not surprisingly, given the economic pain it was inflicting on citizens, the government had not regained the legitimacy it lost in 1968.

As a result, the presidential succession of 1988 proved unusually difficult for the ruling party to manage. Historically the president simply named his successor, who was then duly nominated by the ruling party and ratified by national election. De la Madrid named as his successor Carlos Salinas de Gortari, but rather than rubber-stamping the nomination, party traditionalists protested. When they were overruled, some broke with the party to launch an independent left-wing campaign led by Cuautehmoc Cárdenas, son of Mexico's most revered president, who eventually went on to form a party known as PRD (Partido de la Revolución Democrática). At the same time the center-right mobilized under the banner of an old but revitalized party, the PAN (Partido de Acción Nacional).

These mobilizations against the state and its ruling party proved to be surprisingly popular and successful. In the end Salinas was barely elected to the presidency, officially receiving the slimmest majority in Mexican history (50.4 percent), and this victory was probably achieved only through massive electoral fraud. When the new president assumed office on December 1, 1988, the power and prestige of the state, along with the Mexican economy, seemed at a low ebb. Not only was Salinas widely considered to be illegitimate, but there was growing dissent within the ruling party as the "dinosaurs" vented their displeasure with the neoliberal technocrats who, for the moment, had gained the upper hand.

At the beginning of the Salinas administration, therefore, the new order was far from locked into place. On the contrary, the neoliberal hold on the state and the state's hold on society both seemed tenuous. The ponderous ship of the Mexican political economy would take time to reverse course. The structural changes introduced by de la Madrid were unpopular both inside and outside the ruling party, and their future seemed dubious. Under Mexico's system of centralized presidential power, it was entirely possible for a future president to undo everything accomplished by the neoliberals with the stroke of a pen.

As a former minister of SPP and a Harvard-trained technocrat himself, President Salinas was determined to carry forward the neoliberal agenda, and under his administration the pace of privatization accelerated dramatically, the federal payroll was further slashed, government administration continued to be streamlined, and state participation in the economy was greatly reduced. Still, there was the troubling problem of institutionalizing the reforms and making them permanent. To solve this problem, Salinas broke with tradition and boldly turned toward the United States.

Specifically he proposed joining the free trade agreement that had already been negotiated between Canada and the United States, a move that would tie the neoliberal Mexican economy to a treaty with its powerful northern neighbor. It would be extremely difficult, if not impossible, for a future Mexican president to abrogate a treaty with the United States, no matter how powerful he was. Moreover, the creation of a North American market would bring about permanent institutional changes that would make a return to the old regime costly in practical and financial terms as well.

The structural and fiscal reforms introduced by Presidents de la Madrid and Salinas naturally met with great favor in Washington; indeed, U.S. officials had long recommended many of the changes that they had implemented. The first Bush administration warmly embraced Salinas's overture; after receiving authority from Congress for "fast-track" negotiation, it began talks to create an expanded North American Free Trade Agreement (NAFTA) that would embrace Mexico. The treaty was successfully negotiated and ratified by the U.S. Senate in 1993, with strong support from the new president, Bill Clinton. NAFTA took effect on January 1, 1994, and from that date forward the United States was officially committed to a policy of economic integration between itself and its neighbor to the south.

The imposition of the neoliberal regime after 1986 immediately accelerated cross-border flows of all sorts. In figure 5.1, we show trends in total trade (imports plus exports) and two kinds of international business migration (temporary entries for business purposes and intracompany transferees), all derived from official Immigration and Naturalization Service (INS) and International Monetary Fund (IMF) statistics. We date the beginning of the neoliberal era from Mexico's entry into GATT, and to show trends on a common scale we divide each series by its 1986 value.

Total trade between Mexico and the United States began at relatively modest levels in 1965 and for the next decade changed very little. From 1976 to 1982 trade expanded as Mexico borrowed heavily to finance consumption and investment during the oil boom, causing a surge in U.S. exports. After the onset of the economic crisis in 1982, however, trade ceased to grow and fluctuated around $30 billion, roughly maintaining this value through 1986. Thereafter, trade accelerated at an unprecedented rate, and the rate of increase appears to have received an added boost after the implementation of NAFTA in

Figure 5.1 Cross-Border Business Exchanges, 1965 to 1998 (1986 = 1.0)

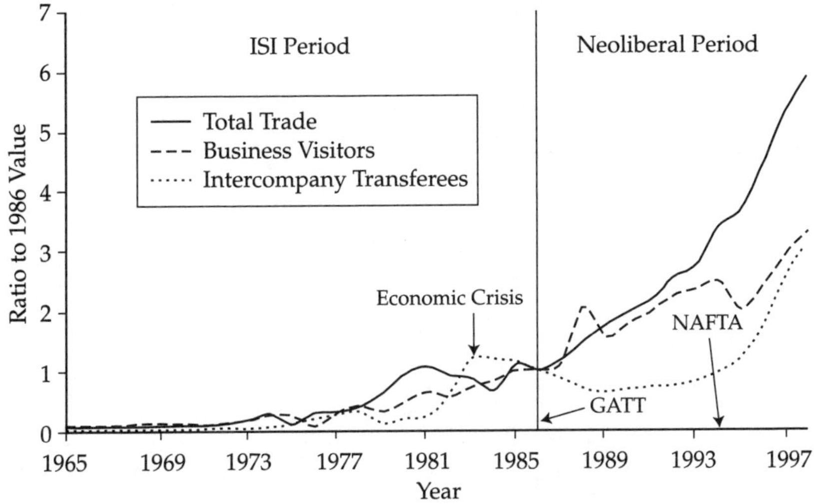

Source: International Monetary Fund; U.S. Immigration and Naturalization Service.

1994. By 1997 total trade stood at record levels and was five times its 1986 value, a rather stupendous increase in little over a decade.

The rise in trade was paralleled by an increase in the cross-border circulation of Mexicans for business purposes. After Mexico joined GATT, the number of Mexicans entering the United States on nonimmigrant business visas increased almost threefold, from 128,000 to 373,000 per year. The number of intracompany transferees coming into the United States also climbed, from 4,300 per year in 1986 to 11,000 in 1997. Although we do not show the data here, the number of Mexican treaty investors admitted to the United States also shot up in the post-GATT period (jumping from 73 to around 1,700 per annum).

The growth of trade promoted other cross-border movements as well, such as exchange visitors and people legally crossing the border in cars and trucks or on foot. Trends in these indicators of binational integration are graphed in figure 5.2, and again the data are divided by 1986 values to create a common scale. As can be seen, the number of people flowing into the United States through legal ports of entry increased very gradually from 1965 to 1979 and then remained fairly constant until 1986, when the number of crossings stood at 114 million per year. With Mexico's entry into GATT, however, we see a very

Figure 5.2 Cross-Border Movements of Visitors, 1965 to 1998 (1986 = 1.0)

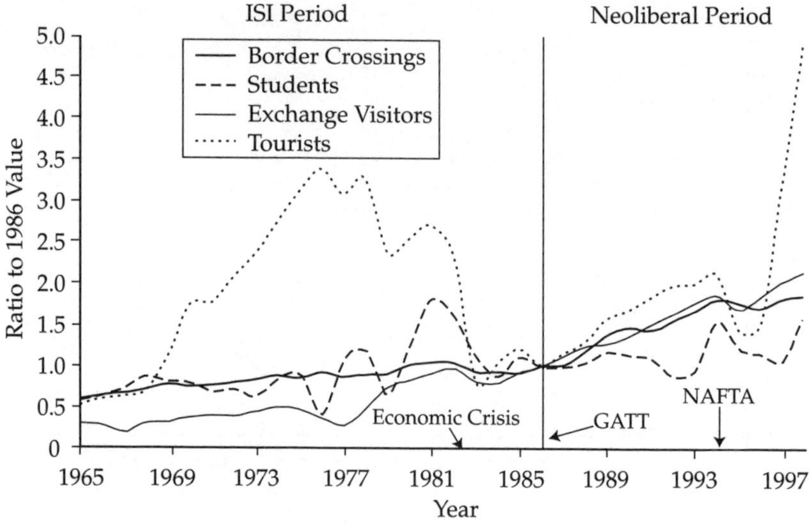

Source: U.S. Immigration and Naturalization Service.

sharp increase in the volume of cross-border traffic, which reached 208 million persons in 1997, nearly twice its 1986 level. The number of exchange visitors similarly changed very little from 1965 to 1977, ranging between 1,000 and 2,000 per year; the number of exchanges rose until 1981, then remained fairly constant (at around 3,000 per year) until 1986. Paralleling the trend observed for border crossings, however, the number of exchange visitors rose rapidly with the onset of the neoliberal period, peaking at 6,100 in 1997, two times its 1986 level.

Figure 5.2 suggests that one form of transnational movement, tourist entry (non-immigrant visitors entering for pleasure), is not a product of the neoliberal era. Indeed, the boom years of Mexican tourism seem to have been from 1970 to 1981, when ISI policies and the oil boom produced an overvalued peso, making U.S. vacations accessible to a large fraction of Mexicans. Tourism crashed along with the economy after the peso devaluation of 1982; it fluctuated at around 600,000 persons through 1986, after which it expanded again. The latter expansion lasted until the peso devaluation of 1994, which initiated another cycle of crash and recovery. Although Mexican tourism has generally expanded under neoliberalism, it has proven to be quite sensitive to exchange rates and always falls markedly after a significant devaluation, the last of which was in 1994.

The movement of Mexican students to the United States also appears to be very sensitive to exchange rates, which determine the relative cost of a U.S. education. Student migration is affected by the fiscal capacity of the Mexican state as well, since the government funds most scholarships used by Mexicans for study abroad. The number of students coming into the United States thus fell sharply in both 1976 and 1982, dates that correspond to major devaluations. The number of students going to the United States remained fairly stagnant from 1982 through 1993. Although the number increased in 1994, it fell once again following the peso devaluation at the end of that year. Today about 11,000 Mexican students enter the United States each year.

The final cross-border flow we consider is the movement of temporary documented workers. Every year the United States admits a large number of migrants with visas that permit work but not permanent settlement. In figure 5.3, we graph the number of Mexicans admitted as contract workers in agriculture (under the H2A visa program) and the total number of Mexicans admitted in any nonimmigrant worker category. As can be seen, the two series show little movement until 1986, when both begin to move rapidly upward. Aside from the surge in 1989, the increase has been steady and has generally accelerated over time. By 1997 the United States was admitting around 37,000 Mexicans per year for renewable periods of short-term labor.

The Politics of Separation

As envisioned under NAFTA, North American integration has thus been proceeding at a rapid pace in recent years, and cross-border traffic has multiplied accordingly. In an era of pervasive globalization, Mexico, Canada, and the United States have come together to compete as a single trading bloc, creating a free trade zone within which national borders will grow increasingly porous. Even as the United States has committed itself to integrating most markets in North America, however, it has paradoxically sought to prevent the integration of one particular market: that for labor. Indeed, since 1986 the United States has embarked on a determined effort to restrict Mexican immigration and tighten border enforcement. U.S. policy toward Mexico is inherently self-contradictory, simultaneously promoting integration while insisting on separation.

Figure 5.3 Cross-Border Movements of Labor, 1965 to 1998 (1986 = 1.0)

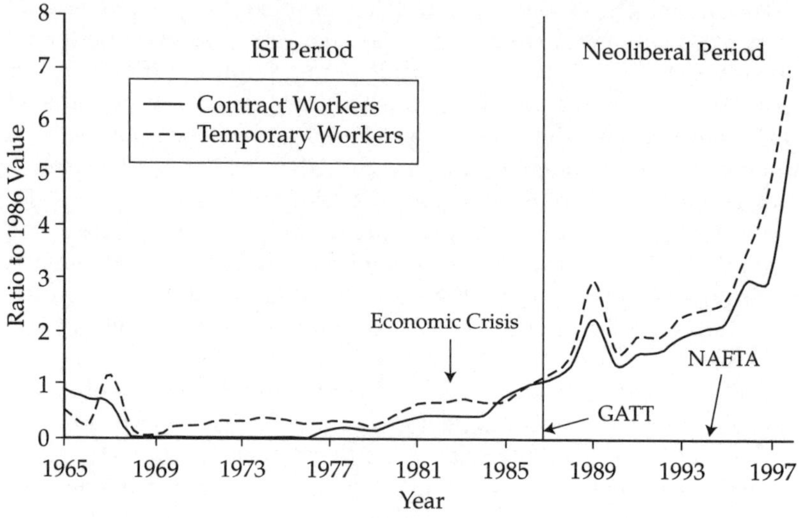

Source: U.S. Immigration and Naturalization Service.

Manufacturing a Border Crisis

This sort of schizophrenia toward Mexico is nothing new. If anything, it is typical. Throughout the twentieth century the United States regularly encouraged or welcomed the entry of Mexican workers while publicly pretending not to do so. Only the mechanism of self-deception has changed over time. The current institutional arrangement has its roots in the late 1970s and early 1980s. As we saw in chapter 4, there is little statistical evidence that undocumented migration was accelerating at this time. What did change was how political and bureaucratic actors framed the issue.

Neither the numbers nor the legal status of immigrants is particularly relevant to understanding the policy regime that emerged after 1986. More important are U.S. political and economic conditions, which provided a context that allowed immigration to be framed in crisis terms. Economically the 1970s were painful for Americans. The Arab oil embargo doubled and then tripled petroleum prices after 1973, sending industrial nations into a deep and prolonged recession. The U.S. dollar lost more than half its real value between 1970 and 1980, the rate of unemployment increased by 50 percent, median income fell by 5 percent in real terms, and income inequality rose by 15 percent. Throughout the decade the economy remained in the doldrums and lost ground to economies in Europe and Asia. By almost any measure, Americans were worse off in 1980 than they had been a decade before (as presidential candidate Ronald Reagan made sure to remind voters that year).

In geopolitical terms, the United States was faring little better: the tide of the cold war seemed to turn against it. In 1973 the U.S. military withdrew from Southeast Asia, and two years later the South Vietnamese government collapsed, resulting in a chaotic exodus that sent hundreds of thousands of refugees streaming toward American shores. At the same time Fidel Castro remained firmly ensconced in Cuba, Eastern Europe continued under Soviet domination, China had not yet turned toward the market, and left-wing guerrilla movements were threatening U.S.-backed governments throughout Latin America and the Caribbean. The 1970s ended with the takeover of the U.S. embassy in Tehran by revolutionary Islamic students and U.S. State Department employees being held hostage.

By 1980, therefore, American confidence was at a low ebb. Successive rounds of recession and inflation and perceived humiliations at home and abroad had accumulated to produce an electorate that was fearful, angry, and looking for someone or something to blame. The Vietnam War had been lost, the Sandinistas were in power, real wages were declining, and the rich were getting richer while most families had to work harder just to stay in place. In reaction, U.S. voters expelled the hapless administration of President Jimmy Carter and turned to the magnetic self-confidence of Ronald Reagan. It was "morning in America," and having gained control of both the White House and Senate, Reagan and the Republicans sought to remake the U.S. political economy.

Faced with voter anger over intractable economic problems that lacked obvious or easy solutions, Reagan fell back on two time-honored strategies—ideology and scapegoating. Ideologically Reagan moved the nation sharply to the right: the new administration put a strong emphasis on anticommunism and had a decided tendency to view all international conflicts through the lens of the cold war. The Soviet Union was "the evil empire," the leftist president of Panama was a "tin horn dictator," and the Sandinistas were a "threat to the regional peace." Enemies of the United States lurked everywhere, national security became the watchword, and much time, effort, and money were put into defending America from enemies at home and abroad.

Under Ronald Reagan, national economic ideology also moved rightward. The free market became the key to prosperity, and barriers to the market were to be dismantled. The statist vision of the New Deal, in which government safeguards the welfare of the people and protects them from the excesses of capitalism, gave way to a new philosophy of individual initiative, self-reliance, and progress through competition. In keeping with this ideological stance, Reagan led the way in downsizing the state, reducing federal employment, lowering taxes, deregulating industry, breaking unions, and cutting back on social spending. Only in the area of national security was the role of the state strengthened through a sharp increase in military spending, which in fact increased the budget deficit in spite of the other cuts.

Although "Reaganomics" eventually produced an economic boom in the latter half of the 1980s, its immediate effect was to aggravate the economic circumstances that had undermined Carter's presidency. By 1983 national unemployment had risen to 9 percent, the dollar had lost another 6 percent of its 1970 value, the poverty rate had risen to 15 percent, median income had declined by another 2 percent, and the rise in income inequality had accelerated. The early 1980s were thus marked by an unusual combination of economic insecurity and cold war hysteria, and it was in the atmosphere of this strange brew that far-reaching changes in U.S. immigration policy took shape.

During the 1980s immigrants increasingly were cast in the role of scapegoats for the nation's ills. Ronald Reagan led the way by framing border control as an issue of national security. As a result of Communist insurgencies in Central America, he foresaw "a tidal wave of refugees—and this time they'll be 'feet people' and not boat people—swarming into our country seeking safe haven from communist repression to the south" (quoted in the *Washington Post,* June 21, 1983). The media immediately picked up on the imagery of the "tidal wave" and extended the metaphor, referring to Latin American migrants as a "steady stream" or a rapidly rising "tide" that was close to becoming a "flood."

The symbolic linkage between immigration and the cold war reached cinematic proportions in 1984 with the release of the movie *Red Dawn,* directed by John Milius. Before any live action appears onscreen, the story is framed by a text scrolling slowly from bottom to top: "The Soviet Union suffers the worst harvest in 55 years. Labor and food riots in Poland. Soviet troops invade Cuba and Nicaragua. They reach troop strength goals of 500,000. El Salvador and Honduras fall. Green Party gains control of West German Parliament. Demands withdrawal of nuclear weapons from European soil. Mexico plunged into revolution. NATO dissolves. The United States stands alone . . ." (quoted from *Red Dawn,* Valkyrie Films).

The scene then opens on a small-town high school located on the plains at the edge of the Rocky Mountains. Classes are just beginning when suddenly the morning sky is filled with hundreds of Russian- and Spanish-speaking paratroopers who, fully armed, take up positions around the school. When a teacher charges outside to investigate, he is cut to pieces by machine-gun fire. The school erupts in pandemonium, and in the ensuing melee a group of high school boys, led by several star athletes, pile into a pickup truck and escape to the mountains (stopping, naturally, at a guns-and-ammo store along the way). There they organize themselves as guerrilla freedom fighters called "the Wolverines," after their school sports team. The rest of the movie covers their valiant armed struggle against the mixed Soviet-Latino army of occupation.

In 1986 President Reagan exacerbated the cold war hysteria by linking border control not only to national security but to the threat of foreign terrorism. In a televised speech, he reminded viewers that "terrorists and subversives are just two days' driving time from [the border crossing at] Harlingen, Texas" (quoted in Kamen 1990). A year later Reagan's cabinet-level Task Force on Terrorism warned that extremist groups could be expected to "feed on the anger and frustration of recent Central and South American immigrants who will not realize their own version of the American dream" (quoted in Dunn 1996). By the late 1980s the tidal metaphor of a "flood" had given way to martial images of threatened "invasion." The border was "under siege," Border Patrol officers were "outgunned," and they constituted a "thin green wall" trying to "hold the line." Loss of control became the dominant narrative used by politicians and the media to discuss the border and movements across it (Andreas 2000). It was in this atmosphere that a new regime of immigration control would emerge.

As early as 1982 the Reagan administration had introduced legislation to give the president new authority to declare "immigration emergencies" of up to 120 days, during which time the border could be sealed by the military and aliens deemed threats to national security could be rounded up and detained without warrant. Although the proposed immigration emergency bill failed to pass Congress, portions of it would resurface later in other legislation. By 1986, however, the Reagan administration had created the Alien Border Control Committee to develop contingency plans for sealing the border and arresting aliens, and the Federal Emergency Management Agency (FEMA) had held roundup exercises with personnel from the Department of Defense (Dunn 1996).

The demonization of Latino immigrants as "invaders" and "terrorists," the linking of border control to national security, and the cultivation of public hysteria about undocumented migration was not lost on enterprising INS bureaucrats, who detected a means of increasing both their prestige and their resources. The rise of the Immigration and Naturalization Service as a powerful and wealthy bureaucracy began in earnest in January 1992. As undocumented migrants were returning to the United States from their Christmas visits home, the Border Patrol chief in San Diego, Gustavo de la Viña, erected a new fence, deployed additional Border Patrol agents, and installed new detection equipment along the westernmost section of the border, which ran from the port of entry at San Ysidro to the Pacific Ocean.

When they encountered these new obstacles to clandestine crossing, undocumented migrants and smugglers did the obvious thing: they attempted to go around them. The closest unbarricaded sector was the San Ysidro crossing station itself, where the fence stopped just short of the port of entry. In essence, the new border policy funneled all migrants within an extended sector to a single crossing point. Clever smugglers quickly recognized an advantage in the new concentration of people and began organizing "banzai runs" of fifty or more immigrants. Swarms of people would suddenly rush the border, overwhelm the small number of immigration inspectors, and dart into the southbound lanes of Interstate 5, disappearing in the traffic and confusion (Rotella 1998).

As hordes of men, women, and children dashed madly across the border, jumped over highway dividers, and darted through traffic, to the consternation of startled native drivers, Border Patrol Chief de la Viña was waiting with a video crew to capture the moment on tape. The images were then assembled into a public relations video entitled *Border Under Siege* that was released to the public (Rotella 1998). The video was a public relations bonanza for the agency. The dramatic images of undocumented migrants running across the border and risking life and limb to cross an eight-lane freeway quickly became a powerful symbol of "a border out of control." Clearly a national boundary was being "invaded" by "desperate" aliens. Lost in the uproar was the fact that the images were a *direct consequence* of the Border Patrol's own policies—neither the number nor the characteristics of migrants had changed in any significant way.

The scenes depicted in *Border Under Siege* became an important resource for aspiring politicians seeking to exploit illegal migration as a political issue, the most blatant of whom was the Republican governor of California, Pete Wilson. With his state mired in a deep recession triggered by the end of the cold war and the corresponding reduction of defense spending, his 1994 reelection campaign was floundering. He was well behind in the polls when he devised a new campaign strategy explicitly designed to inflame public anxieties and fears about immigration: blaming the state's economic woes on the federal government's failure to control the border. Using footage taken directly from the Border Patrol video, he produced a television advertisement that featured images of immigrants dashing into traffic as a narrator intoned: "They keep coming. Two million illegal immigrants in California. The federal government won't stop them at the border, yet requires us to pay billions to take care of them." To symbolize his determination to "stop the invasion" of immigrants, Governor Wilson called up California's National Guard, and as the TV cameras rolled, he dispatched them to patrol the border near San Diego. Voters had apparently forgotten that just a few years earlier, as a U.S. senator, Wilson had sponsored legislation to *relax* border controls, and indeed, he regularly employed undocumented workers himself (see Dunn 1996; Andreas 2000).

Lines in the Sand

The framing of border control as an issue of national security, and illegal migration as a military invasion, created a climate in which elected representatives came under increasing pressure to "do something" about the "problem" of undocumented migration. As a result, between 1986 and 1996 the U.S. Congress, three presidents, and several states undertook a remarkable series of actions to reassure citizens that they were working to "regain control" of the Mexico-U.S. border. After 1986 border control became ritualized as a mandatory public performance, and U.S. politicians competed with one another to offer symbolic gestures of how much they cared about undocumented migration. In the words of Peter Andreas (2000, 144, emphasis added), "From the political perspective, the way the media and the public *see* the border is more important than actual deterrence."

The Immigration Reform and Control Act The arrival of a new era of Mexican migration was heralded by the passage, in October 1986, of the Immigration Reform and Control Act. Given an economically vulnerable and fearful electorate, rising hysteria about an alien invasion, and the perceived risk to national security posed by an uncontrolled border, Congress felt compelled to act. Late in the year Senator Alan Simpson (R-Wyo.) and Representative Peter Rodino (D-N.J.) surprised everyone by overcoming the roadblocks to a bill that most observers had long considered to be dead (Fuchs 1990). Through a series of backroom deals, historic compromises, and a delicate balancing of interests, they succeeded in crafting legislation that gave something to everyone and permitted Congress to go on record as taking visible and forceful action to stop illegal migration.

IRCA sought to combat undocumented migration in four ways. To eliminate the attraction of U.S. jobs, it imposed sanctions on employers who knowingly hired undocumented workers. To deter people from trying to enter the United States illegally in the first place, it allocated additional resources to expand the Border Patrol. To wipe the slate clean and begin afresh, it authorized an amnesty for undocumented migrants who could prove continuous residence in the United States after January 1, 1982; the amnesty program was combined with a special legalization program for undocumented farmworkers that was added to appease agricultural growers. Finally, the legislation incorporated most of Reagan's earlier proposed legislation, giving the president new authority to declare an "immigration emergency" if large numbers of undocumented migrants had or were soon expected to embark for the United States—in essence creating the legal foundations for another Operation Wetback.

By enacting employer sanctions, IRCA repealed the famous Texas Proviso, which for years had protected from prosecution persons and firms that hired illegal aliens (Teitelbaum 1986). The new law required employers to verify that workers carried documentation that established identity and the right to work in the United States. Failure to do so could result in harsh penalties, including fines of up to $10,000 and criminal prosecution for repeated offenses (Bean et al. 1989; U.S. Department of Labor 1991). In addition, the Border Patrol received a $400 million supplement to hire additional officers in 1987 and 1988. New funds were also made available to the U.S. Department of Labor to undertake workplace inspections, and a $35 million contingency fund was established to cover costs associated with future "immigration emergencies" (Bean et al. 1989).

IRCA's legalization programs ultimately provided residence documents to more than 3.0 million persons: 1.7 million "legally authorized workers" (LAWs—those demonstrating a long-term residence in the United States) and 1.3 million "special agricultural workers" (SAWs—people showing prior employment in U.S. agriculture). Of those legalized, 2.3 million (three-quarters of the total) were Mexicans—1.3 million LAWs and about 1 million SAWs. In Los Angeles County alone, some 800,000 former undocumented migrants were legalized, and in six other metropolitan areas the tally exceeded 100,000 (U.S. Immigration and Naturalization Service 1992). Unlike most legal resident aliens, however, those who were legalized under IRCA were required to take English-language and civics classes. Reflecting the cold war hysteria and national security obsessions of the time, Congress chose to push the new immigrants very deliberately and forcefully toward U.S. citizenship. To placate growers and ethnic lobbies, Congress was grudgingly prepared to let them in—but they damn well better learn how to speak English and be good Americans.

The Immigration Act of 1990 Despite expectations that IRCA would somehow slow Mexican immigration, by 1990 it was clear that the legislation was not working as planned. Although border apprehensions fell in the period 1987 to 1989, by 1990 they were once again on the rise, increasing 26 percent over the prior year. Moreover, it turned out that the 2.3 million Mexicans who had been legalized under IRCA all had relatives in Mexico, and legalization would dramatically increase the odds that these relations would themselves migrate to the United States without documents (Massey and Espinosa 1997). Legalization also had a ripple effect on legal immigration as spouses and dependents of IRCA-legalized migrants suddenly qualified for visas under the preference system. It also became apparent that a large share of the 1.1 million SAW legalizations had been based, in all likelihood, on fraudulent claims. According to Philip Martin, Edward Taylor, and Philip Hardiman (1988), the number of people who were legalized in California under the SAW program (672,000) was *three times* the size of the state's entire agricultural workforce during the qualifying period. Rather than discouraging illegal migration, IRCA actually promoted it.

With both legal and illegal migration from Mexico still on the rise, Congress returned to the drawing board and in 1990 passed another major revision of U.S. immigration law. The 1990 Immigration Act focused more strongly on border control, authorizing funds to hire another one thousand Border Patrol agents. It also tightened employer sanctions, streamlined criminal and deportation procedures, and increased penalties for numerous immigration violations. The act did not, however, focus entirely on the border, for it also sought to impose limits on the total number of immigrants who could be admitted in any single year.

The perceived need for limits stemmed from the fact that a growing fraction of immigrants were entering the United States through categories that were not subject to numerical limitation. Of the 1.5 million legal immigrants admitted to the United States in 1990, for example, only 298,000 (just under 20 percent) were subject to numerical limitation; the rest were spouses, minor children, or parents of U.S. citizens, or they were refugees. Clearly immigration was exceeding the worldwide ceiling of 270,000 that Congress had envisioned in 1980.

In response, the 1990 act sought to cap total immigration to the United States. It fixed a temporary cap of 700,000 immigrants per year through 1994, at which point the cap fell to 675,000 per year. More pointedly, the act sought to cap family immigration (the category under which most nonquota immigrants entered) at just 480,000 per year. Under the 1990 act, immediate relatives of citizens could still enter the United States without numerical restriction, but rather than entering *in addition to* those admitted under numerically restricted categories, in the future they would be *subtracted from* the following year's family quota of 480,000. Although lawmakers sympathetic to immigrants opposed these caps, they were unable to block them. They did succeed, however, in inserting language that made the caps "flexible" in that no more than 226,000 visas could be subtracted from the family quota in any given year. In essence, it permanently subtracted these from numerically limited categories, further lengthening already long waiting times.

The 1990 act also sought to influence the national origins of immigrants. By the late 1980s immigrants were coming overwhelmingly from Asia and Latin America. In 1990, for example, 22 percent of those legally admitted came from Asia, and 63 percent came from Latin America, with Mexico alone accounting for 44 percent of the total. The dominance of Mexico stems from the fact that a majority of those admitted in 1990 came in under IRCA's legalizations, among whom Mexicans were predominant. When IRCA immigrants are subtracted, the prevalence of Mexicans drops to 8 percent and Latin Americans to 20 percent, with Asians rising to 46 percent.

Under any scenario, however, the vast majority of immigrants in 1990 were definitely not Europeans. Although reluctant to admit an actual preference for immigrants of European origin, there was substantial talk in Congress about certain regions being "underrepresented" in the immigrant flow (and they were not thinking of Africa). Thus, in addition to capping the number of family visas, Congress expanded the number of visas going to skilled, well-educated jobseekers, who were expected to come mainly from developed nations. The 1990 act also created a new category of "diversity" visas. Set at 55,000 per year, visas in this category were to be distributed randomly to applicants from countries that had been "adversely affected" by the 1965 Immigration and Nationality Act (those whose share of total immigration had fallen after 1965—in other words, European nations). Senator Edward Kennedy of Massachusetts was even able to insert a special provision that from 1992 through 1994, stated that

48,000 of these diversity visas had to be reserved for natives of Ireland. During this brief period it was virtually impossible to migrate illegally from Ireland!

State Initiatives Although immigration is mostly a matter of federal policy, during the 1980s a variety of states jumped onto the anti-immigrant bandwagon. Most state actions were symbolic gestures with few practical consequences; they simply provided voters or legislators with a tangible means of registering their dislike of foreigners. By far the most common vehicle was the circulation of an initiative to make English a state's official language. Prior to 1980 only five states had enacted such a provision, but by 1998 the number had swollen to twenty-five (according to the website www.us-english.org). Most of these referenda were passed in the brief period between 1984 and 1988, with particularly heavy activity in 1987 (when five states made English their official language).

Although such gestures, as intended, irritated Latinos and Asians, they had virtually no effect on their daily lives, and Los Angeles did not end up being renamed "The Angels." The anti-immigrant hysteria stirred up by Governor Pete Wilson in California, however, did lead to the circulation and passage of Proposition 187, a referendum that aspired to more concrete actions. This law proposed to prohibit undocumented migrants from using publicly provided social services, including public schools. It also required state and local agencies to report suspected illegal aliens to the California attorney general and the INS, and it made the manufacture, distribution, sale, or use of false citizenship or residence documents a felony under the law. After its lopsided passage by voters, the terms of the proposition were immediately challenged in court by the American Civil Liberties Union (ACLU) and other groups. Although most of its provisions were ultimately declared unconstitutional and never went into effect, the proposition provided an important rallying point for mobilization against immigrants and sent a strong signal to officials in the nation's capital.

Prevention Through Deterrence Early in the Clinton administration (in 1993 and 1994), the INS developed a new border strategy that came to be known as "prevention through deterrence." The idea was to prevent Mexicans from crossing the border illegally in order to avoid having to arrest them later (Andreas 2000). The strategy began in September 1993, when the Border Patrol chief in El Paso, Silvestre Reyes, on his own initiative launched "Operation Blockade" as an all-out effort to prevent illegal border crossing within El Paso, Texas. Within a few months immigrants had been induced to go around Silvestre's imposing wall of enforcement resources, and traffic through El Paso itself was dramatically reduced.

The policy was extremely popular with El Paso's residents. Although they were overwhelmingly of Mexican origin themselves, they had grown weary of the unwelcome visitors. A survey carried out by a local nonprofit organization revealed that what bothered El Paso residents was not undocumented migrants per se, but the fact that they frequently stopped in yards to drink water and rest. It was thus the invasion of private space that people did not like; if the migrants had been invisible or remained in public areas, few would have cared.

As a result of the operation, Reyes was lauded as a local hero and ultimately went on to be elected to Congress. Naturally his superiors in Washington, D.C., took note of the favorable publicity and the apparent success of Operation Blockade. After being renamed "Operation Hold-the-Line," to assuage Mexican sensibilities, its strategy and tactics were incorporated into the Border Patrol's strategic plan for 1994 (U.S. Border Patrol 1994). In October of that year the INS launched a second operation using the approach pioneered by Silvestre Reyes in El Paso, this time along the busiest stretch of border in San Diego.

"Operation Gatekeeper" saw the installation of high-intensity floodlights to illuminate the border day and night, as well as an eight-foot steel fence along fourteen miles of border from the Pacific Ocean to the foothills of the Coast Ranges. Border Patrol officers were stationed every few hundred yards behind this formidable wall (which came to be known as the "tortilla curtain"), and a new array of sophisticated hardware (motion detectors, infrared scopes, trip wires) was deployed in the no-man's-land it fronted (see Dunn 1996). As in El Paso, the operation was a huge success. From being the busiest point on the entire border, San Diego became positively tranquil, even boring, for Border Patrol officers who were forced to sit in their vehicles staring at a blank wall for hours on end. Operation Gatekeeper put an end to the chaotic images of migrants running through traffic that had so troubled California's voters. Once again, the border appeared to be "under control."

Of course, throwing up blockades in El Paso and San Diego did not really stop undocumented migrants from entering the United States; it simply channeled them to other, less visible locations along the two-thousand-mile border. Passage through remote mountains, high deserts, and raging rivers had been too costly and risky to undertake as long as San Diego and El Paso remained relatively open, but once Operation Hold-the-Line and Operation Gatekeeper made these sectors difficult to traverse, the prospect of crossing in more distant and dangerous areas did not look so bad. Indeed, crossing in remote areas, which tended to be lightly patrolled, had certain advantages.

One immediate result of the Border Patrol crackdowns, therefore, was to deflect undocumented migrants to new crossing points. As a result, the agency was soon compelled to expand its operations geographically and to launch additional operations in other sectors. In 1995 "Operation Safeguard" was unleashed in Nogales, Arizona; in 1996 Operation Gatekeeper was extended to another sixty-six miles of border; in 1997 Operation Hold-the-Line was extended ten miles west into New Mexico; in August 1997 "Operation Rio Grande" was implemented along thirty-six miles of border in southeast Texas; and in 1999 Operation Safeguard was extended east and west from Nogales to Douglas and from Douglas to Naco, Arizona.

The Illegal Immigration Reform and Immigrant Responsibility Act of 1996 The buildup of enforcement resources was further accelerated by Congress through its passage of the Illegal Immigration Reform and Immigrant Responsibility Act of 1996. Once again, legislation focused heavily on deterrence, authorizing funds for the construction of two additional layers of fencing in San Diego and enacting tougher penalties for smugglers, undocumented migrants, and visa overstayers. It also included funding for the purchase of new military technology (magnetic footfall detectors and an electronic finger-printing system) and provided funds for hiring one thousand Border Patrol agents a year through 2001 to bring the total strength of the Border Patrol up to ten thousand officers (Andreas 2000).

Once again, however, an immigration act's provisions were not confined to the border. Taking a cue from California's Proposition 187, the 1996 act declared illegal aliens ineligible to receive Social Security benefits and limited their eligibility for educational benefits, even if they had paid the requisite taxes. It also gave authority to states to limit public assistance to aliens (both legal and illegal) and increased the income threshold required for a legal resident alien to sponsor the immigration of a family member. The latter provision represents another attempt to scale back family immigration: Congress did not expect that many poor immigrant families would be able to meet the new income threshold.

The Personal Responsibility and Work Opportunity Reconciliation Act of 1996 Although billed as a reform measure to "end welfare as we know it," the Personal Responsibility and Work Opportunity Reconciliation Act (PRWORA) of 1996 also contained provisions with far-reaching effects on immigration. Again, it copied Proposition 187 in barring illegal migrants from most federal, state, and local public benefits. It also required the INS to verify the immigration status of aliens before they could receive any federal benefit, and it placed new restrictions on the access of legal immigrants to public services, barring them from receiving food stamps or Supplemental Security Income (SSI) and prohibiting them from qualifying for means-tested programs for five years after their admission. Paralleling the 1996 immigration act, it provided states with greater flexibility in setting eligibility rules for legal immigrants and gave them the statutory authority to exclude them from both federal and state programs.

Together the 1996 welfare reform and immigration acts accomplished nationally what Proposition 187 had been unable to do in California—they definitively barred undocumented migrants from Social Security coverage and means-tested programs. But the federal lawmakers went the Californians one better by also drastically reducing the access of *legal* immigrants to public programs. Although unintended, these new provisions suddenly gave legal Mexican immigrants—who historically had displayed very low rates of naturalization—a strong incentive to acquire U.S. citizenship, which would put them in position to sponsor the unrestricted entry of their immediate relatives.

Militarizing the Border

The string of restrictive policies enacted between 1986 and 1996 proved to be bureaucratically beneficial to the Immigration and Naturalization Service, particularly to its enforcement branches. In the space of ten years the Border Patrol went from a backwater agency with a budget smaller than that of many municipal police departments (Teitelbaum 1980) to a large and powerful organization with more officers licensed to carry weapons than any other branch of the federal government save the military (Andreas 2000). By February 1999 the Border Patrol had grown to nearly eight thousand agents and inspectors and was seeking to hire new officers at the rate of more than eighty per month. The agency was so desperate for bodies that it offered a signing bonus of $2,000, and a 1997 article in the *Federal Times* reported that "Border Patrol agent" and "immigration inspector" were among the top ten categories for job growth in the federal workforce (Rivenbark 1997). The INS budget, meanwhile, had reached $4.2 billion by 1999, with over $900 million going to the Border Patrol alone. In the course of this remarkable expansion, the

Figure 5.4 Size and Budget of the Border Patrol and the INS, 1978 to 1998 (1986 = 1.0)

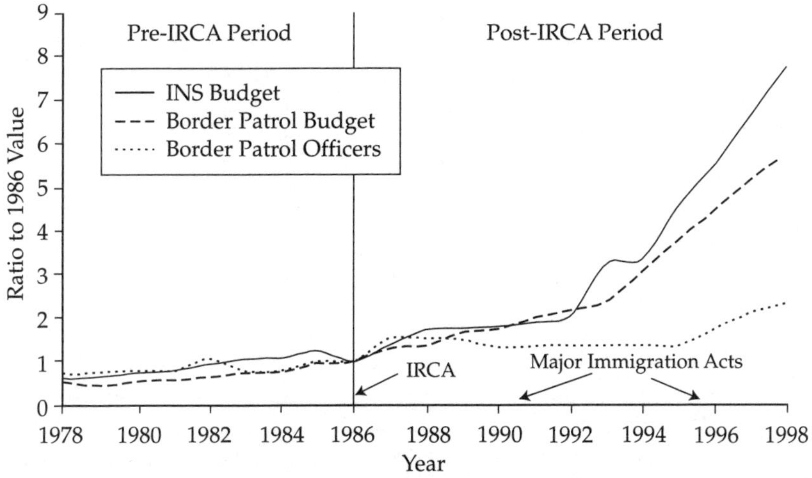

Source: U.S. Immigration and Naturalization Service.

agency acquired a large array of expensive new hardware, including 58 helicopters, 43 airplanes, 355 night-vision scopes, and a host of high-tech devices such as electronic intrusion-detection sensors, closed-circuit TV systems, infrared radar, electronic fingerprinting systems, and microwave communications (Dunn 1996).

The explosive growth in the size and importance of the INS and the Border Patrol is clearly revealed in figure 5.4, which presents the nominal budgets for the two entities as well as the number of Border Patrol officers in the years from 1978 to 1998. To capture trends on the same scale, we once again divide numbers in each series by their 1986 values. As can be seen, the INS and the Border Patrol budgets changed little in the years before IRCA. Then suddenly they doubled between 1986 and 1992 and accelerated exponentially thereafter. By 1998 the INS budget was nearly eight times its 1986 level, and the Border Patrol budget was almost six times its former level. The number of Border Patrol officers more than doubled between 1986 and 1998, reaching around 8,500 in the latter year.

The additional resources and personnel allocated to the INS after 1986 had a pronounced effect on the agency's enforcement efforts. In figure 5.5, we graph the number of linewatch-hours and the number of deportations reported by the Border Patrol, again expressing each

Figure 5.5 Indicators of Immigration Enforcement Effort, 1965 to 1998 (1986 = 1.0)

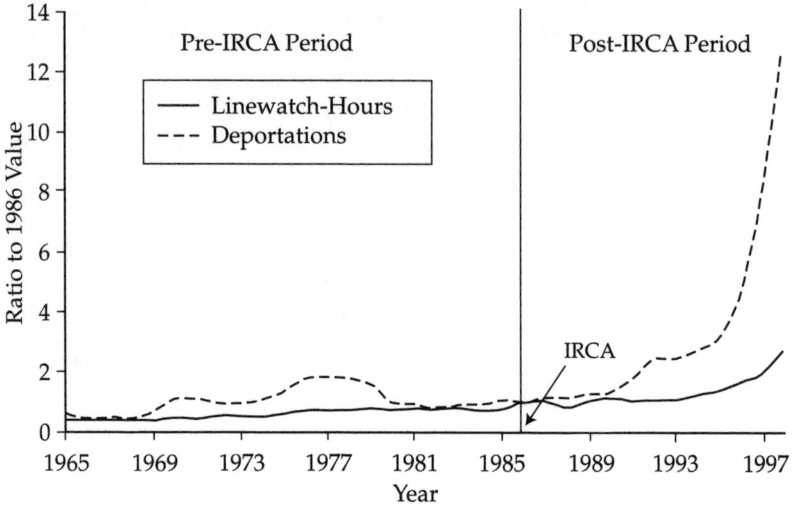

Source: U.S. Immigration and Naturalization Service.

series relative to its 1986 value. Linewatch-hours are the number of person-hours spent by agents patrolling the Mexico-U.S. border. After 1986 linewatch-hours began to grow, and after 1992 this growth accelerated rapidly. By 1997 the Border Patrol was devoting twice as much time to patrolling the border as in 1986. Deportations of Mexicans surged briefly in the late 1970s but then fell in the early 1980s. After 1986, however, the number of Mexicans deported once again rose very rapidly, increasing by a factor of thirteen over the next ten years.

Enlisting in the War on Drugs

As Mexico and the United States became more integrated and the border grew more porous in the wake of trade liberalization, it became easier not only for people to enter the United States but also for drugs and other contraband. With the invention and popularization of crack cocaine, the demand for drugs soared in the United States in the early 1980s. Initially cocaine was transported through smugglers based in south Florida, but a massive interdiction effort mounted by the U.S. Drug Enforcement Agency (DEA) successfully disrupted the

Caribbean routes and displaced the bulk of the traffic to Mexico. Once smugglers had established operations along the border, U.S. efforts to harden the frontier with respect to drugs came into direct conflict with the goal of softening the border with respect to trade (Andreas 2000).

With the deregulation of the Mexican trucking industry and the implementation of NAFTA, an increasing number of long-distance trucks crossed into the United States, along with thousands of cars and buses. Today an average of 220,000 vehicles cross into the United States from Mexico each day, and if trade is to flourish, very few of them can be detained at the border for a thorough inspection and search. In 1995 the DEA estimated that 85 percent of illegal drugs entered the country through regular ports of entry in commercial trucks and passenger vehicles (Dunn 1996; Andreas 2000). Thus, the NAFTA-induced surge in cross-border traffic necessarily made drug smuggling easier than ever.

During the mid-1980s Ronald Reagan broadened his list of national security threats to include not only immigrants but also drugs. In 1986 he signed a secret National Security Decision Directive that named drugs as a threat to national security and authorized the military to cooperate with civilian law enforcement agencies to launch a new "war on drugs." In an era of expanding free trade and economic deregulation, of course, it was neither realistic nor feasible to clamp down seriously on cross-border traffic through ports of entry, even though the vast majority of illegal drugs entered the country through these routes. Nonetheless, something visible had to be done to signal the government's resolve to win the newly declared war.

The means chosen—to launch a massive interdiction effort concentrated largely *between* ports of entry—once again framed the issue as one of border control. In the words of a Reagan-era drug enforcement official, "We are engaged in something akin to a guerrilla war along the border against well-entrenched and well-organized trafficking groups" (quoted in Dunn 1996, 3). Once again the U.S. border was subject to invasion by dangerous foreigners who posed a threat to national security.

The framing of drugs as an issue of border control played directly into the hands of entrepreneurial bureaucrats at the INS and the Border Patrol. In 1984 Reagan administration officials formed the Southwest Border Drug Task Force to coordinate federal, state, and local agencies in developing an interdiction strategy; the Border Patrol was designated as the lead agency in the new effort. The 1986 Anti–Drug Abuse Act officially broadened the Border Patrol's duties to include narcotics as well as immigration enforcement, and soon one-third of

Figure 5.6 INS Involvement in Drug Enforcement, 1965 to 1998

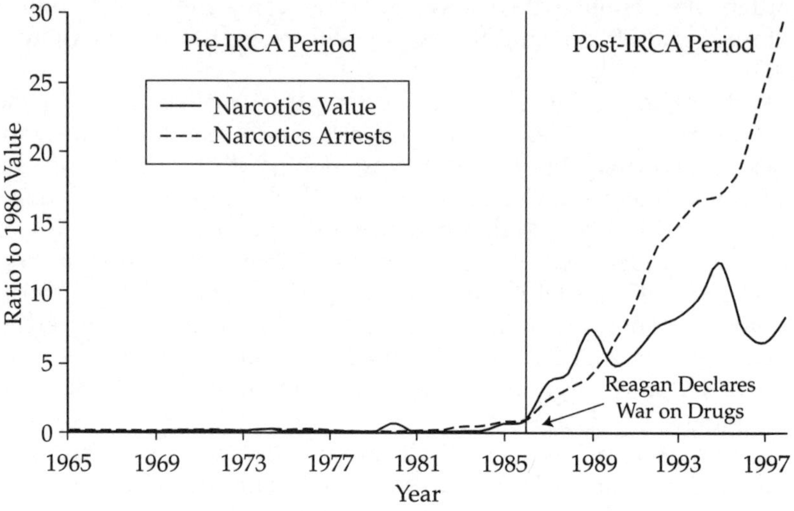

Source: U.S. Immigration and Naturalization Service.

all Border Patrol agents were cross-deputized to enforce U.S. drug laws (Dunn 1996).

After 1986 the Border Patrol's involvement in drug enforcement activities skyrocketed, as revealed by figure 5.6, which shows trends in the value of narcotics seized and the number of narcotics arrests made from 1965 to 1998 (expressed relative to their 1986 values). As with the other indicators we have examined, 1986 was the turning point. Before that date the INS was hardly involved at all in drug enforcement, but after 1986 the agency's involvement rose exponentially. Between 1986 and 1998, arrests for narcotics violations increased almost thirty fold, and the dollar value of the narcotics seized grew by a factor of twelve through 1995 before declining and then recovering to reach eight in 1998. (Narcotics value is highly subjective and less reliable as an indicator than narcotics arrests.)

As a result of these trends, the Border Patrol's linewatch-hours increased rapidly after 1986, but increasingly these hours were spent in tracking drug smugglers, not in chasing undocumented immigrants or those who smuggled them. Moreover, whereas immigration enforcement yields a large number of arrests with little effort and little staff time, catching drug smugglers and confiscating their wares is much more time- and labor-intensive. Although participation in the war on drugs brought the INS new power, prestige, and resources, increasingly these resources were divided between two mutually exclusive and competing activities.

The Symbolic Politics of Border Control

By the early 1980s Mexico-U.S. migration had evolved into a stable system based on the circulation of undocumented labor. This migratory system began to take shape in 1965 to replace the bracero system that had prevailed between 1942 and 1964. Movements under the undocumented regime were governed by stable parameters, which yielded relatively steady probabilities of first migration, border crossing, remitting, return, and remigration. Border enforcement selected for working-age males who were married but traveling without dependents. Migrants were very likely to remit money home and to return after limited sojourns north of the border. As documented in chapter 4, there is little evidence that the likelihood of undocumented migration was rising before 1986, or that the total rate of Mexico-U.S. migration exceeded that which had prevailed during the bracero era.

Nonetheless, actors inside and outside of government found it politically useful and materially profitable to make undocumented migration and drugs salient political issues during the 1980s. Framing them as issues of border control and national security, they offered U.S. citizens two new "enemies" upon which their insecurities could be projected. Both were seen to emanate from malevolent foreign sources, and both constituted grave threats to national security. Drugs were foisted upon Americans by sinister foreign cartels and malicious traffickers who were taking advantage of America's openness to flood it with cheap drugs, bringing a wave of addiction, violence, and mayhem to U.S. cities. Immigrants, especially those without documents, were depicted in one of two ways: as desperate people fleeing poverty and despair at home, or as potential terrorists who, if they did not already have terrorist aspirations when they arrived, would become easy prey for the Communist provocateurs and agents loose among them.

Having positioned drugs and immigrants as dire threats to national security, politicians created a political dynamic wherein it became difficult *not* to take some kind of dramatic action. Framing drugs and immigrants in terms of border control, the proposed solutions focused almost exclusively on creating a militarized, defensive perimeter along the nation's border with Mexico in an effort to seal off the unauthorized flows. The crucial date was 1986, when Congress passed IRCA and President Reagan signed the national security directive declaring drugs a threat to national security.

Meanwhile, those responsible for U.S. drug demand were let off lightly. Americans were exhorted to "just say no," while large amounts of money, equipment, and personnel were thrown into interdiction efforts. These efforts concentrated on stretches of border between the points of entry through which most drugs were known to be entering. Likewise, U.S. demand for undocumented labor received short shrift compared with border defense and interdiction. Although IRCA did outlaw the hiring of undocumented workers, all that an employer had to do to escape prosecution was to show that he had seen two easily falsifiable documents: one proving identity (a driver's license) and another demonstrating the right to work (a Social Security card). The employer was under no obligation to take any steps to authenticate the documents.

Moreover, after IRCA's initial authorization of new funds for the Department of Labor to undertake work-site inspections, internal enforcement of U.S. immigration laws was quietly but steadily reduced (Andreas 2000), then all but abandoned in the late 1990s. Whereas by 1999 more than 2,000 INS agents patrolled the San Diego–Tijuana border, the number of agents stationed north of Los Angeles had fallen from 65 to 22. In 1999 only 2 percent of the INS budget was devoted to the enforcement of employer sanctions, and of the 1,700 investigators assigned to the interior, only one-fifth of their time was devoted to work-site enforcement, yielding only 340 full-time person-equivalents to monitor all jobs in the United States (Andreas 2000). In contrast, during the 1990s the Border Patrol's budget increased by a factor of six, and the number of agents doubled. As a result of this allocation of resources, INS investigations of employers for immigration violations fell from around 15,000 in 1989 to 888 in 1997, while deportations of Mexicans increased by a factor of three (Andreas 2000).

The anti-immigrant hysteria reached its peak in the mid-1990s and crested with the passage of additional "reform" legislation in 1996. With the end of the cold war and the opening of China, the foreign menaces that had dominated the American imagination since 1945 suddenly disappeared, making immigrants and drugs more salient as foreign threats and yielding an exponential growth in resources for border enforcement. The remarkable concentration of effort at the border occurred despite reports from the General Accounting Office (GAO) that "interdiction has not had—and is unlikely to have—a significant impact on the national goal of reducing drug supplies to the United States" (cited in Andreas 2000, 82). The GAO's assessment of Operation Gatekeeper and Operation Hold-the-Line was that they were, at best, "inconclusive": data failed to indicate "whether the increased difficulty of entry has deterred the flow of illegal entries into the country . . . [or] . . . whether there had been a decrease in attempted reentries by those who had previously been apprehended" (General Accounting Office 1997, 4).

Nonetheless, political leaders in the United States prefer border policing over other approaches to dealing with the issues of drugs and immigration. This seeming contraction persists because border enforcement represents more of a ritualistic performance than an actual strategy of deterrence. As Andreas (2000, 11, emphasis in original) puts it:

> The popularity of the border as a political stage is based as much on the *expressive role* of law enforcement (reaffirming moral boundaries) as it is on the *instrumental goal* of law enforcement (effective defense of physical boundaries). High profile law enforcement campaigns that fail in their instrumental purpose can nevertheless be highly successful in their expressive function. Border control efforts are not only *actions* (a means to a stated instrumental end) but also *gestures* that communicate meaning. Even as the enforcement performance has failed to deter illegal border crossings significantly, it has nevertheless succeeded in reaffirming the importance of the border.

Thus, the border enforcement strategy that evolved in the United States after 1986 had little to do with the reality of immigration or the actual operation of a migration system whose roots could be traced back to 1942 and even before. It had much more to do with domestic fears and insecurities than with any real upsurge in undocumented migration or change in the nature of Mexican immigration. It was related more to the nervousness felt by many Americans at the increasing volume of cross-border movements of people, goods, ideas, and products—a direct result of U.S. trade policies. As the United States grew increasingly integrated with its North American neighbors, its political leaders felt a need to reassure citizens of the continued salience of the Mexico-U.S. border, and enterprising bureaucrats in the INS found it very much worth their while to provide the necessary imagery.

If this bit of political theater had had few practical consequences, then there would be little to criticize. If the only problem with pursuing integration while insisting on separation was that it was self-contradictory, hypocritical, and a waste of public money, then perhaps no one would really care. Unfortunately, however, the latest attempt by the United States to have its cake and eat it too has incurred serious costs and led to a host of unforeseen and largely negative consequences for people on both sides of the border. Not only have the instrumental goals of border control (deterring undocumented immigration) not been achieved, but the net effect of America's self-contradictory policies has been to promote rather than restrict Mexican immigration, and these policies have done so under circumstances that exacerbate the negative consequences for both nations.

Chapter 6

Breakdown: Failure in the Post-1986 U.S. Immigration System

IF THERE is one constant in U.S. border policy, it is hypocrisy. Throughout the twentieth century the United States has arranged to import Mexican workers while pretending not to. With the sole exception of the 1930s, when the Great Depression effectively extinguished U.S. labor demand, politicians and public officials have persistently sought ways of accepting Mexicans as workers while limiting their claims as human beings. Only the formula by which this sleight of hand is achieved has changed over time, shifting from the legerdemain of a legal guest-worker program between 1942 and 1964, to the Potemkin Village of circular undocumented migration from 1965 to 1985, to the smoke and mirrors of "prevention through deterrence" after 1986.

Despite these charades, the benefits of Mexico-U.S. migration have historically exceeded the costs for all concerned. Since 1986, however, the self-contradictory policy of working to consolidate North American markets while blocking the integration of one particular market has needlessly driven up the costs and reduced the benefits of transnational migration. Although the balance may still be positive, the ratio is far from optimal, and in many ways the United States is doing serious damage to the social and economic fabric of both nations. In an era of massive state-sponsored integration and continent-wide free trade, the costs of U.S. hypocrisy have become unaffordable.

The Sham of Border Control

"If a tree falls in the forest and no one hears it, has it really fallen?" That is the well-known conundrum posed for meditation by Zen Buddhism. It seems that politicians and officials in charge of U.S. border policy have meditated extensively on this thought, for post-IRCA border policies have had less to do with stopping undocumented migrants than with pushing them into remote sectors of the border where they will be neither seen nor heard, and most important, where they will not be videotaped.

During the undocumented era the brunt of Mexican immigration was directed toward California. According to an analysis of census data by Jorge Durand and his colleagues (2000), 63 percent of all Mexicans who arrived in the United States from 1985 to 1990 went to California, more than four times the number of those who went to the next most popular destination, Texas, which accounted for just 15 percent of all arrivals (followed by Illinois at 5 percent). Given that California is the nation's largest state, that Los Angeles is the nation's second-largest city and the world's media capital, and that San Diego is a large and politically conservative metropolitan area, the geography of undocumented migration practically guaranteed that it would become politically salient and socially visible in the context of a severe economic recession on the West Coast.

By far the most active sector of the border during the 1980s was that separating San Diego from Tijuana, followed in order of importance by El Paso–Juarez and Laredo–Nuevo Laredo. Among undocumented migrants apprehended for illegal entry by the INS in 1986, for example, 45 percent were arrested in the San Diego sector alone, 21 percent in the El Paso sector, and 17 percent in the San Antonio sector (which includes Laredo). Through 1986, in other words, 85 percent of all undocumented migrants entered the United States through three narrow corridors, which together made up only a tiny fraction of the two-thousand-mile border (U.S. Immigration and Naturalization Service 1987).

Reflecting the geographic concentration of undocumented migration, the Border Patrol's enforcement resources were likewise distributed unequally. Historically agency operations focused overwhelmingly on the San Diego and El Paso sectors; when the massive militarization of the border began in 1993, these two districts naturally led the way. Operation Blockade was launched in El Paso in 1993, and Operation Gatekeeper followed in San Diego in 1994. As the new "tortilla curtain" of deterrence went up in these cities, migrants naturally began to go around the reinforced portions of the border, prompting U.S. authorities to extend their lines of enforcement outward. This pattern of deployment, response, and counterdeployment influenced the geography of migration in two ways. First, Operation Gatekeeper, by far the largest deployment of enforcement resources, deflected migrants

Figure 6.1 Apprehension Probabilities and Border-Crossing Locations, 1980 to 1998

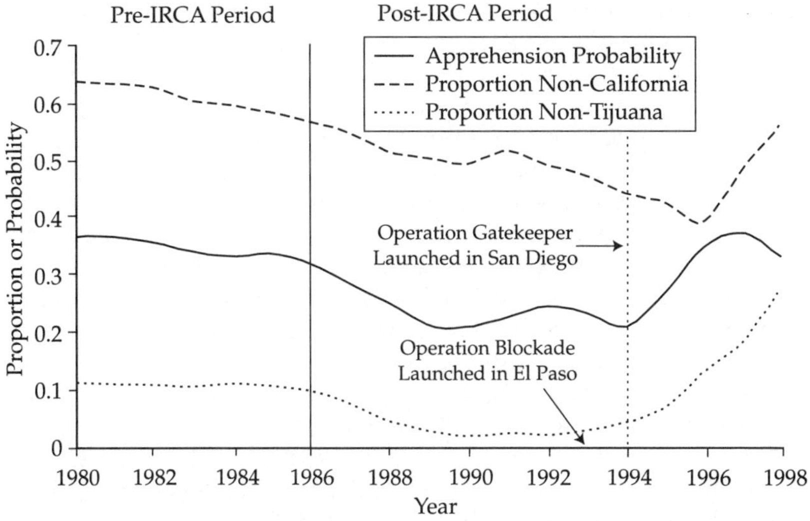

Source: Mexican Migration Project.

away from California and toward new crossing points in Arizona, New Mexico, and more remote sections of the Rio Grande Valley in Texas. Second, within heavily traversed corridors, such as those in San Diego–Tijuana and El Paso–Juarez, the new militarization channeled migrants away from built-up, settled areas and redirected them to more remote and desolate country.

Figure 6.1 illustrates the changing geography of Mexican immigration using data from the Mexican Migration Project, which compiled complete histories of border crossing for 4,881 undocumented household heads (see appendix A). This data series is indicated by the dashed line at the top of the figure, which represents the proportion of migrants entering the United States outside of California. As can be seen, from 1980 through 1996 undocumented migration focused increasingly on Californian crossing points. The proportion of undocumented migrants crossing into other U.S. states fell steadily from 64 percent in 1980 to 39 percent in 1996. By the mid-1990s, in other words, nearly two-thirds of the traffic in undocumented migrants entered the United States by way of California. Two years after the launching of Operation Gatekeeper in San Diego, however, there was a sudden and very sharp upswing in the proportion crossing into other states: from 1996 to 1998 the share of non-California crossings jumped from 39 percent to 58 percent, a swing of nineteen points (49 percent) in just three years! This shift is highly significant in statistical terms ($p < .001$). (To perform this and subsequent statistical tests we estimated a multivariate model that controlled for the respondent's age, education, state of origin, community size, and, when appropriate, the respondent's sex and number of prior U.S. trips. The models are included in appendix B.)

Not only were undocumented migrants deflected away from California, but those who continued to cross into California entered the state at more remote points along the border, away from the built-up portions of Tijuana and San Diego. The dotted line at the bottom of figure 6.1 shows the proportion of California-destined migrants who crossed at points outside of the Tijuana–San Diego corridor. Prior to Operation Gatekeeper, Tijuana was the crossing point of choice for the overwhelming majority of undocumented migrants. Fewer than 11 percent of all undocumented migrants chose another crossing point before 1994, and during the early 1990s nearly all (98 percent) California-bound migrants chose to cross at Tijuana.

The dramatic post-1994 expansion of enforcement activities within San Diego brought a swift and instantaneous reaction on the part of migrants. With the construction of a solid wall of enforcement stretching from the Pacific Ocean inward to the mountains of the Coast Ranges, migrants logically began to go elsewhere, and the proportion of non-Tijuana crossings skyrocketed, rising from just 3 percent in 1993, the year before Operation Blockade, to nearly 30 percent by 1998, a tenfold increase in five years (also highly significant, $p < .001$). As the border through Tijuana was increasingly reified as a three-layered iron fence backed by ground sensors and troops, border traffic simply shifted eastward into empty desert, rugged mountains, and lonely ranch country. By the late 1990s the San Diego sector had grown quiet, and to citizens of southern California and the rest of the nation the border once again seemed under control.

It was not long, however, before border stations in Arizona, which had experienced no significant migration since the 1920s, suddenly reported a sharp increase in cross-border traffic. Sleepy border communities in the state of Sonora overnight became boomtowns, while on the U.S. side, inhabitants of towns such as Douglas, Arizona, grew increasingly alarmed by the rising tide of migrants crossing their yards, traversing their fields, clogging their bus stations, packing into cheap motels, and congregating at street corners on their way to new destinations throughout the United States. To residents of small, backwater communities on both sides of the border, it must indeed have seemed like an "invasion," albeit one manufactured by U.S. border policy. As in El Paso, however, what residents objected to was the local visibility of the migrants, not their presence in the country per se.

In response to the ensuing local outcry, the Border Patrol extended its strategy of targeted enforcement to other population centers along the Mexico-U.S. border, launching missions comparable to Operation Blockade in the Arizona gateway towns of Douglas and Nogales, as well as in Columbus, New Mexico, and Laredo, Brownsville, and McAllen in Texas. At each port of entry, essentially the same scenario was played out: the selective hardening of the border within town deflected the flow of migrants outward into more sparsely populated country, rendering the flows less visible, both socially and politically.

With the border perceived by citizens to be under control and U.S. unemployment rates reaching record lows by the late 1990s, undocumented migration evaporated as a political issue. The absence of public controversy did not mean, however, that the Border Patrol's strategy of "prevention through deterrence" was really working. On the contrary, by pushing migration away from urbanized areas and toward sparsely populated sectors, the Border Patrol had effectively channeled migrants toward portions of the border where they would be less likely to be caught, for in addition to being less inhabited, the new crossing points were also less patrolled. In other words, the enforcement strategy pursued by the United States after 1993 functioned to *reduce* the odds of arrest by directing larger numbers of migrants toward border locations where enforcement resources were scarce and apprehension was less likely.

To demonstrate this fact, figure 6.1 also plots annual probabilities of apprehension, which were computed from MMP border-crossing data using an estimation procedure developed by Massey and Singer (1995). Historically studies have shown the odds of apprehension for undocumented migrants to be about one in three (Espenshade 1990; Espenshade and Acevedo 1995; Singer and Massey 1998). On any given attempt at clandestine border crossing, in other words, the likelihood of capture was 33 percent, compared with a 67 percent chance of entering the United States undetected. These are indeed the relative odds revealed by our calculations during the pre-IRCA period. As indicated by the solid line, the probability of apprehension held fairly steady at .32 to .36 through the early 1980s. After 1986, however, the probability fell steadily to reach record lows of .20 to .25 in the period 1990 to 1994. (We discuss the reasons for this decline later in the chapter.)

The launching of Operation Blockade in El Paso in 1993 and Operation Gatekeeper in San Diego in 1994 produced an immediate upsurge in the probability of apprehension, which by 1996 had restored the odds of arrest to historic levels. But thereafter the probability of apprehension fell once again, and by the end of the 1990s it was moving rapidly downward. There is little evidence, therefore, that the Border Patrol's string of post-1993 enforcement operations was successful in raising the probability of apprehension. On the contrary, a formal statistical test reveals that, on average, the post-1986 probability lies significantly below the pre-IRCA standard ($p < .001$; see appendix B). If anything, relative apprehension probabilities have fallen in the years since IRCA.

Together the graphs presented in figure 6.1 relate a very simple story. The massive increase in enforcement at the two busiest crossing points during 1993 and 1994 was initially successful in raising the probability of apprehension. Caught unawares, migrants were arrested in large numbers. According to official statistics, the number of apprehensions increased by 300,000 from 1994 to 1995, and by another 250,000 between 1995 and 1996 (U.S. Immigration and Naturalization Service 1997). As figure 6.1 shows, however, migrants quickly learned that crossing in Tijuana or El Paso was no longer fruitful and that the rules of the border game had changed. Migrants passing through Baja California immediately began to go around Tijuana (indicated by the upswing in the dotted line beginning in 1994), and about two years later they started to avoid California entirely (indicated by the upswing in the dashed line beginning in 1996). Once these evasive actions had been taken, the probability of apprehension once again began to fall and by 1998 was moving rapidly downward.

Given that post-IRCA apprehension probabilities were, with the exception of a brief period from 1995 to 1996, well below historic values, one would not expect much of a deterrent effect stemming from Operation Gatekeeper and its extensions. This expectation is indeed borne out by MMP data on the initiation of undocumented migration. To compute the probability of taking a first undocumented trip, we followed men and women, age fifteen to thirty-five, year by year from 1980 through 1998. If they had never been to the United States in a particular year, they were included in the denominator; if they departed on a first undocumented trip in that year, they were counted in the numerator, and all later years were excluded from consideration. Performing this operation across person-years yields a series of first-trip probabilities, which are plotted for men as the solid line in figure 6.2.

From 1980 through 1984 the probability that a Mexican male age

Figure 6.2 Probability of Taking First Undocumented Trip to the United States, 1980 to 1998

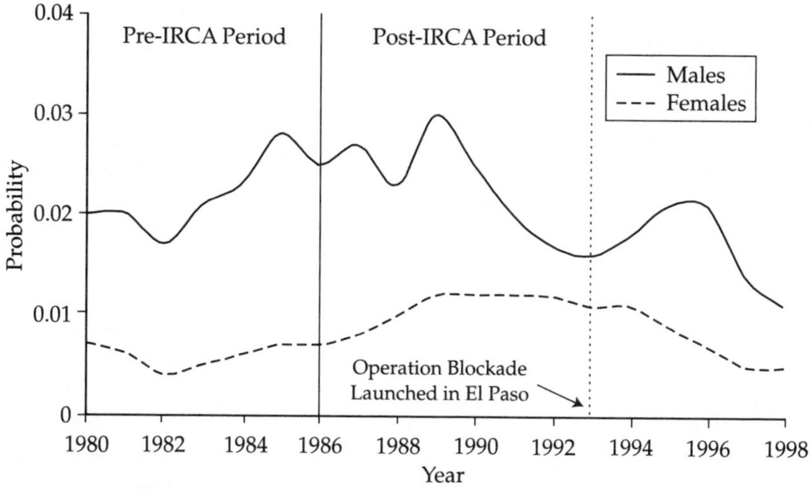

Source: Mexican Migration Project.

fifteen to thirty-five would undertake a first undocumented trip remained fairly steady at around .02 per year. In 1985 the likelihood of migrating illegally shifted upward slightly to fluctuate between .025 and .030. After 1989, however, it declined, reaching .018 in 1993. Then it rose to .021 in 1996 before falling back to .011 in 1998. This trend suggests neither a border out of control before 1986 nor much of a deterrent effect afterward. On the whole, the shifts have been relatively minor, and the overall trend is one of constancy, with year-to-year fluctuations in the probability of undocumented migration that are not obviously connected to U.S. border policies.

If anything, the shifts in the probability of male migration are more closely connected to the ebbs and flows of the Mexican economy than to U.S. border policies. Hence, they dipped after the onset of the economic crisis in 1982, then rose as the crisis deepened in the mid-1980s, shooting up again during the second round of hyperinflation in 1987 and 1988. Then they fell markedly with the onset of the economic boom of the early 1990s before rising again after the peso devaluation crisis of 1994. If we classify observations into three periods—pre-IRCA (1980 to 1986), transition (1987 to 1992), and post-IRCA (1993 to 1998)—we find that the probability of leaving for the United States without documents was significantly higher during the transition and post-IRCA periods than during the pre-IRCA period ($p < .001$; see appendix B).

Trends in the likelihood of female migration are plotted in figure 6.2 as the dashed line. Obviously, the likelihood of female migration is much less than that of males, but similarly there is little evidence of a deterrent effect of border enforcement. During the pre-IRCA period the probability of female migration generally fluctuated around a value of 0.005 per year. From 1987 to 1993 the probability of initiating undocumented migration increased significantly and came to exceed 0.01 per year in the years between 1989 and 1993. This surge in female migration probabilities reflects the movement of wives to join husbands who had been legalized under IRCA. After 1994, however, the probability of female migration returned to its historic level of around .005 per year and leveled off. A statistical test once again shows that the probability of first undocumented migration was greater in the transition and post-IRCA periods than before ($p < .001$). A careful analysis thus leads to the conclusion that both Mexican men and Mexican women were more likely to begin migrating without documents after the border build-up than before. Despite all the fanfare along the border, the deterrent effect has been nil.

The Costs of Self-deception

Although the strategy of "prevention through deterrence" may have failed to achieve its manifest goal, it has nonetheless been a marvelous public relations success from the viewpoint of the Border Patrol. As undocumented migrants have been shunted off into sparsely populated territory, they have become socially invisible and politically inconspicuous. Jarring images of undocumented Mexicans darting through traffic have been replaced by scenes of order and tranquillity at ports of entry, which are the only portions of the border that most U.S. citizens ever see. Elected officials and the public thus have felt reassured that the border is once again under control, and both the INS and the Border Patrol have been rewarded with new prestige, resources, and respect.

So what is the problem? If politicians, public officials, and citizens of the United States wish to deceive themselves into believing that North American labor markets will remain separate while other markets move toward integration, what is the harm? U.S. border policy has always been hypocritical. What is new is not the hypocrisy but the formula by which it is achieved. Self-deception always comes at a price, and whereas the price may have been acceptable in earlier times, during an era of North American free trade and massive market integration, the costs have become exceedingly high, not just in dollars but in human lives.

Wasted Lives

The diversion of undocumented migrants into rugged terrain between well-defended ports of entry has lowered the odds of apprehension, but it has also increased the risks of injury and death. These desolate sectors may be less populated and less patrolled, but they are also more dangerous. According to the authors of the most complete study of deaths along the border, "illegal border crossing patterns have been spatially restructured to circumvent areas of high border enforcement, and the whole border region, from Texas to California, has become a more dangerous area to cross than before the new enforcement efforts of the 1990s" (Eschbach, Hagan, and Rodriguez 2001, 1).

Using cause-of-death statistics from vital statistics registries in both Mexico and the United States, Karl Eschbach and his colleagues (1999, 2001) compiled a count of migrant deaths along the border for the years 1985 to 1998. We combined this time series with our own estimates of the number of undocumented entries to derive a series of death rates. The number of entries was computed by multiplying the expression $(1 - p)/p$ by the annual count of border apprehensions, where p is the annual probability of apprehension (see Massey and Singer 1995). Eschbach and his colleagues (2001) noted that deaths from suffocation, drowning, heat exhaustion, and exposure were most sensitive to shifts in border enforcement, so we computed a death rate for these causes combined, along with unknown causes. Unknown causes are included because the cause of death is often unspecified when people die alone in remote country and leave remains that are found days, weeks, or sometimes even months later.

Figure 6.3 shows the trend in the death rate from 1986 through 1998. In the years immediately after IRCA's passage the border death rate stood at 3 to 4 per 100,000 crossings, but during the early 1990s it dropped below 2 per 100,000. Following the implementation of Operation Blockade and Operation Gatekeeper in 1993 and 1994, however, the rate of death from suffocation, drowning, heat, cold, and unknown causes increased *threefold* to plateau at around 6 per 100,000 in 1997 and 1998. This difference of 4 deaths per 100,000 in the rates that prevailed immediately before and after the launching of Operation Blockade provides a precise means of assessing the cost of U.S. border policies in human lives. During 1998 around 4 million persons are estimated to have attempted to cross the border without documents

Figure 6.3 Death Rate from Suffocation, Drowning, Heat Exhaustion, Exposure, and Unknown Causes Along the Mexico-U.S. Border, 1986 to 1998

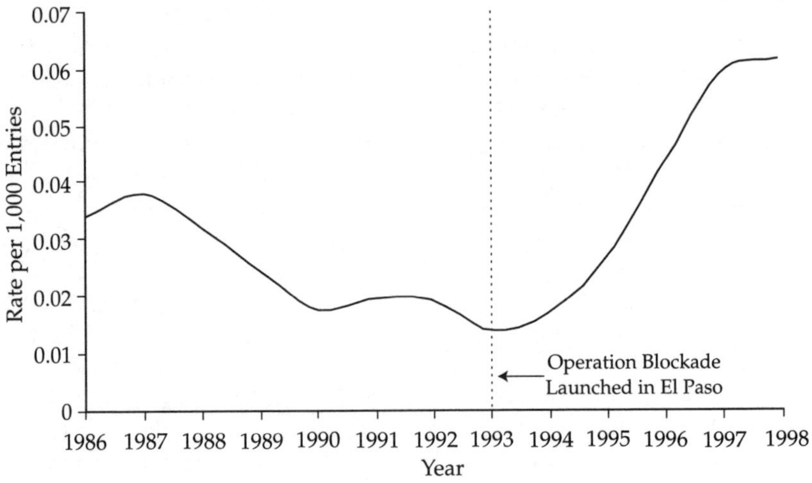

Source: Mexican Migration Project; Border Deaths Project.

(computed using the method of Massey and Singer 1995). Four million crossings multiplied by a death rate of 4 per 100,000 yields 160 extra deaths per year.

This figure represents the number of deaths that would not have occurred under the enforcement regime that prevailed before 1993. Every year the new regime remains in place, in other words, 160 people lose their lives needlessly, which seems a rather high price to pay simply to maintain the pretense of a border under control. Moreover, it is a rather conservative estimate of the lives lost: it is based only on the difference between pre- and post-1993 death rates for selected causes. Even before Operation Blockade, border crossing was no cakewalk, and one might argue that no one should have to die for the "crime" of seeking work in the United States. According to Eschbach and his colleagues (2001), 347 people lost their lives on the border in 1998; thus, at current migratory volumes, the true toll in human life is closer to 350 needless deaths per year.

Wasted Money

While undocumented migrants suffer mightily under the new policy regime, the Border Patrol itself profits handsomely. From being an

Figure 6.4 Apprehension Rate for Border Patrol, 1980 to 1998

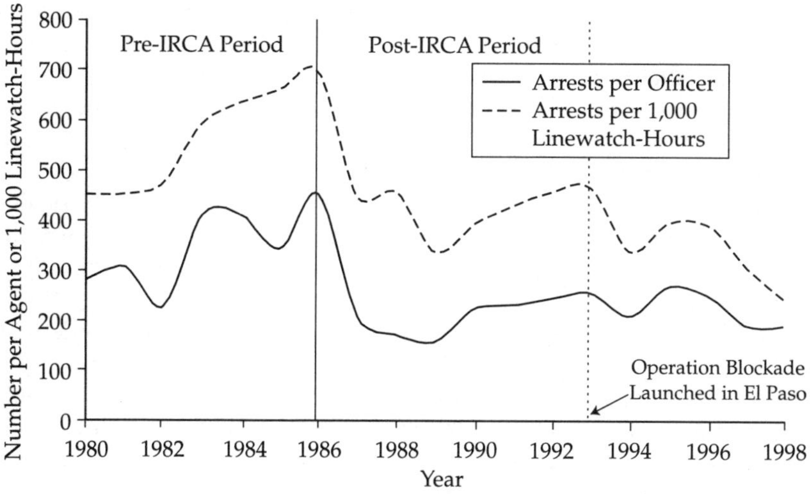

Source: U.S. Immigration and Naturalization Service.

institutional backwater with a budget of $151 million in 1986, the Border Patrol has grown to become the nation's largest civilian police force, with more than ten thousand officers in uniform and an annual budget in excess of $1 billion. As already noted, however, the new infusion of resources has neither raised the odds of apprehension nor lowered the likelihood of initiating undocumented migration. Together these facts suggest that U.S. citizens have been spending more but getting less in the way of actual border enforcement, and in the process they have been wasting a lot of public tax money.

The declining efficiency of border enforcement is suggested by the data in figure 6.4, which presents two indicators of enforcement productivity. The first is the number of apprehensions divided by the number of Border Patrol agents, indicated by the solid line in the lower part of the figure. This index measures the workload handled by the average Border Patrol officer each year. Despite some fluctuation, the index generally rose from 1980 through 1986. Whereas the typical Border Patrol officer made 280 arrests in 1980, by 1986 the figure had risen to 450, a 61 percent increase in efficiency. With the implementation of IRCA, however, the number of arrests per officer plummeted to just 160 in 1989. Thereafter it increased slightly but never again reached the level it had attained in 1986.

Border enforcement is not simply a matter of having enough officers; it also depends on what those officers do. Are they busy with paperwork, for example, or actually patrolling the border? The INS records the annual number of "linewatch-hours" to measure the total person-hours spent by agents patrolling the Mexico-U.S. border, providing an alternative measure of Border Patrol efficiency: the number of apprehensions per linewatch-hour. To produce a series on the same scale as the prior index, we multiplied this ratio by 1,000 and plotted the trend as the dashed line in figure 6.4.

In general, the pattern of change closely parallels the pattern depicted earlier. Efficiency increased sharply from 1980 to 1986, with arrests going from 450 per 1,000 linewatch-hours to around 700, a gain of 56 percent. As before, however, the implementation of IRCA after 1986 was associated with a sharp decline in the effectiveness of enforcement. For every 1,000 hours spent patrolling the border, the number of arrests dropped from 700 in 1986 to just 340 in 1998. Although the index rose somewhat in the mid-1990s, it declined thereafter to reach a record low of 240 per 1,000 in 1998, roughly one-third of the peak value achieved in 1986.

Despite the 176 percent increase in linewatch-hours from 1986 to 1998, and the 130 percent increase in Border Patrol officers, the number of undocumented aliens actually apprehended, either per person or per linewatch-hour, has fallen dramatically. According to the analysis of Singer and Massey (1998), the primary reason for this drop in efficiency was the growing involvement of the Border Patrol in drug interdiction. Whereas guarding the border from unlawful entry is a relatively efficient operation that yields a large number of arrests per unit of agency resources, patrolling the border for drug traffickers is a labor-intensive process that yields a small number of arrests per input of time and personnel. During a time (1986 to 1998) when the number of immigrant apprehensions per officer decreased from 450 to 200, the number of narcotics arrests increased from 0.7 to 7.6 per officer. Likewise, the decline of 360 alien apprehensions per 1,000 linewatch-hours was offset by an increase of just six points in the relative number of drug arrests.

Whether Border Patrol officers are arresting undocumented migrants or drug traffickers, however, is beside the point. A more fundamental question is what kind of deterrence U.S. taxpayers are buying with their money. This subject is examined in figure 6.5, which documents a trend of rising inefficiency with respect to the cost of border enforcement. The first index we consider is the ratio of the Border Patrol budget to the underlying volume of undocumented migration. This ratio assesses the degree to which the supply of enforcement dollars matches the agency's ostensible workload, as measured

Figure 6.5 Relative Cost of Border Patrol Enforcement, 1980 to 1998

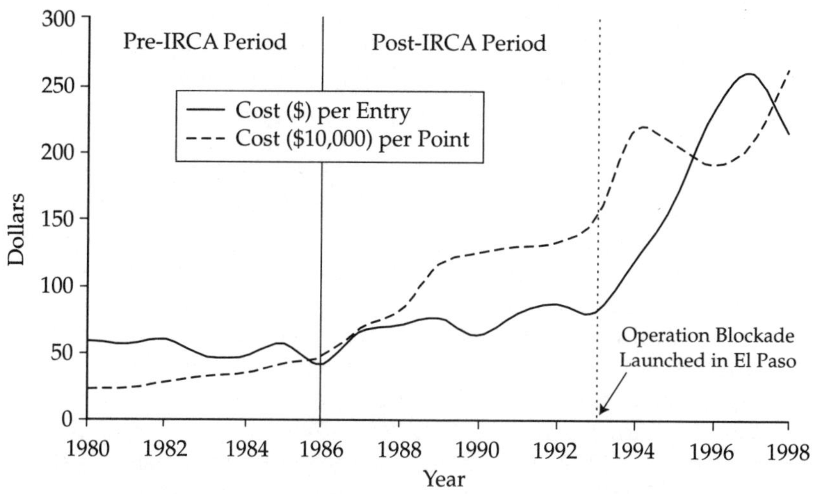

Source: U.S. Immigration and Naturalization Services; Mexican Migration Project.

by the estimated number of undocumented entries (see the solid line). The second index is the ratio of Border Patrol expenditures to the probability of apprehension, which may be interpreted as the marginal cost of border enforcement: what it costs to raise the probability of apprehension by one point (see the dashed line).

In earlier chapters, we asserted that increases in enforcement resources roughly kept pace with increases in the volume of undocumented migration during the years leading up to IRCA, thus yielding a constant probability of apprehension (.33) through 1986. The data in figure 6.5 confirm this assertion. From 1980 through 1986 the ratio of Border Patrol expenditures to entries remained virtually constant at $50 per entry. Although the marginal cost of apprehension rose slowly, it stayed below $500,000 throughout the period. In other words, the cost to U.S. taxpayers of border enforcement was $50 per undocumented entry, or around $500,000 per point of apprehension probability.

In the immediate aftermath of IRCA, however, both indicators began to rise rapidly. The cost of border enforcement rose from $50 per entry in 1986 to around $85 per entry in 1993. As the Border Patrol increasingly involved itself in drug interdiction and the underlying volume of undocumented migration actually *fell* in the wake of IRCA's massive legalization, the Border Patrol's budget grew in a way that was disconnected from its underlying workload. As a result, the marginal cost of apprehension accelerated rapidly after 1986, essentially tripling, going from around $500,000 per probability point in 1986 to roughly $1.5 million in 1993. With the launching of Operation Blockade and its various extensions after 1993, agency inefficiency really began to soar. The cost per entry went from $80 in 1993 to $260 in 1997, and over the same period the marginal cost of apprehension jumped from $1.5 million to $2.6 million per probability point.

Border enforcement involves not only the Border Patrol, of course, but a host of other people and facilities operated by the Immigration and Naturalization Service: immigration inspectors, detention facilities, guards, ports of entry, maintenance crews, administrators, clerical workers, and so forth. We therefore calculated two alternative measures of agency productivity by using the entire INS budget. Once again the cost ratios were flat through 1986 and climbed thereafter (data not shown). Total INS expenditures averaged around $200 per entry before IRCA, and the marginal cost of apprehension stood at about $1.75 million per probability point. Over the next twelve years both indices rose sharply, and by 1998 the former had reached $1,100 per entry and the latter $9 million per probability point. In other words, by the end of the 1990s U.S. taxpayers were buying apprehension probabilities that were no higher than they had been in the early 1980s, but they were paying five times as much!

How much money has been wasted in feckless border enforcement since 1986? The amount that should have been spent to maintain apprehension probabilities at historic levels can be estimated by taking the figure of $200 per undocumented entry that was the norm for the INS through 1986 and multiplying it by the number of entries estimated to have occurred from 1987 through 1998. This operation yields a total projected expenditure of $4.2 billion under the pre-IRCA enforcement regime. In fact, the actual budget for the INS from 1987 through 1998 totaled $20.7 billion, meaning that $16.5 billion was spent to no apparent effect. That is, the same probability of apprehension and the same degree of deterrence could have been purchased for $16.5 billion less than was actually spent. This figure represents the bill that taxpayers paid to maintain the illusion that the border was under control during a period of massive North American integration. At current rates of undocumented entry, Americans continue to pour at least $3 billion into useless border enforcement *each year.*

Declining Wages

IRCA sought not only to deter undocumented migrants by expanding border enforcement but also to neutralize the magnet of U.S. jobs by criminalizing the hiring of undocumented workers. IRCA required that prospective employees, for the first time, present documents that confirmed their identity and right to work in the United States. Employers, in turn, had to fill out an "I-9 Form," which identified the prospective worker and listed the documents he or she had presented. Although employers were not required to file I-9 forms with either the INS or the U.S. Department of Labor, they were required to keep them on file and to present them to an immigration inspector upon request. Failure to prepare and keep appropriate records would result in harsh penalties, including fines of up to $10,000 and criminal prosecution for repeated offenses (Bean et al. 1989; U.S. Department of Labor 1991).

IRCA sought to apply sanctions only against employers who knowingly hired undocumented migrants, and the I-9 forms were devised as a means to define "knowingly." As long as an employer inspected some reasonable-looking documents and completed an I-9 form, he or she had satisfied his or her duties under the law. An employer was under no obligation to verify the authenticity of the documents or to check with Washington about a person's legitimacy. If a work site was raided by the INS and the status of an employee found to be undocumented, as long as the employer had filled out and kept an I-9 form he or she was not liable to prosecution under IRCA. That employer had not *knowingly* hired the undocumented worker according to the letter of the law.

This procedure for implementing employer sanctions had two predictable consequences. First, it created a black market for bogus documents. Whereas before 1986 all that Mexicans had to do to be hired was to show up at a work site and offer their labor, after 1986 the rules changed: a worker now had to appear *with documents.* Within a short time entrepreneurs on both sides of the border were putting the latest desktop publishing techniques to work to create facsimiles of driver's licenses, Social Security cards, voter registration forms, birth certificates, and even permanent resident visas ("green cards"). Although price and accessibility varied with the complexity of the document and the quality of the reproduction, the black market was soon awash in fraudulent papers, which were sold openly by street vendors in towns and cities throughout Mexico and surreptitiously in Mexican neighborhoods throughout the United States.

The widespread availability and use of fraudulent documents markedly reduced IRCA's effectiveness in eliminating the demand for undocumented labor. Lindsay Lowell and Zhongren Jing (1994) estimated that as many as half of all unauthorized hires between 1986 and 1993 were made by employers who had in fact complied with IRCA's provisions, a finding generally corroborated in other studies

(U.S. Department of Labor 1991; Donato 1994; Lowell, Teachman, and Jing 1995). In the wake of employer sanctions, therefore, it was not really a question of whether a migrant could obtain documents and find a job; it was more a matter of how much he or she was willing to pay to get them and the quality of reproduction for which he or she was willing to settle.

A second consequence of IRCA's formula for implementing employer sanctions was more subtle but ultimately more serious. Even though I-9 forms offered a huge loophole to employers seeking to evade IRCA's restrictions, such evasion came at a price. In sectors of the labor market characterized by rapid turnover, seasonality, and small profit margins, the need to fill out and retain I-9 forms for every worker created a significant paperwork burden that dramatically raised the costs of hiring. Moreover, even if employers seemed to be protected by the I-9 form, they could not be sure that they would avoid prosecution, especially in the early days, when it was not clear exactly how the new law would work. Although the objective risks to employers may have changed little as a result of IRCA, the subjective risks were much higher, at least initially.

As a result of the increased costs and risks, some employers lowered the wages of their employees, thus compensating themselves for their added paperwork costs and new perceived risks. Employer sanctions in essence imposed a "tax" on the hiring of workers in sectors of the economy characterized by significant undocumented employment, and bosses then extracted that tax from their workers in the form of lower wages (Cobb-Clark, Shiells, and Lowell 1995; Bansak and Raphael 1998). If an employer knew for a fact that a worker was undocumented, he or she would have a special incentive to lower the wages of that person, and research clearly indicates the opening up of a gap in rates of pay between documented and undocumented workers, one that did not exist prior to 1986 (Phillips and Massey 2000). Contrary to what Congress had intended, therefore, employers continued to hire undocumented migrants; they simply transferred the costs and risks of doing so to the workers themselves in the form of lower pay.

Other employers took a different route to ensure their continued access to undocumented labor. Whereas before IRCA most employers hired undocumented workers directly, afterward they shifted to a pattern of indirect hiring through labor subcontractors. Under a subcontracting arrangement, a U.S. citizen or resident alien contractually agrees with an employer to provide a specific number of workers for a certain period of time to undertake a defined task at a fixed rate of pay per worker. Since the workers themselves are technically not employees of the firm but of the subcontractor, the employer avoids the need to comply with IRCA's burdensome paperwork requirements and escapes liability under the law. In return for providing this legal buffer, the subcontractor retains a portion of the workers' wages as income.

Such arrangements quickly became standard practice in industries characterized by high turnover, such as agriculture, construction, gardening, and custodial services (Martin and Taylor 1991; Taylor and Thilmany 1993; Taylor 1996; Martin 1996; Durand 1997; Taylor, Martin, and Fix 1997). As a result, the hiring process was completely restructured in sectors of the economy where immigrants worked. As indirect hiring became established after 1986, moreover, it was imposed on *all workers* regardless of legal status or citizenship. If citizens or legal resident aliens wished to get a job in agriculture or construction, they too had to work through a subcontractor and forfeit a portion of their wages in return for the opportunity to work. IRCA thus served to encourage outsourcing and to exacerbate the broader shift toward income inequality in the United States.

Thus, a perverse consequence of IRCA's employer sanctions was to lower the wages and undermine the working conditions not only of undocumented migrants but of documented migrants and U.S. citizens as well. This shift is illustrated in figure 6.6, which shows the trend in real wages earned by documented and undocumented Mexican migrants on their last U.S. trip. The data once again come from the MMP, but in this case the figures have been adjusted to constant 1983 U.S. dollars. As can be seen, IRCA had a relatively modest effect on the wages of undocumented migrants (see the dashed line). From 1980 through 1986 their wages trended slowly downward, going from around $4.10 per hour in 1980 to around $3.90 in 1986, a drop of about 3.3 cents per year. Over the next six years, however, the rate of decline accelerated to 8.3 cents per year as wages fell to around $3.40 in the immediate post-IRCA period, for a total decline of 13 percent from 1986 to 1992.

Among documented migrants, in contrast, the post-IRCA decline was much more serious. As with illegal migrants, those with documents experienced declining wages before the implementation of IRCA. Over the entire six-year period the wages of legal immigrants fell from $6.75 to $5.50 per hour, a drop of 21 cents per year. However, a very large portion of the decline occurred between 1982 and 1983, a period in Mexico of economic crisis and peso devaluation, which in the space of a few months made the perceived value of U.S. wages skyrocket and hence dramatically reduced Mexicans' reservation wages in dollar terms. If we exclude this one year from our cal-

Figure 6.6 Wages (1983 U.S. Dollars) Earned on Last U.S. Trip, 1980 to 1998

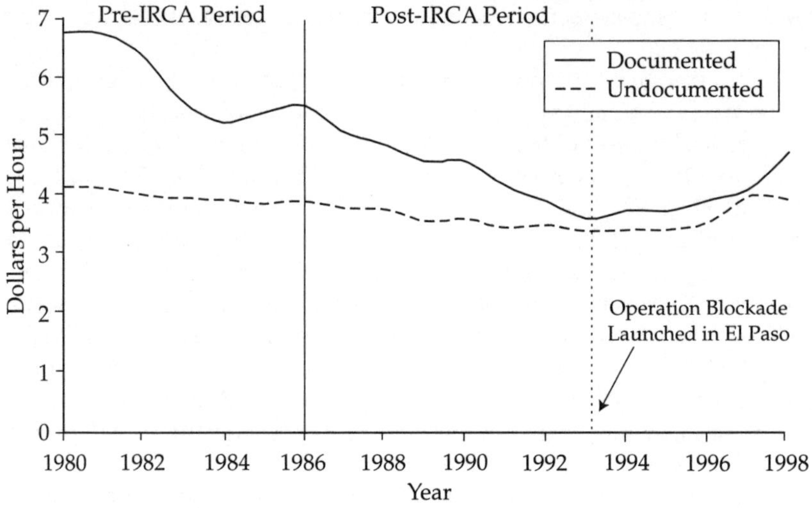

Source: Mexican Migration Project.

culations, the average decline over the period is only 9 cents per year. Whatever situation prevailed before IRCA, after 1986 the rate of decline accelerated to around 27 cents per year, causing a 35 percent erosion of value by 1993, a significant drop ($p < .001$).

After 1993 the decline in migrant wages bottomed out; starting in 1996, wages began to rise once again, both for those with documents and for those without, reflecting broader trends in the U.S. economy. The late 1990s witnessed the first upturn in wages among unskilled workers in several decades, owing to record low rates of unemployment and strong labor demand (Uchitelle 1997). Given such a tight labor market, Doris Meissner, the commissioner of the Immigration and Naturalization Service, made official in March 1999 what had for some time already been the de facto INS policy: the agency would cease internal inspections at work sites and enforce immigration laws only at the border and ports of entry (Billings 1999). Under these circumstances, the wages of documented and undocumented migrants rose in the late 1990s, although as of 1998 they had not yet recouped the ground lost in the period 1986 to 1992.

The shift from direct hiring to labor subcontracting also brought about a growing informalization of employment, which is observed in

Figure 6.7 Wages Paid in Cash on Last U.S. Trip, 1980 to 1998

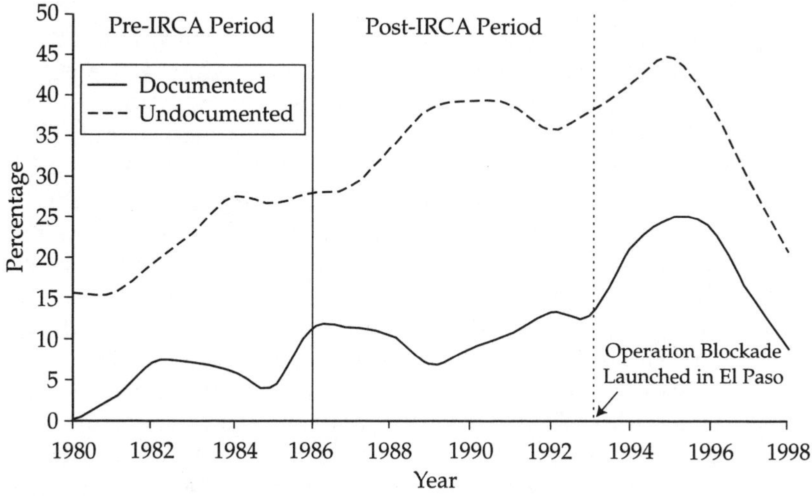

Source: Mexican Migration Project.

the MMP data as a growing tendency to be paid in cash rather than by check. Whereas most businesses pay their workers by check so as not to run afoul of the IRS and other federal agencies, subcontractors are much less likely to do so. Subcontractors themselves may be paid by check, but they generally cash such checks and then distribute the money among their "crew" of workers. Cash payment is a good indicator of informalization because those paid in cash tend not to have taxes withheld and are very unlikely to be eligible for social benefits, either public or private. Subcontracting arrangements and cash payments also make it easier for employers to skirt occupational safety and health regulations, minimum-wage laws, and other worker protections.

Figure 6.7 shows the percentage of documented and undocumented migrants who were paid in cash on their most recent U.S. trip from 1980 to 1998. As one would expect, undocumented migrants are more likely than legal immigrants to be working informally. Nonetheless, in the early 1980s the practice of cash payment was rare for both groups. In 1980 and 1981, for example, only 16 percent of undocumented migrants reported cash wages, and among documented migrants the figure was close to zero. After 1982 informalization began to increase among undocumented workers, and the percentage paid in cash nearly doubled within two years, rising to 28 percent. Although the percentage also increased for legal migrants over this period (from 3 to 7 percent), on the eve of IRCA's passage in 1985 it had once again dropped back to around 4 percent. In contrast, the rate of cash payment remained fairly constant for undocumented migrants in the years immediately preceding IRCA, holding at around 27 percent.

IRCA's passage in 1986 was associated with a jump from 4 to 11 percent in the rate of cash payment among documented migrants; that rate fell back to around 7 percent in 1989 before reaching 13 percent in 1992. In other words, between 1985, the year before IRCA, and 1992, the year before the launching of Operation Blockade, the rate of informalization among documented migrants tripled, albeit from a low base. Among undocumented migrants, meanwhile, the rate of informalization rose dramatically in the years following IRCA. From the plateau of 27 percent that held from 1984 to 1987, the rate of cash payment rose to 39 percent by 1989 and fluctuated between 35 and 39 percent through 1993. From a situation in 1980 where virtually no documented migrants and just a tiny minority of undocumented migrants were paid in cash, by 1993 cash payment had become relatively common, characterizing the employment terms of nearly 40 percent of undocumented workers and 13 percent of documented workers.

The launching of repressive border enforcement operations in 1993 was associated with another acceleration in the rate of informalization for migrant workers. Between 1993 and 1995 the frequency of cash payment reached 25 percent for legal immigrants and 45 percent for those without documents. Only the very tight labor markets that emerged after 1996 brought relief; by 1998 the degree of informalization was falling sharply for both groups, dropping to 20 percent for undocumented migrants and 9 percent for documented migrants.

Nonetheless, in the years from 1986 to 1993, Mexican migrants—legal as well as illegal—increasingly worked for lower wages under more precarious circumstances, and the decline in wages was especially sharp for documented migrants. Under these circumstances, one might expect migrants to make up for falling wages by increasing their hours of work (see Dávila, Pagán, and Grau 1998). As figure 6.8 reveals, this is indeed what happened, and given the relatively greater loss suffered by documented migrants, the increase was especially dramatic for them. From 1980 to 1984 documented migrants worked between forty-two and forty-three hours per week, compared with forty-five to forty-seven hours for undocumented migrants. Given the higher wages earned by the former, they were in a position to receive the same total earnings as the latter while working fewer hours. After 1984, however, documented migrants increased their la-

Figure 6.8 Hours Worked per Week on Last U.S. Trip, 1980 to 1998

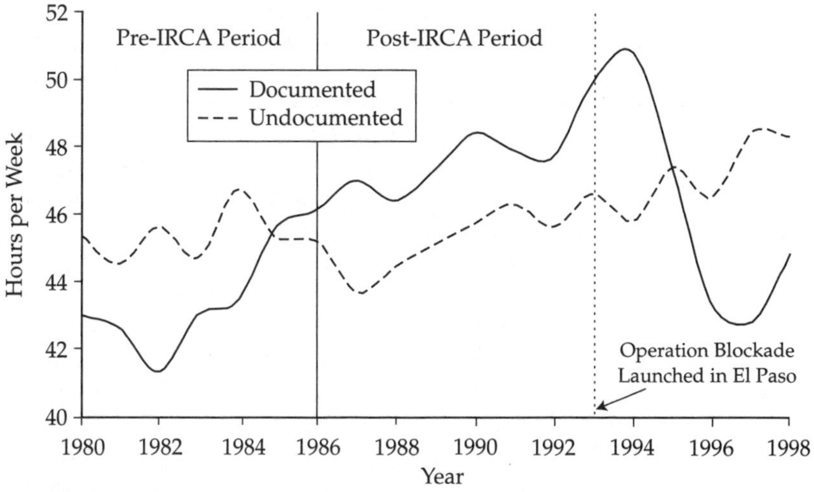

Source: Mexican Migration Project.

bor supply in response to the sharp decline in their wages, with the number of hours worked jumping from forty-three to forty-six hours per week by 1986. In contrast, hours of work dropped from forty-seven to around forty-four hours per week for undocumented migrants, representing the rather flat trend in wages for them.

Thus, with the advent of IRCA in 1986, documented migrants for the first time worked more hours than their documented counterparts, and over the next eight years the gap widened. During 1990 and 1991 hours worked per week fluctuated around forty-eight hours for legal immigrants and around forty-six hours for those without documents. With the launching of the border buildup in 1993, moreover, the gap of two hours per week turned into a chasm of five hours as the hours of labor supplied by documented migrants shot up to fifty-one per week in 1994, compared with under forty-six hours for those without documents. As the free fall in wages bottomed out during the latter half of the 1990s and formalized employment practices returned to U.S. labor markets, the relative amount of labor supplied by documented versus undocumented migrants once again returned to its historical norm. Among documented migrants, hours of work plummeted to forty-three hours per week and then rose to forty-five hours by 1998. In contrast, labor supply for undocumented migrants oscillated upward unsteadily to reach forty-eight hours in the same year.

Despite the partial recovery of the late 1990s, as of 1998 both documented and undocumented migrants were working longer hours for lower pay under more vulnerable circumstances than they had in either 1980 or 1986, and if we had considered the situation in 1994, before the remarkable expansion of the 1990s had significantly tightened labor markets, the situation would have looked markedly worse. It is perhaps unsurprising that undocumented migrants were worse off in the post-IRCA period. After all, Congress *sought* to make their lives miserable. What is more disconcerting is that, in relative terms, the deterioration in wages and working conditions was far more severe for legal residents, and presumably for the naturalized and native citizens who worked alongside them. Thus, rather than eliminating the magnet of U.S. jobs and reducing undocumented migration, the post-IRCA regime of immigration enforcement lowered wages and working conditions for people with a legal right to live and work in the United States. Rather than protecting domestic workers, the criminalization of undocumented hiring ended up marginalizing them by exacerbating income inequality, encouraging subcontracting, and generally promoting the informalization of hiring.

Maximizing the Pain

The massive wastage of lives, money, and wages has been bad enough, but the consequences of the post-IRCA enforcement regime are actually worse than we have indicated so far. Not only have recent immigration and border policies produced a host of negative consequences, but they have ensured that such consequences will befall the largest number of people in the widest variety of U.S. regions. Although the post-IRCA enforcement regime may not have deterred many migrants, it did succeed in transforming a circular flow of short-term migrants entering just three states into a nationwide diaspora of long-term residents settling within all states of the Union. Whereas before 1986 Mexican immigration was a regional issue affecting a handful of states, post-IRCA policies guaranteed that it would grow to become national in scope.

The Geographic Diversification of Mexican Migration

As we have already shown, the vast majority of border crossings prior to 1986 occurred in California, and not surprisingly the bulk of these migrants simply proceeded to jobs and opportunities in that state. If migrants did not go to California, they generally went to Texas or Illinois. The massive buildup of enforcement resources in southern California, El Paso, and around other ports of entry, however, diverted the migratory flows away from traditional points of destination. The deflection of migrants away from California was especially pronounced, for the militarization of the San Diego–Tijuana sector was accompanied by an unusually deep recession and a nasty anti-immigrant mobilization in southern California. At the same time IRCA's massive legalization program liberated 2.3 million former undocumented migrants, some 55 percent of whom lived in California, from the enforced servitude of illegal status and gave them, for the first time, the confidence and freedom to strike out in search of better opportunities elsewhere.

The net effect of the border buildup, the legalizations, the recession, and the anti-immigrant mobilization was to transform Mexican immigration from a regional into a national phenomenon. The progressive "nationalization" of Mexican migration is indicated in figure 6.9 by the rising percentage of Mexican migrants going to a nontraditional destination (defined as anyplace outside of California, Texas, or Illinois). Once again the data come from the MMP.

During the period 1980 to 1986 the vast majority of both documented and undocumented migrants were going to traditional receiving states: 85 to 90 percent of those with documents and 90 percent of those without. Although the relative number of legal immigrants going to nontraditional states had begun to rise before 1986, it surged in the years immediately after IRCA to reach 25 percent in the late 1980s before dropping back to 12 percent in 1992. The bulge from 1986 to 1992 reflects the behavior of newly legalized immigrants who, given the bleak situation in California, sought out new opportunities in different regions. Although we would not expect legal migrants to be much affected by the border buildup launched in 1993, we would certainly expect them to respond to the nativist mobilization and anti-immigrant hysteria that occurred at the same time. The passage of Proposition 187 in 1994 thus led to another surge in the movement of documented migrants away from California and toward nontraditional destination states, and as the economy heated up and labor shortages appeared in the Northeast, the Midwest, and the Southeast in industries such as meatpacking, poultry processing, seafood canning, construction, and agribusiness, the trend accelerated. By 1998, 30 percent of legal immigrants were avoiding the traditional "big three" destinations.

In the immediate post-IRCA period, undocumented migration was

Figure 6.9 Workers Going to a Nontraditional Destination on Last U.S. Trip, 1980 to 1998

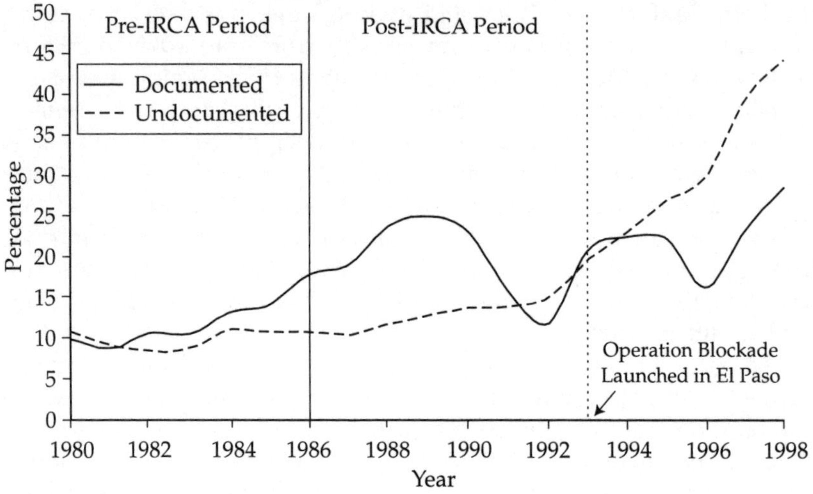

Source: Mexican Migration Project.

only modestly affected by the escalation of border enforcement, which proceeded rather slowly through 1992. Most migrants continued to make their way to California, Texas, or Illinois. As of 1992, on the eve of Operation Blockade, only 15 percent of undocumented migrants had gone to a nontraditional destination. With the massive militarization of border enforcement in 1993, however, the stream of undocumented migrants immediately shifted away from traditional receiving states and toward new destination areas. The share going to a nontraditional destination tripled between 1992 and 1998, rising from 15 to 45 percent. With this remarkable spreading out of Mexican migration, the newly created negative consequences of repressive immigration enforcement—falling wages, rising job informality, and a greater marginalization—would affect a larger number of Americans than ever before.

The Shift Toward Permanence

Not only were undocumented migrants dispersing more widely in the wake of the new enforcement regime, but they were staying longer north of the border. A perverse consequence of draconian border enforcement is that it does not deter would-be migrants from trying to enter the country so much as it discourages those who are already here from returning home. The end result of a border buildup is typically longer trip durations, lower probabilities of return migration, and a shift toward permanent settlement. Geographic diffusion combined with a shift toward permanence guarantees that the effects of Mexican immigration—positive or negative—on the United States and its people are maximized.

Border enforcement pushes undocumented migrants toward longer trips and lower return probabilities for two reasons. First, even though the costs of border crossing are not increased to the point where migration becomes uneconomical, they are nonetheless increased, both in practical and monetary terms. We have already seen the rising toll in human life brought about by the militarization of the border after 1993; for every death there were also many injuries and serious mishaps that went undetected. Having run the gauntlet of border enforcement and survived, it is hardly surprising that migrants are loath to repeat the experience.

At the same time tougher enforcement increases the out-of-pocket costs of border crossing. As more people turned to border smugglers (*coyotes*) and were forced to undertake longer trips over more hazardous terrain, the financial costs of border crossing began to rise. The growing cost of border crossing is indicated in figure 6.10, which shows the average cost, by year, of hiring a coyote in Tijuana and elsewhere from 1980 to 1998. If a migrant did not use a paid smuggler in crossing, the cost was coded as zero. In this way we capture changes in the rate as well as the price of border smuggling. All prices are expressed in constant 1983 dollars.

Prior to IRCA, the cost of coyote rental was fairly constant and did not differ much between Tijuana and elsewhere. In Tijuana the average cost fluctuated narrowly between $210 and $220, whereas at other crossing points the average cost trended slowly downward from $250 in 1980 to around $190 in 1986. Not much changed in the immediate post-IRCA period. From 1986 through 1991 Tijuana coyote prices remained steady at $210 to $220, while non-Tijuana prices fluctuated between $150 and $200.

With the escalation of enforcement after 1992, however, the world changed significantly for undocumented migrants, and the cost of renting a smuggler began to inflate rapidly. Geographic diversification also contributed to increases in coyote fees, which came to incorporate transport costs to ever more distant locations. In Tijuana the price rose from its historical average of around $215 to reach $359 in 1998, representing an annual inflation rate of more than 7 percent. Away from Tijuana, the situation was even more dramatic. As sleepy

Figure 6.10 Cost (1983 Dollars) of Hiring a Coyote, 1980 to 1998

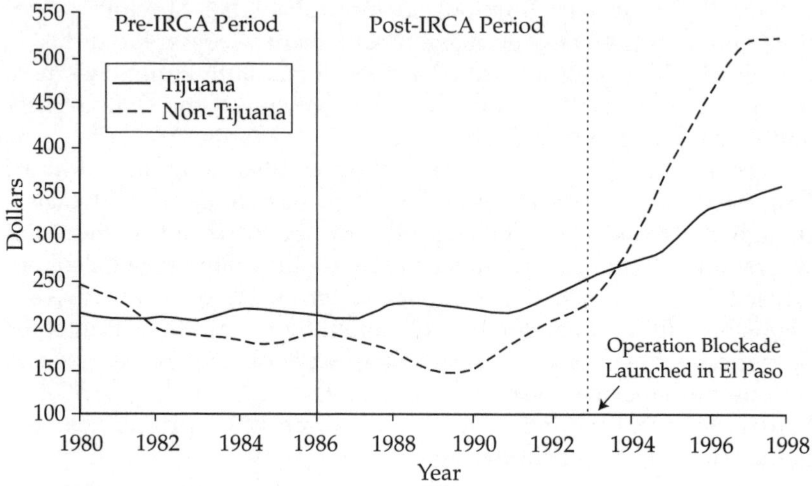

Source: Mexican Migration Project.

Mexican border towns overnight became major staging areas for clandestine border crossing, the sudden imbalance between the demand for and the supply of smuggling services caused the average price to skyrocket from a low of $150 in 1990 to $525 by 1998—a remarkable price inflation of 250 percent in just eight years (averaging 11 percent per year).

As we have already shown, the percentage of crossings that took place at points other than Tijuana also increased dramatically after 1992. As a result of this trend, a growing share of migrants were paying the highest and most rapidly inflating smuggling fees. Considering Tijuana and non-Tijuana crossings together, the average price of a coyote rose from $189 in 1990 to $482 in 1998. To pay off this higher debt and move the trip toward profitability, migrants after 1990 had to work longer. However long it had taken to amortize coyote fees before 1990, by 1998 it was taking two to three times longer.

The higher fees also contributed to the growing prevalence of family-financed migration, which led to more secure service and lower probabilities of apprehension. When fees were under $250, migrants generally saved or borrowed the needed funds themselves. As fees rose to $600—and even higher when greater transportation costs were factored in—coyotes were increasingly financed by family or friends already in the United States. The U.S. resident would contract with a coyote to meet a specified relative on the Mexican side of the border and transport him or her to a prearranged meeting point in the United States. The agreement was secured with a down payment made in the United States, and the balance was paid with the delivery of the specified person at the agreed-upon meeting point. In this way, delivery was guaranteed, safety was increased, and migrants and their families achieved some protection against fraud. It represents yet another instance of social capital translating directly into U.S. access to build self-perpetuating momentum into the migratory process.

The most accurate way to measure the shift from circulatory migration toward permanent settlement is to compute annual probabilities of return migration. Using life history data compiled for household heads in the MMP, we counted all person-years in which subjects spent any time north of the border and divided this total into the number who went back to Mexico during the person-year in question, yielding an annual probability of return migration. We then plotted these yearly probabilities for documented and undocumented migrants, as shown in figure 6.11.

Undocumented migrants are indicated by the solid line at the top of the figure. As one might predict, the likelihood of returning home is much greater for undocumented than for documented migrants (who are indicated by the dashed line at the bottom of the figure). Before IRCA, the annual probability of return migration for undocumented migrants varied between .25 and .30 per year. If 1,000 migrants were to enter the United States subject to a 25 percent chance of returning each year, 763 would return home within five years, yielding an average trip length of around 3.0 years and a median duration of 2.4 years. During the immediate post-IRCA period, the annual probability of return migration rose slightly, fluctuating around .32 in the years from 1986 through 1990. Given this return probability, 86 percent of all migrants would be expected to return home within five years, yielding an average trip length of 2.0 years and a median duration of just 1.8 years.

Beginning in 1990, however, the likelihood of return migration began to fall and then plunged massively with the border buildup that commenced in 1993. By 1998 the annual probability of return migration had fallen to just .10, some 70 percent below the 1990 figure. Such a probability implies an average trip length of 8.9 years and a median duration of 6.6 years. After five years, only 40 percent of migrants would be expected to have left the United States. In short, U.S. immigration and border policies after 1990 transformed what had been a circular flow of temporary migrants into a settled immigration of permanent residents, as indicated by the shift in mean trip length from two to nine years.

Although documented migrants were not directly affected by the

Figure 6.11 Probability of Returning Within Two Years of Entering United States on First Trip, 1980 to 1998

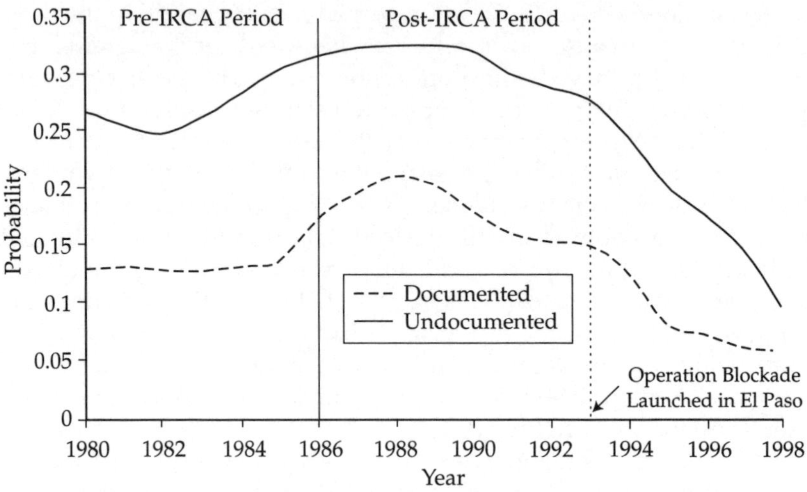

Source: Mexican Migration Project.

massive increase in border enforcement during the 1990s, they were affected indirectly. Among households in the MMP sample that contained documented migrants, 46 percent also contained someone without documents. With an undocumented migrant in a household, family members could not circulate together freely, since legal immigrants were reluctant to leave their undocumented relatives behind. As a result, the rate of return migration for legal immigrants, which was already much lower than that of undocumented migrants, fell even further after 1990. From a peak of around .20 per year in the late 1980s, the annual return probability reached .06 in 1998. However, return probabilities were falling more slowly for documented than for undocumented migrants, and by the late 1990s the two groups were converging toward a figure somewhere between .05 and .10.

Thus, post-IRCA immigration policies were instrumental in promoting the permanent settlement of Mexican migrants in three ways: first, by legalizing a huge number of migrants and thereby shifting them from a higher to a lower probability of return; second, by increasing the costs of border crossing in a way that discouraged return trips by undocumented migrants; and finally, by lowering the already low probabilities of return for legal immigrants. When documented and undocumented migrants are considered together, we find that the total probability of return migration dropped from a high of .260 in 1986 to just .075 in 1998.

The pre-IRCA probability yields an average trip length of 3.3 years and a median duration in the United States of 2.3 years. If 100,000 Mexican migrants were to enter the United States each year subject to this rate of departure (.26), in the long run we would observe the formation of a stationary population of 3.343 million Mexicans in the United States. In contrast, assuming the 1998 rate of return migration (.075) yields an average trip length of 12.8 years and a median duration of 8.9. Under this circumstance, the annual entry of 100,000 Mexican migrants would yield a permanent stationary population of 12.821 million persons. In other words, by significantly reducing the probability of return migration, the post-IRCA regime of border enforcement dramatically increased the ultimate size of the Mexican population in the United States, raising it by a factor of nearly four!

When figures from the 2000 census first became available, they revealed a dramatic increase in the size of the Hispanic population: Latinos had overtaken blacks to become the nation's largest minority group almost a decade earlier than expected. Although the rapid growth of the Hispanic population took most demographers, the media, government officials, and the public by surprise, in reality there was no mystery about it: the dramatic increase in the size of the Mexican population was entirely predictable and followed axiomatically from immigration and border policies instituted by the United States after 1986.

The Shift Toward Dependency

Even if the rate of Mexican entry into the United States had remained constant, the rate of growth in the Mexican population of the United States would have increased substantially because of the drop in return probabilities. But as we saw in figure 6.2, the wave of legalizations that transpired between 1986 and 1990 was followed by an *increase* in the odds of female undocumented migration, essentially doubling it over its pre-IRCA average. A similar increase in the odds of female migration occurred among documented migrants. As male migrants began to extend their trips to avoid the necessity of recrossing the border, they naturally began to send for their wives. Accompanying the increase in permanence, therefore, was a new feminization of migration.

Table 6.1 presents selected characteristics of documented and undocumented migrants leaving for the United States on their first trip before and after the implementation of IRCA. Not surprisingly, legal

Table 6.1 Characteristics of Migrants on First U.S. Trip Before and After IRCA

Category and Characteristic	Pre-IRCA: Migrated 1980 to 1986	Transition Era: Migrated 1987 to 1992	Post-IRCA: Migrated 1993 or Later
Undocumented migrants			
Female	25.7%	34.4%	32.5%
Under age thirteen	4.2	4.1	3.1
Not working[a]	11.5	18.5	19.5
Documented migrants			
Female	44.7	46.9	45.9
Under age thirteen	56.2	57.1	55.1
Not working[a]	15.9	22.4	29.1

Source: Mexican Migration Project.
a. Migrants age sixteen or older.

immigration has always been substantially female, and there is little trend over time. The percentage of women among documented migrants fluctuated around 46 percent before IRCA (1980 to 1986), during the post-IRCA transition period (1987 to 1992), and after IRCA (1993 onward). What has changed over time has been the propensity for women to migrate in *undocumented* status. Before IRCA, women constituted only one-quarter of undocumented migrants, whereas during the transition and post-IRCA periods that figure rose to one-third.

In concert with the feminization of undocumented migration, the percentage of migrants who were not working also increased. The proportion of undocumented migrants not holding a U.S. job nearly doubled between the pre-IRCA and post-IRCA periods, going from 11.5 to 19.5 percent. Although there was no trend toward feminization among documented migrants, the percentage of nonworkers likewise nearly doubled, going from 16 to 29 percent between the two periods. Many of these nonworkers were undoubtedly children, since at all times a clear majority (55 to 57 percent) of documented migrants were under the age of thirteen.

In contrast, only a tiny fraction (3 to 4 percent) of undocumented migrants were age twelve or younger. Although undocumented migration may increasingly include adult women, through 1998 there was little sign of any "greening" of undocumented migration. Mexican parents are understandably reluctant to expose their children to the dangers of undocumented border crossing and the rigors of clandestine life in the United States.

Table 6.2 Use of U.S. Social Services on Last Trip Before and After IRCA

Category and Characteristic	Pre-IRCA: Migrated 1980 to 1986	Transition Era: Migrated 1987 to 1992	Post-IRCA: Migrated 1993 or Later
Undocumented migrants			
Children in school	11.2%	9.8%	6.2%
Receiving unemployment	6.3	3.5	2.6
Receiving food stamps	4.2	4.4	2.9
Receiving welfare	2.9	3.2	4.0
Documented migrants			
Children in school	46.5	33.3	21.5
Receiving unemployment	32.9	33.6	23.9
Receiving food stamps	10.3	13.7	4.9
Receiving welfare	9.0	6.5	8.1

Source: Mexican Migration Project.

In sum, the shift in Mexican migration from short-term circulation to long-term settlement has been accompanied by a feminization of the undocumented flow and a doubling of the relative number of nonworkers, but not by an increase in the migration of children, a step that usually comes only with legalization. The shift toward feminization and dependency might be thought to augur a greater use of U.S. social services, but this does not seem to be the case. If anything, utilization rates have gone down over time, at least according to MMP data compiled from migrant household heads on their last U.S. trip.

As table 6.2 indicates, as we move from the pre-IRCA period through the transition era to the post-IRCA period, lower proportions of both documented and undocumented migrants reported having children in U.S. schools, receiving unemployment, and getting food stamps. The rate of welfare receipt shows no significant trend. These trends may be interpreted positively as reflecting a gradual improvement in economic circumstances or negatively as a progressive disenfranchisement of Mexican migrants—both legal and illegal—from publicly provided services in the United States. No doubt both occurred to some extent.

As we have shown, however, wages and working conditions generally deteriorated through 1996, suggesting that economic improvements could have played a role only toward the end of the series. In contrast, anti-immigrant mobilizations occurred in the early 1990s and culminated in 1996, suggesting a greater weight toward disenfranchisement. Considered together, the feminization of migration, the rise in dependency, and the abrupt drop in the use of public services indicate the growing marginalization of an increasingly permanent population of the United States.

The Future of an Illusion

To summarize what we have demonstrated so far, post-IRCA immigration policies have failed to stop undocumented migration; they have produced a host of negative consequences for immigrants and natives alike; they have spread these unfortunate effects as widely as possible throughout the country; and they have maximized their negative impact by transforming a permanent flow into a permanent settlement that includes increasing proportions of dependents rather than productive workers. If this were not enough, the post-IRCA regime of immigration policy has actually *encouraged* additional migration from Mexico to the United States. By sponsoring a massive legalization campaign and pushing Mexicans decisively toward naturalization, U.S. policies have sowed the seeds for an even larger migration in the future, guaranteeing that the illusion of a controlled border will become ever more difficult and costly to maintain.

The schizophrenic nature of U.S. immigration policy toward Mexico was built into the IRCA legislation itself, for this act simultaneously contained provisions that were narrowly restrictive and wildly expansive. To enact employer sanctions and secure funding for border militarization, IRCA's backers had to placate civil libertarians, Latino advocacy groups, humanitarian organizations, and employers by authorizing two large-scale legalization programs: an amnesty for undocumented settlers and a special legalization program for undocumented farmworkers. Between 1987 and 1990 Congress authorized persons who believed they qualified for either program to apply for temporary legal status. As figure 6.12 shows, there was an immediate surge in applications for temporary protected status, which peaked at around 1.2 million in 1988 (see the solid line).

Although it admitted them to temporary legal status, IRCA deliberately pushed these former undocumented migrants toward U.S. citizenship by requiring them to take special courses in English and U.S. civics *before* receiving their permanent visas. Those who obtained a green card through the usual channels did not have to take such classes. Despite the additional barriers, in the end some 2.3 million Mexican immigrants dutifully complied with the requirements, took their English and history courses, and were admitted to permanent

Figure 6.12 Post-IRCA Legalization of Mexican Migrants

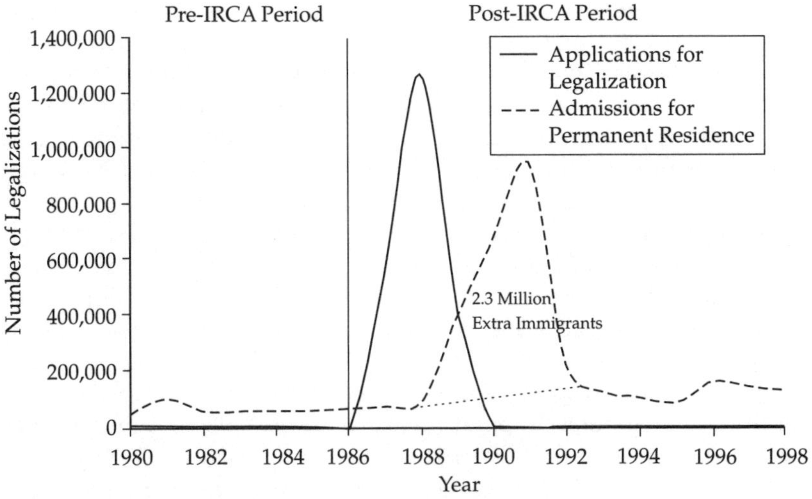

Source: U.S. Immigration and Naturalization Service.

resident status between 1989 and 1993 (see the dashed line in figure 6.12).

IRCA's legalization programs did more, however, than simply change the legal status of people who were already migrating. It seems actually to have *pulled into migration* many Mexicans who otherwise would never have left for the United States. The special agricultural worker (SAW) program, in particular, was so loosely administered, so nebulous in its criteria for qualification, and so plagued with opportunities for fakery that it induced many Mexicans who had never worked in U.S. agriculture, or even been in the United States, to cross the border in hopes of being legalized through fraudulent means. According to one study, the number of SAW applicants in California alone was *three times* the size of the state's entire agricultural workforce during the period in question (Martin, Taylor, and Hardiman 1988). In short, IRCA for a brief period actually *expanded* legal migration, increasing the rate of documented out-migration from Mexico to levels not seen since the 1920s.

If requiring English and civics lessons had not been enough to drive home the message that even legalized migrants were not so welcome in the United States, the early and middle 1990s witnessed an upsurge of nativist sentiment that proved to be more convincing. After achieving success at the state level through a variety of referenda, the nativist movement went national in 1996 when the U.S. Congress passed legislation that stripped legal immigrants of their right to many federal and state entitlements. At about the same time the Mexican government moved toward accepting dual nationality and in 1998 officially recognized the right to retain Mexican citizenship even after naturalizing in the United States. In other words, during the short period from 1993 to 1998 the costs of becoming a U.S. citizen were dramatically lowered by Mexican authorities while the benefits were markedly increased by U.S. policies.

The result was predictable: a massive movement of Mexicans toward naturalization, ultimately producing half a million more new U.S. citizens than would have otherwise been the case. As figure 6.13 shows, there was an exponential increase in the number of naturalizations by Mexicans during the early 1990s, with the annual number rising from just 13,000 in 1992 to 217,000 in 1996. Although the number of naturalizations dropped thereafter, as of 1998 the annual number was still in excess of 100,000, six times the 1980 to 1993 average. Between 1992 and 1998 some 480,000 more Mexicans had naturalized than would have been expected under the pre-1992 regime.

These successive waves of legalization and naturalization had important consequences for the future of Mexican immigration, since U.S. immigration law allocates the vast majority of its annual quota of numerically limited visas to relatives of citizens and resident aliens. The second family preference category, for example, reserves some 114,200 green cards per year for the spouses, minor children, and unmarried adult sons and daughters of permanent resident aliens, subject only to the country quota of 20,000 visas per year. We determined that each migrant in the MMP who was legalized under IRCA had an average of 4.0 relatives who qualified for entry in this preference category. If we apply this figure to the 2.3 million persons who were legalized under IRCA, we estimate that an additional 9.2 million entitlements for immigration visas were created as a result of the legalization. Although these people may have to wait in line for a long time, owing to the country quotas, if they can wait long enough they will ultimately get a green card that will enable them to live and work in the United States.

Although legalization generates some potential for future immigration, even more entitlements for entry are created by naturalization. To begin with, 112,000 visas are reserved for the adult sons and daughters and brothers and sisters of U.S. citizens, subject only to country quota limitations. The average naturalized person in the MMP data had 1.8 nonmigrant siblings and 0.6 nonmigrant adult children, for a total of 2.4 potential immigrants in this numerically limited

Figure 6.13 Naturalizations of Mexican Immigrants, 1980 to 1998

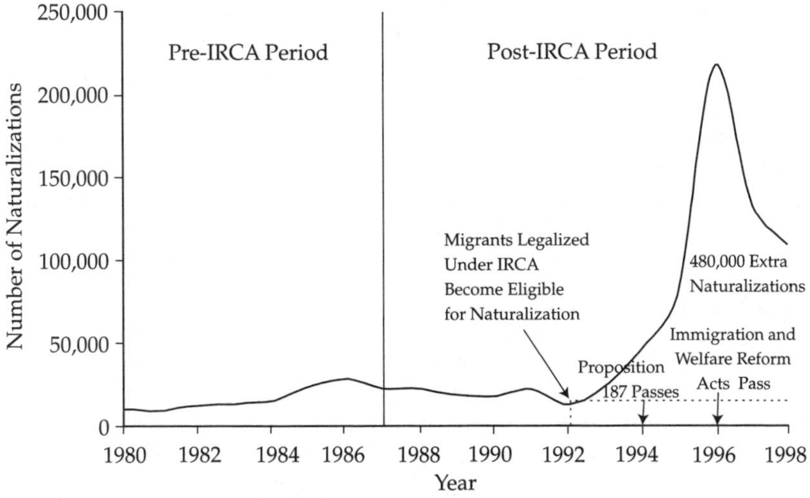

Source: U.S. Immigration and Naturalization Service.

category. In addition, every U.S. citizen has the right to sponsor the entry of his or her spouse, minor children, and parents *without any numerical restriction whatsoever.* According to MMP data, each naturalized person had an average of 0.4 nonmigrant spouses, 1.2 nonmigrant minor children, and 0.6 living nonmigrant parents, for a total of 2.2 potential additional immigrants.

Applying these figures to the 480,000 naturalizations induced by U.S. policy through 1998, we estimate that the new regime of immigration enforcement created 11.5 million potential new immigrants subject to numerical limitation and another 10.5 million subject to no restrictions at all. In short, the schizophrenic policy regime that began with the passage of IRCA and culminated with the twin 1996 immigration and welfare reform bills created a tremendous potential for future *legal* migration from Mexico to the United States.

Legalization and naturalization not only have important implications for legal migration but also affect the future of undocumented migration. Although the acquisition of documents or citizenship may not confer a "right" to illegal entry by friends and relatives, it does put a migrant in a better position to sponsor them unofficially. Through legalization, former undocumented migrants gain not only access to higher wages, more geographic mobility, and better housing but greater confidence. The new freedoms and resources make it easier for them to pay the costs of border smuggling, provide shelter, purchase documents, make contacts, and find jobs for their friends and relatives who wish to migrate illegally. According to MMP-based estimates published by Douglas Massey and Kristin Espinosa (1997), being in a household in which someone had been legalized under IRCA increased the likelihood of migrating illegally by a factor of almost nine, raising it from .04 per year to .35 per year. Thus, by granting 2.3 million green cards to former undocumented migrants, IRCA made it easier for millions of their undocumented friends and relatives to migrate to the United States.

The Worst of All Possible Worlds

If the United States had set out to design a dysfunctional immigration policy, it could hardly have done a better job than what it did between 1986 and 1996. U.S. taxpayers now waste at least $3 billion annually in essentially useless border enforcement while the efficiency of Border Patrol operations is in rapid decline. Despite its extravagance, the expensive post-IRCA enforcement regime has had no detectable effect, either in deterring undocumented migrants or in raising the probability of their apprehension. It has been effective, however, in causing at least 160 needless deaths each year. It has also lowered wages for workers—both native and foreign, legal and illegal—and exacerbated income inequality in the United States. Furthermore, it has guaranteed that these negative externalities are widely felt by transforming a seasonal movement of male workers going to three states into a national population of settled families dispersed throughout the country. Later attempts to ban noncitizens from receiving social services have marginalized both documented and undocumented migrants and undermined the health, education, and welfare of future American citizens. These attacks on social rights have only served to accelerate the movement of Mexicans toward naturalization, setting the stage for even larger migrant flows in the future. In the end, we have the worst of all possible worlds: continued and growing Mexican migration under conditions that are detrimental to the United States, its citizens, and the migrants themselves.

All of these negative consequences fundamentally stem from the unwillingness of the United States to accept the reality of North American integration. In NAFTA the nation committed itself to a joint framework for the continent-wide integration of markets for goods, capital, information, commodities, and services, but since then it has refused to recognize the inevitable fact that labor markets also merge in an integrated economy. In practical if not logical terms, it is impossible to create a single North American market characterized by the free movement of all factors of production except one. Rather than bringing labor migration into the open and managing it in ways that might maximize the benefits and minimize the costs, the United States has employed increasingly repressive means and growing amounts of money to drive the flows underground to maintain the illusion of a controlled border—one that is miraculously porous with respect to all movements except those involving labor and drugs.

As this chapter has clearly shown, however, maintaining this pretense has become increasingly costly, and given the seeds for future migration that U.S. authorities have already sown, it will only grow more costly in years to come. The time is thus ripe for the United States to abandon its illusions, stop deceiving itself, and to accept the reality, indeed the necessity, of North American integration. It is not as though there is another choice. Canada, Mexico, and the United States are one another's primary trading partners, and all three nations are increasingly bound together by dense networks of transportation, communication, trade, friendship, kinship, and multifarious association. Integration is so advanced that stopping it now would be sheer folly, far more costly to all parties than simply allowing it to continue. It is far more practical and painless to attempt to manage the process of integration for the benefit of all concerned rather than to pretend to stop it from proceeding. To do so, however, requires a revolutionary change in thinking about Mexican immigration and a fresh approach to U.S. border policy, our subject in the next and final chapter.

Chapter 7

Repair Manual: U.S. Immigration Policies for a New Century

IMMIGRATION policy is often cast as a Hobson's choice between open and closed borders, between the free and unhindered movement of immigrants and the imposition of strict limitations on their numbers and characteristics. Public officials and citizens alike generally think about immigration using the conceptual apparatus of neoclassical economics, whether they realize it or not. They see a developing world filled with millions of desperately poor people who, unless they are forcibly blocked or at least strongly discouraged, will surely seek to improve their lot by moving to developed nations such as the United States. This view focuses not only on the gulf in living standards but also on a contrasting demography. Whereas the developing world is large (5 billion people) and growing rapidly (by 1.7 percent per year), the developed world is much smaller (1.2 billion people) and growing more slowly (just 0.1 percent per year). Unless wealthy countries keep up their defenses, it seems logical to conclude, they will be "flooded" or "invaded" by impoverished migrants from the Third World.

When framed in these stark terms, the necessity of a strict immigration policy seems self-evident, and given the conceptual tools offered by neoclassical economics, the only realistic policy is to attempt to raise the costs and lower the benefits for both documented and undocumented migrants. Such has been the logic employed by U.S. policymakers in recent years. By militarizing the border, penalizing employers who hire unauthorized workers, barring immigrants from social programs, limiting their rights to housing, health care, schooling, and employment, and generally making life unpleasant for foreigners in the United States, U.S. policy has sought to tilt the cost-benefit calculation to make immigration seem less attractive.

We have seen, however, that the causes of international migration are by no means limited to those theorized under neoclassical economics. Although some migrants do indeed move to take advantage of a wage gap to maximize lifetime earnings, it does not follow that wage differentials necessarily "cause" immigration. Indeed, the largest migration streams are generally *not* associated with the widest wage gaps, and large differences in living standards frequently do not yield significant migration streams, even in the absence of formal barriers.

It is not that the theory of neoclassical economics is wrong, but that by itself it is seriously incomplete. As our review here has shown, international migration stems as much from the mechanisms specified by the new economics of labor migration, social capital theory, segmented labor market theory, and world systems theory as from those described by neoclassical economics. If a comprehensive understanding of international migration requires a synthesis of different theoretical viewpoints, so too does the formulation of an enlightened and efficacious immigration policy.

In this final chapter, we lay out a vision for immigration reform intended to lead policymakers and the public away from the costly and self-destructive policies of the past. Our vision offers a third way between the extremes of an open border and draconian restrictions on international movement. It is grounded in a broad conceptualization of international migration that recognizes its multi-causal nature. Rather than attempting to discourage immigration through unilateral repression—seeking to stamp out flows that U.S. policies otherwise encourage—we propose to recognize immigration as a natural part of North American integration and to work *to manage it more effectively*. Much as flows of capital, commodities, and goods are managed for the mutual benefit of trading partners by agreements such as NAFTA, labor migration can also be cooperatively managed to maximize the benefits and minimize the costs for both sending and receiving societies.

Foundations of a New Policy

To be successful, any policy must be grounded in certain realities. First and foremost, it must be grounded in scientific truth. During the 1940s and 1950s, for example, Soviet authorities built an agricultural policy around the theories of T. D. Lysenko, whose ideas on the inheritance of acquired characteristics were consistent with Stalinist ideology but ran counter to the basic principles of scientific genetics (Sheehan 1985). The end result was not a triumph of Soviet socialism but a series of disastrous harvests and needless famines. In the same way, immigration policies grounded in ideology rather than scientific understanding can be expected to yield bitter fruits—perhaps not massive famine, but wasted money, lost lives, depressed wages, and missed opportunities.

A good public policy is not simply a matter of science, of course. It must also recognize concrete political interests and be grounded in a broadly defensible morality. With respect to immigration policy in particular, it is important to understand clearly the interests of people in sending as well as receiving societies and to state forthrightly the moral strictures against which potential policies are to be evaluated. Although not everyone may agree with the ethical principles so adumbrated, once they are made explicit at least they can be discussed and debated.

Basic Scientific Truths

In the foregoing chapters, we outlined a synthetic theory of international migration that was well supported by empirical research. We then employed it to explicate and interpret the history of Mexico-U.S. migration over the course of the twentieth century. We showed how the mechanisms specified under various theoretical models continue to promote and sustain international migration within North America today. This conceptual and empirical groundwork puts us in a position to identify some basic scientific truths about international migration as it currently transpires on the stage of a globalized, post-industrial economy.

First of all, contrary to common perceptions, *international migration does not stem from a lack of economic development, but from development itself.* As industrialization spread across Europe from 1800 to 1929, it triggered waves of emigration in country after country (Massey 1988; Hatton and Williamson 1994, 1998). Likewise, at present the poorest and least developed nations do not send out the most international migrants. If that were true, international migration would be dominated by sub-Saharan Africa, yet apart from within-continent refugees, this region accounts for a tiny fraction of international movements (Zlotnik 1998). The fact of the matter is that no nation has yet undergone economic development without a massive displacement of people from traditional livelihoods, which are mainly located in the countryside; in the vast majority of cases a large fraction of these people have ended up migrating abroad.

A second basic truth is that *immigration is a natural consequence of broader processes of social, political, and economic integration across international borders.* Those who adapt to the upheavals of market creation and industrialization through emigration do not scatter randomly, nor do they necessarily head for the nearest wealthy society. Rather, they go to places to which they are *already linked* economically, socially, and politically. Economic links reflect broader relations of trade and capital investment. Political links stem from treaties, colonialism, military incursion, or simply solidarity in the face of a common enemy (as during the cold war). Social ties stem from institutional arrangements that bring people into contact with one another on a regular, sustained basis, such as overseas troop deployments, student exchange programs, diplomatic missions, tourism, trade, and multinational corporations.

Third, when they enter developed countries such as the United States, *immigrants are generally responding to a strong and persistent demand that is built into the structure of post-industrial economies.* Owing to shifts in the technology of production, the emergence of the welfare state, and the embedding of market relations in broader social structures, labor markets in developed nations have become increasingly segmented into a primary sector containing "good" jobs that are attractive to natives and a secondary sector of poorly paid "bad" jobs that natives shun. To fill the latter, employers turn to immigrants, often initiating flows through direct recruitment. If there were no demand for their services, immigrants, particularly those without documents, would not come, since they would have no means of supporting themselves.

A fourth basic fact about immigration that surprises many people is that *migrants who enter a developed country for the first time generally do not intend to settle there permanently.* Settlement intentions reflect the underlying motivations for migration. The motivation that most people attribute to immigrants is a desire to maximize lifetime earnings, which indeed involves a permanent relocation abroad, but as we have seen, other motivations are equally if not more important. Those seeking to overcome incomplete markets for capital, credit, insurance, and futures move not to maximize earnings but to solve economic problems *at home.* Rather than moving abroad permanently to maximize earnings, they seek to leave *temporarily* to generate earnings that can be repatriated to diversify risks, accumulate capital, and circumvent a lack of credit. These motivations imply that, initially at least, most migrants *expect to return.*

The diversity of immigrant motivations yields another basic observation: *international migration is often less influenced by conditions in la-*

bor markets than by the state of other markets. Assuming that immigrants come to maximize earnings, policies to date have sought to influence labor markets, yet if migrants are actually moving to self-insure, acquire capital, or substitute for a lack of credit at home, then lowering expected wages may not eliminate or even reduce the impetus for international migration. More leverage on migration decisions might well be had by influencing other markets, particularly those in sending regions and notably those for capital, credit, futures, and insurance. Neoclassical economics begins with the assumption that markets exist and function well, but in fact they must be constructed, often at considerable societal cost.

Whatever a migrant's original intentions, a sixth basic truth is that *as international migrants accumulate experience abroad, their motivations change, usually in ways that promote additional trips of longer duration, yielding a rising likelihood of settlement over time.* Neoclassical economic theory assumes that people's preferences are exogenous—not influenced by the economic processes being explained. Although most migrants may begin as target earners, they are typically changed by the migrant experience itself. Living and working in an advanced, post-industrial economy exposes them to a consumer culture that inculcates new tastes and motivations that cannot be satisfied through economic activities at home. Rather, the easiest path to their satisfaction is through additional foreign labor. As migrants spend more time abroad, they acquire social and economic ties to the host country and begin to petition for the entry of immediate family members. Over time temporary migrants thus have a way of turning into permanent settlers.

A seventh basic fact about international migration is that *it tends to build its own infrastructure of support over time.* As a result, migratory flows acquire a strong internal momentum that makes them resistant to easy manipulation by public policies. As politicians in country after country have discovered to their chagrin, immigration is much easier to start than to stop. The most important mechanism sustaining international migration is the expansion of migrant networks, which occurs automatically whenever a member of a social structure emigrates to a high-wage country (Massey and Zenteno 1999). Emigration transforms ordinary ties such as kinship or friendship into potential sources of social capital that aspiring migrants can use to gain access to a high-paying foreign job.

Finally, despite strong tendencies toward self-perpetuation and settlement, *immigrant flows do not last forever—they have a natural life that, whether long or short, is necessarily of limited duration.* Drawing on observations originally made by Akerman (1976), Hatton and Williamson (1998) used historical data for fifteen European nations from 1850 to 1914 to develop a stylized curve for the emigration transition—the pattern of out-migration rates experienced by European nations as they underwent economic development. They found a standard pattern of transition that occurred over eight or nine decades: from low to high rates of emigration, then back to low rates. The level and timing of the transition was approximated by a simple quadratic equation: $ER = -0.35 + 2.66{*}t - 0.27{*}t^2$, where ER represents the annual emigration rate and t represents the number of decades since the beginning of out-migration.

Figure 7.1 plots this curve to show the stylized emigration transition that prevailed during the classic "age of migration" in Europe from 1800 through 1914. As can be seen, the transition lasted roughly nine decades, a period that Hatton and Williamson (1998) refer to as "emigration time." The initial phase is characterized by rapid acceleration in the rate of emigration, which reaches a peak of just over 6.0 per 1,000 in the fourth decade, followed by an equally rapid decline to zero during the ninth decade. The precise shape of this curve naturally varies somewhat from country to country depending on underlying factors such as the rate of demographic increase, the pace of industrialization, and the stock of co-nationals already abroad (an indicator of the extent of network development). As industrialization proceeded across Europe, however, wages eventually rose relative to those in the New World while fertility and mortality levels dropped. The growing equalization of wages and the lessening of demographic pressures, combined with the emergence of well-functioning markets, led to the progressive reduction of incentives for international movement after the fourth decade. By the ninth decade of emigration time it was all over: mass migration had ended.

Ninety years may seem like a long time for a country to accept immigrants while waiting for economic conditions to improve in sending regions. It is unlikely that today's governments would be willing to accept mass immigration for such a long period of a time. However, out-migration from Europe occurred under very different technological, governmental, and international circumstances. Transportation and communication were slower, productive technologies were less transportable, economies were more ponderous, and there were few international institutions to promote international development, such as the World Bank, the International Monetary Fund, the World Trade Organization, the Agency for International Development, and the host of UN agencies that support everything from family planning to improved health and education.

By the end of the twentieth century the transition to economic de-

Figure 7.1 Emigration Transition in Europe, 1800 to 1914, and in Postwar South Korea, 1965 to the Present

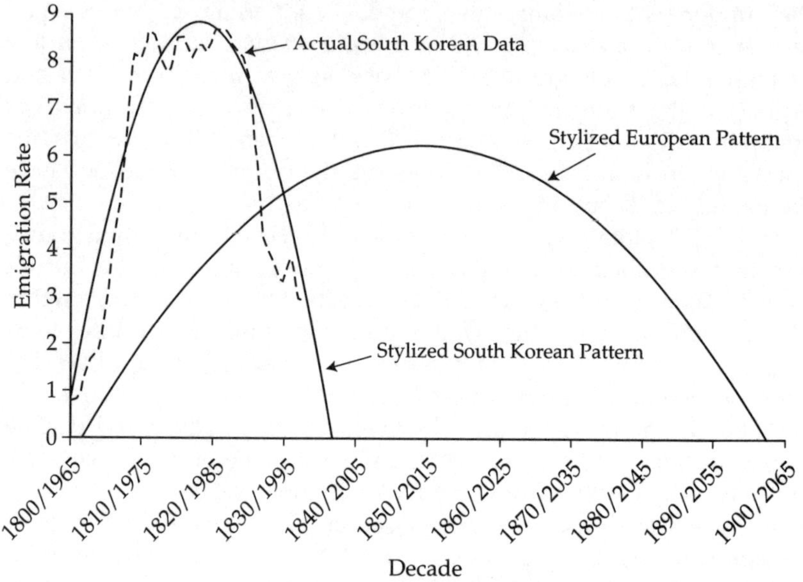

Source: Hatton and Williamson 1998; U.S. Immigration and Naturalization Service.

velopment seems to have been occurring much more rapidly than it did before 1914. A good example is South Korea. In 1965 it ranked among the world's poorest nations with a per capita income of only $159, a mere 4 percent of U.S. per capita income. By inserting itself into the global trading regime, however, and adopting a disciplined monetary strategy that encouraged a high rate of savings and investment, South Korean officials built a modern industrial economy in just thirty years. In 1995 South Korean per capita income was $9,700.

Despite its rapid economic growth and the accompanying sharp reduction in fertility, the South Korean economy was not able to absorb all of the workers entering the non-agricultural workforce each year through natural increase and structural displacement. As in Europe, many of these "surplus" workers ended up becoming international migrants; the vast majority went to the United States. Fortunately for South Korea, in 1965 the United States repealed its historical ban on Asian immigration, and between 1965 and 1995 some 768,000 Koreans entered the country as legal immigrants. Because South Korea's population grew from 28.4 million to 45.1 million over the same period, we can draw the implication that the nation exported around 4 percent of its demographic increase to the United States.

Such a level of emigration during development is not at all exceptional by historical standards. Between 1846 and 1924, for example, Britain and Ireland together exported some 17 million persons, representing nearly *half* of their total demographic increase. Over the same period Italy sent out some 9.5 million persons—roughly 37 percent of its total growth. What is remarkable about South Korea, therefore, is how *little* emigration occurred in the course of its economic development.

Even more remarkable than the modest scale of South Korean emigration was its speed. Whereas European nations took eight or nine decades to complete their transition, South Korea did it in three or four. To document this fact, figure 7.1 plots the rate of South Korean emigration by emigration time (where 1965 = 0). The smaller scale of South Korean emigration is not readily apparent from this graph, because rates are expressed as emigrants per 10,000 persons, whereas Hatton and Williamson (1998) expressed European rates per 1,000 people. Nonetheless, as can be observed, following the liberalization of U.S. laws, South Korean emigration rapidly rose to a peak, reaching a value of 8.5 after two decades (around 1985). Thereafter, the rate fell quite rapidly, reaching 2.9 by the middle of the third decade (the late 1990s).

The South Korean emigration transition corresponds roughly to the quadratic equation of $ER = 0.75 + 9.00*t - 2.4*t^2$, meaning that the rise and decline of emigration occurred roughly *three times faster* in twentieth-century South Korea than in nineteenth-century Europe. Thus, not only is mass emigration a temporally limited phenomenon, but recent evidence suggests that contemporary emigration peaks at levels well below those observed earlier and that the time required for transition has shortened dramatically.

Political and Economic Interests in Receiving Societies

As with all public policies, those regulating international migration create winners and losers. It is therefore important to consider explicitly the costs and benefits of international migration and how they are distributed among people in receiving and sending societies. Within the former, people with an economic interest in immigration can be divided into two broad categories: those who possess economic inputs that are *complements* to those owned by immigrants, and those who possess inputs that are *substitutes* for those of immigrants.

Immigrants carry as many as three kinds of resources with them when they leave: financial capital, human capital, and labor power. Financial capital, of course, is fully mobile with or without the movement of people, and not surprisingly, relatively few immigrants migrate as investors. In contrast, the productive use of human capital generally requires the presence of the person bearing it, and the number of skilled international migrants has consequently increased sharply in recent years. In practical terms, however, immigrants bearing human capital do not undermine the economic welfare of well-educated natives. Indeed, owing to the global scarcity of skills and training, the financial returns to education have risen sharply in the past decade despite the growth in immigration (see Massey 2000a). Consequently, most governments in developed countries have moved to *increase* the number of visa slots reserved for the entry of immigrants with skills and education, and in doing so they have encountered little opposition from well-educated natives.

Most of the world's international migrants do not move to invest their human capital, however, but to offer their labor. Consequently, it is in their capacity as workers that immigrants are most widely considered. As unskilled laborers, immigrants generally serve as substitutes for unskilled natives. Although substitutability may be less than perfect owing to differences in language and culture, the entry of immigrant workers generally serves to increase the supply of labor and put downward pressure on wages. To the extent that wages are downwardly "sticky" for institutional or other reasons (see Bewley 1999), the increased competition is expressed as unemployment. For this reason, poorly educated natives and labor unions have generally favored more restrictive immigration policies.

Residents of receiving societies also have an interest in immigration as taxpayers and consumers. As consumers, natives reap significant benefits from immigration in the form of lower prices, a benefit they enjoy every time they purchase a product to which immigrant labor has contributed. Fruits and vegetables, for example, would undoubtedly be more expensive in the United States were it not for the fact that virtually all harvesting is performed by immigrant (mainly Mexican) labor. Immigrants also pay taxes and consume public services. To the extent that immigrants join natives in paying taxes, the latter benefit because the financial burdens of government are spread over a larger number of people. To the extent that immigrants use public services, however, natives incur an additional tax burden.

The net balance between the tax contributions of immigrants and the value of the public services they consume has been the subject of a controversial and inconclusive debate. (For recent reviews, see MaCurdy, Nechyba, and Bhattacharya 1998; Garvey and Espenshade 1998; Clune 1998; and Lee and Miller 1998.) What is not in dispute, however, is the sharp disconnect between the level of government where public services are consumed and the level of government where taxes are paid. The highest rates of taxation—income taxes combined with those for Social Security and Medicare—occur at the federal level. State and local taxes pale by comparison, and strong local opposition to property and sales taxes has historically held them to low rates as well. As a result, a disproportionate share of immigrant tax revenues flow into federal coffers.

In contrast, the costs of absorbing immigrants are paid almost entirely at the state and local levels. As we have seen, the geographic distribution of immigrants is highly uneven. A mere six states (California, New York, Texas, Florida, Illinois, and New Jersey) and less than a dozen localities (New York City, Newark, Miami, Los Angeles, San Diego, San Francisco, Chicago, Dallas, and Houston) thus pay a hugely disproportionate share of the national costs of absorbing immigrants and seeing to their health, education, and welfare and that of their children. It is no coincidence that the 1980s revolt against property taxes and the 1990s mobilization against immigrants both erupted in California, by far the largest immigrant-receiving state.

Naturally, natives have interests that are not simply economic in nature. Inevitably, some natives just do not like foreigners for social or cultural reasons. They are made uncomfortable by people speaking a different language, expressing unfamiliar attitudes, and comporting themselves in strange ways. Others fear that immigrants will undermine widely shared social values and political ideals, or that the presence of too many foreigners will fragment society along linguistic, racial, or ethnic lines. A few people are just plain prejudiced—they dislike immigrants on the basis of race, ethnicity, or religion. In the real world, it is difficult to disentangle such social and cultural motivations from purely economic motivations. Those who express the strongest anti-immigrant sentiments tend to be those with little education, few skills, and low incomes—precisely the people who are most likely to compete economically with immigrants.

Political and Economic Interests in Sending Societies

Although most people in developed countries may stop at some point to think about how immigration affects them, their family, and their society, rarely do they consider the nature and distribution of interests in migrant-sending countries, nor do they consider how the sending society's interests might be intertwined with those of their own society. To the extent that international migration affects the social, political, and economic welfare of a sending nation, moves to expand or restrict immigration may affect its stability, and to the extent that its stability is important to the receiving society, immigration policies may have important boomerang effects. Whatever the nature of immigration's direct costs and benefits to the United States, for example, policies that undermine the political and economic stability of Mexico are clearly *not* in U.S. interests.

The effects of emigration within sending nations depend on what resources migrants take with them when they leave and how those resources would have been deployed had they stayed. Again, it is important to make a fundamental distinction between those who leave bearing only their labor power and those who depart with various forms of capital. Given that the movement of financial capital has now been decoupled from the movement of people, capital flight through emigration is no longer a serious concern. More attention has been focused on the "brain drain": the overseas flight of human capital. To the extent that emigrants take away valuable human capital that could have been used productively to promote economic growth and development at home, the sending society suffers a clear loss.

The effect of this loss must be evaluated, however, in light of two additional considerations. The first is what the emigrants would have done with their skills and education if they had stayed. If an electrical engineer is unable to find work in a company, nonprofit organization, or university and ends up driving a cab, then the potential loss of his or her skills does not represent a serious constraint on development, because there are many other less-educated people who could drive cabs equally well. The loss of human capital through emigration would not affect development because that capital was not being productively used anyway. A second consideration focuses on what emigrants do after they leave. If they leave for good and never send any money home, then emigration may indeed constitute a deadweight loss. If their foreign labor generates a stream of remittances and repatriated savings, however, then the loss of human capital may be more than offset by a return flow of financial capital.

To the extent that remittances provide developing nations with a critical source of foreign exchange, therefore, labor migration may *positively* influence the prospects for economic development and constitute an important resource for growth. In 1989, for example, Turkey received $3 billion in remittances from migrants working in Germany and other European nations. This figure constituted 4 percent of Turkey's total GDP and was sufficient to finance three-quarters of its trade deficit. The development potential of remittances is underscored by the fact that they exceeded Turkey's direct foreign investment by a factor of four (Massey et al. 1998).

Thus, the consequences of human capital flight depend substantially on conditions in sending-country labor markets. If, on the one hand, markets for people with skills and education are competitive, then emigration will increase the scarcity of human capital and drive up the returns to education, thus working to the advantage of those who possess human capital but to the detriment of those who own complementary inputs such as financial capital and land. On the other hand, if sending-country labor markets are not competitive but are characterized by a glut of educated workers who experience substantial underemployment, then the loss of human capital will have few, if any, distributional effects. As long as markets for skilled labor are not pushed into competitive equilibrium, emigration simply removes a resource that would otherwise be unproductively engaged.

Public officials and scholars have worried less about the effects of emigration on sending regions when the main resource that emigrants take with them is the power of their own labor. If markets for unskilled workers are in competitive equilibrium, then the emigration of workers reduces labor supply to drive up wages, thus benefiting the workers left behind but lowering the returns for owners of land, human capital, and financial capital. Given that developing countries are typically characterized by an oversupply of workers and high levels of underemployment, the loss of labor does not significantly reduce production or constrain economic growth.

For most developing societies, therefore, the potential loss of human capital and labor through emigration does not constitute a serious threat to economic welfare, and to the extent that emigrants generate remittances and repatriated savings, it represents a potentially important economic resource to be tapped. In 1995, for example, Fernando Lozano Ascencio (1998) estimated that 3.6 billion migradollars (Durand 1988) were remitted back to Mexico from workers in the United States. In contrast to petrodollars and other sources of foreign exchange, migradollars have particularly dynamic effects on sending nations because they are spent rapidly and have large multiplier effects (Durand et al. 1996).

A model of the Mexican economy developed by Irma Adelman and Edward Taylor (1992) suggests that the arrival of 3.6 billion migradollars would actually have a $9.7 billion effect on national income. Because migradollars are spent on goods and services produced in Mexico, they create income for other Mexicans. Moreover, even if most remittances are spent on consumption, some fraction is always invested productively, yielding even larger effects on national output. According to the Adelman-Taylor model, $3.6 billion in remittances would have an $11.7 billion effect on Mexican GDP once the effects of investment and consumer spending are allowed to work their way through the economy.

Interests and Ethics

The political and economic interests associated with international migration are thus fairly clear. Within receiving nations, owners of land and capital (human and financial) generally benefit from international migration, whereas native workers benefit only to the extent that immigrants possess skills and education and are thus complements in production. To the extent that immigrants are unskilled and substitutes for native workers, the latter suffer from downward pressure on their wages and employment. Given that a majority of the world's international migrants (including the vast majority of those from Mexico) are unskilled, most observers conclude that the latter effect predominates and that workers' interests lie in restricting immigration.

Within sending countries, the clearest beneficiaries are the migrant households themselves, which use international migration strategically as a means of enhancing family income, diversifying risks, self-insuring in the absence of effective insurance markets, and acquiring cash in the absence of good markets for capital or credit. In developing countries such as Mexico, where both labor and human capital are in relative oversupply, emigration does not inhibit economic growth or strongly influence the distribution of economic welfare. To the extent that it yields a return stream of remittances and repatriated savings, emigration constitutes an important and potentially powerful resource for national development.

In addition to the economic interests of particular individuals, governments also have important stakes in international migration. The principal interest of sending-country governments is to protect the rights of citizens working abroad, to maximize the annual flow of remittances back home, and to use the resulting funds optimally to promote national economic development. The interests of receiving-country governments are more complex. In theory, political leaders should attempt to optimize the welfare of the largest number of citizens. In practical terms, however, the immediate goal of most politicians is to stay in power, which they do by formulating and implementing policies that satisfy—or at least do not antagonize—a majority of voters.

With respect to immigration, this balancing act generally involves weighing the interests of workers against those of asset-owners. Although the latter may be more economically and politically powerful, the former are more numerous, yielding a dialectical politics of immigration that varies strongly with the business cycle (Foreman-Peck 1992; Goldin 1994; Meyers 1995; Timmer and Williamson 1998). During recessionary times a populist politics prevails and the interests of workers come to the fore; during boom times a client politics takes place behind the scenes, and the interests of landowners, employers, and consumers take precedence (Freeman 1995; Joppke 1998).

Whatever policies are ultimately adopted by government, they must be consistent with moral principles that can be defended on both a national and a world stage (Heyman 1998). Increasingly, public policies are evaluated against a regime of international human rights, as formalized in the 1948 United Nations Universal Declaration of Human Rights, later the Helsinki Accords (see Cornelius, Martin, and Hollifield 1994; Freeman 1994, 1995; Jacobson 1997; Joppke 1998). We see the rights conferred on international migrants by virtue of such international accords as boiling down to five principles:

1. People should be free to leave their country of birth or citizenship for whatever reason without state interference.
2. Once migrants are accepted into a receiving nation in a recognized status, they should receive full legal rights and access to the judiciary system. Specifically, they should receive labor rights equivalent to those of natives, social entitlements from which they would otherwise benefit as native taxpayers, and reasonable access to citizenship and full political participation.
3. Although clandestine migration cannot be eliminated, reasonable steps should be taken to minimize the number of people living and working in undocumented status through a combination of regularization programs, temporary work visas, and moderate border and immigration enforcement.
4. Sending nations should guarantee reciprocal rights of entry and legal protection to citizens of receiving societies.
5. Immigration policies should not be imposed unilaterally but developed cooperatively through multilateral agreements similar to those used to govern international flows of capital, goods, commodities, and information. In an integrated world, nations have

responsibilities beyond their borders, and unilateral actions taken by one nation can have serious negative repercussions for others linked to it in the global system.

The Philosophy of Immigration Management

Immigration policy in most developed countries has so far involved little more than drawing a line in the sand and defending it with increasing allocations of money, equipment, and personnel, at a growing marginal cost. In chapter 6, we showed how this approach has failed in the United States. Immigrants have not been deterred from coming, apprehension probabilities have fallen, trip durations have lengthened, settlement has increased, and immigration has shifted from being a regional to a national phenomenon. U.S. policies have also worked to undermine wages and working conditions in U.S. labor markets, exacerbate income inequality, increase mortality along the border, and expand the potential for future immigration, financed all the while by ever-growing amounts of tax money spent in increasingly inefficient ways. The time is thus ripe for a fundamental rethinking of basic approaches to immigration policy.

The most fundamental tenet of our philosophy of immigration management is that international migration is not an aberrant pathological condition to be stamped out. On the contrary, it follows naturally from the entry of developing nations into the global economy and their consequent social and economic transformation. People seeking to enter developed nations as immigrants are generally not desperate people seeking to escape horrendously poor circumstances, as might be inferred from the works of Robert Kaplan (1996, 2000) and others. Very poor countries, in fact, contribute few migrants to international flows. International migrants typically come from dynamic regions in the throes of rapid economic development. These regions use foreign labor as an instrument to adapt to the structural transformations going on around them. Large-scale emigration was a natural part of European economic development in the nineteenth and early twentieth centuries, and it is a normal part of economic development in the Third World today.

International migrants do not scatter evenly across potential destination countries but follow well-established pathways created through prior relations of trade, investment, military occupation, and colonialism. It does not make any sense, therefore, for immigrant-receiving societies to treat all countries equally. The demand for entry will inevitably be higher in some nations than in others. An equal allocation of visas across countries only generates long backlogs and excessive clandestine migration from a nation's closest trading partners and political allies. In the United States the allocation of 20,000 visas per country was implemented to end discriminatory national-origins quotas that were blatantly prejudiced against Asians, Africans, and southern and eastern Europeans. But evenly distributing visas across nations is only one way of eliminating ethnic bias from an immigration system. Other ethnically neutral criteria based on trade relations, treaties, or historical ties could also be developed.

International migration should be approached not simply as a domestic political issue but as an international issue linked to broader matters of trade and geopolitics. Most nations undergoing economic development and the transition to a market economy end up exporting a significant share of their people as emigrants during a transition period of limited duration. The emigration transition follows a characteristic trajectory, moving from low to high to low rates of out-migration, yielding an inverted U-shaped curve that Philip Martin and Edward Taylor (1996) have called the "migration hump." The strategy that policymakers should adopt is not to prevent such a hump from occurring, but to manage the flows effectively so as to minimize its height and duration. While European countries historically took eight or nine decades to undergo the emigration transition, evidence from the late twentieth century suggests that the hump can now be traversed in as few as thirty years.

Immigrant policies should also recognize that most international migrants are not initially motivated to settle permanently in developed nations, and that hardening the border through repressive police actions only undermines the inclination to return, ultimately reducing the flow of people and migradollars back to sending regions to choke off their development. A smarter strategy would be to cultivate the natural inclination of migrants to remain abroad temporarily by facilitating return migration and the repatriation of funds. Receiving societies would work with sending countries to create binational institutions capable of maximizing the positive effects of migradollars and fully harnessing their development potential. In the long run such an approach would promote a quicker transition over the migration hump and a smaller total out-migration, thus maximizing the gains to the sending society and minimizing the costs to the receiving nation.

The Case of Mexico

By any criterion, Mexico constitutes a special case for U.S. policymakers. The fates of the two countries are clearly bound together by an unusual history and geography. Until 1848 the states of California,

Arizona, New Mexico, Nevada, Utah, and Texas, as well as portions of Wyoming and Colorado, were part of Mexico. In 1853 the United States annexed additional Mexican territory, and since then it has invaded the country three times, most recently in 1917. The two nations share a two-thousand-mile frontier, and the borderlands region, with its string of rapidly growing twin cities and booming manufacturing sector, constitutes one of the most dynamic areas of North America. With total trade at nearly $200 billion per year, Mexico and the United States are among each other's largest trading partners, and together they have joined with Canada to create an integrated, continent-wide market under the North American Free Trade Agreement.

As a result, by mutual agreement, the Mexico-U.S. border will become increasingly permeable to flows of all sorts: capital, information, services, goods, commodities, and, ultimately, people. The two nations already share a sixty-year history of uninterrupted migration, launched in 1942 by a U.S.-sponsored guest-worker program that ultimately imported some 4.6 million laborers. The Mexican-born population of the United States now stands at 8 million, and annual legal immigration runs in excess of 130,000 persons. Another 3.4 million Mexicans enter the country annually on non-immigrant visas, and another 213 million short-term border crossings occur each year. Net undocumented migration from Mexico is currently estimated to be around 150,000 persons per year, and the total stock of undocumented Mexicans stands at about 3 million (U.S. Immigration and Naturalization Service 2000).

In practical terms, the issue is not *whether* Mexico and the United States will integrate—we are already well down that road. The only real issue is *how* the integration will occur. To a substantial degree, the ease and length of the process will be determined by migration policies pursued by the United States and Mexico over the next decade. Up to now, the immigration policies imposed unilaterally by the United States have been counterproductive and have worked to retard Mexican development rather than speed it. In doing so, it has slowed down the emigration transition in Mexico and hindered that country's transition to equal economic partnership.

Our first proposal for change concerns Mexico's immigration quota. It is abundantly clear that the demand for entry from Mexico significantly outstrips the supply of immigrant visas offered by the United States. The number of numerically restricted visas allocated to Mexico, which has a population of 100 million, is the same as that for the Dominican Republic, whose population is only 8.2 million: both countries are allowed 20,000 visas. As a result, the Dominican Republic is actually permitted a *higher* rate of legal emigration (2.5 per 1,000 in 1998) than Mexico (1.4 per 1,000 in the same year), even though, as a partner in NAFTA, Mexico is far more closely linked to the United States and more vital to its interests. The time has come to increase Mexico's absurdly low quota of 20,000 immigrants to a more realistic figure of, say, at least 60,000 per year, a figure that would still yield an annual rate of emigration that is quite modest by historical standards.

Yet even this expansion is unlikely to meet the demand for entry emanating from Mexico. To a great extent, Mexicans seek permanent resident visas because it is the only door left open to them. If another option were available—such as a temporary worker visa—more people would opt for it. Evidence of the desire of Mexicans to return home is abundant. Rather than making it more difficult for migrants to come and go, a more enlightened policy would facilitate it by creating a visa that permits Mexicans to enter, live, and work in the United States without restriction for a period of two years. The visa would be renewable once in the lifetime of the migrant, but only after he or she had returned home for at least a year. The visas would be distributed by a binational agency managed by the U.S. and Mexican governments, to which aspiring migrants would apply directly, thus getting employers and middlemen out of the self-serving business of labor recruitment and limiting the possibilities for corruption.

To ensure the labor rights of migrants, visas would not be tied to specific employers or jobs but issued directly to the migrants themselves. A work visa tied to a particular job leaves the migrant vulnerable to exploitation. Under such circumstances, that person cannot exercise the worker's most fundamental right: the right to withdraw his or her labor. Granting visas to migrants themselves and permitting them to change jobs would not only prevent unscrupulous employers from exploiting migrants but make it difficult for them to use immigrants to lower the wages of natives or cut corners with respect to occupational, safety, and health regulations. This policy would also leave migrants free to participate in unions, and they might be more willing to report violations of their labor rights.

Making such temporary work visas generously available to Mexicans would go a long way toward reducing undocumented migration and the ills that accompany it. If 300,000 two-year visas were issued annually, there would be 600,000 temporary migrants working in the United States at any time—a small share of the U.S. workforce, but a large fraction of all undocumented migrants. We have already seen historically how the provision of 450,000 bracero visas annually reduced undocumented migration to near zero during the late 1950s.

A new guest-worker program would obviate the need for employer sanctions, allowing Congress to repeal the provisions of IRCA that criminalized the hiring of unauthorized workers. As we have seen, employer sanctions have done nothing to reduce undocumented hiring but have functioned to drive down wages and erode working conditions in the United States, thus creating an underground labor market for immigrants and natives alike. As a final step to eliminating this underground economy, the United States should work to regularize the status of undocumented migrants with a record of peaceful, long-term residence in the United States. These people are already present, so regularization would have no immediate effect on U.S. population growth—it would simply facilitate the assimilation of the immigrants and their citizen children into U.S. society.

Enacting a temporary visa program would also provide U.S. authorities with an opportunity to raise funds that might be used to offset the costs of international migration and help Mexico to travel over the migration hump more rapidly on the road to development. Temporary migrants could be charged a $300 fee for each visa, to be paid to the U.S. Treasury in cash or over time in installments. We already know that Mexicans are more than willing to pay this amount to gain access to the United States, and $300 is less than the current cost of renting a coyote along the border. Paying such a fee would obviously be much safer, more secure, and considerably less anxiety-provoking as a way of entering the country.

A $300 fee paid by 300,000 temporary migrants would yield annual revenues of $90 million per year. Another source of revenue would come from federal taxes withheld from the paychecks of temporary workers. If we assume that 600,000 temporary migrants earned annual incomes of only $15,000 and had taxes withheld at a rate of just 15 percent (very conservative assumptions), the resulting revenue stream would be $1.35 billion per year. A more important source of revenue gain would come from a drastic reduction in the personnel and resources devoted to border enforcement. In chapter 6, we estimated that the *same degree of deterrence* could be purchased with a much smaller investment in INS operations, yielding $3 billion in annual savings.

Under this scenario, therefore, a total of around $4.4 billion would become available to mitigate the costs of migration for the United States and to facilitate Mexico's economic development. A portion of these funds could be earmarked for federal revenue sharing to states with large immigrant populations. Because immigration imposes substantial costs on receiving states, the federal government should include the number of foreign-born in its basic formula for revenue sharing. A transfer of resources from the federal government to immigrant-receiving states would do much to assuage the sort of anger and resentment that surged in California in the late 1980s and early 1990s.

The remainder of the funds would be used to benefit the migrants, to facilitate the improvement of markets in Mexico, and to assist that country in building a social welfare net to support its citizens in the event of market failure. Such investments would follow the successful example of Spain and Portugal's integration into the European Union in 1986. During the 1960s and 1970s these nations sent out hundreds of thousands of emigrants for work in the wealthier countries of northern Europe, particularly Germany. Officials in the latter countries were initially worried that admitting poor Iberians into the European labor market would unleash even larger waves of emigrants northward. But in preparation for their integration into the union, substantial EU funds were invested in Spain and Portugal to improve their social, economic, and material infrastructure. As a result, when unification occurred, further emigration did not occur. On the contrary, both countries experienced a large net *return* migration from northern Europe, despite the fact that per capita income in Spain is still only half that in Germany.

Similar investments in Mexico by the United States and Canada, as part of Mexico's integration into the North American common market, would go a long way toward mitigating the incentives for outmigration. For example, a binational insurance agency might be established to allow migrants to purchase low-cost insurance for a variety of purposes, giving them a means of risk management other than migration. Another possibility might be the creation of a binational development bank that would offer matching grants to Mexican communities for the construction or improvement of local infrastructure. Such an institution would give local community leaders a way of multiplying the positive benefits of the 3.6 billion migradollars by pooling them for local development and doubling them in a dollar-for-dollar match. Various existing initiatives have already shown considerable promise (such as "Proyecto 2x1" and "Proyecto 3x1" in the state of Zacatecas). These programs should be evaluated, improved, and applied more widely throughout Mexico.

A particularly important initiative is the expansion of the banking services available to Mexicans of modest economic circumstances, by either modifying existing financial institutions or creating new ones. Two persistent problems that migrants face are the high cost of remitting and the unfavorable rates of exchange they receive in Mexico. At present the discount rate charged against remittances by the oligopoly of firms controlling international transfers is as high as 20 percent; Mexican banks offer favorable exchange rates to investors, firms, and special clients, but they do little for ordinary consumers. The technical and institutional means to create secure and inexpensive channels for migrant remittances clearly exist. It is simply a matter of political will to deploy them effectively.

The extension of banking services to more Mexicans would also go a long way toward improving access to capital and credit. Dollar-denominated accounts could be established to protect migrants against instability in exchange rates, and peso accounts could offer above-market rates to attract funds. Loans could also be made from these deposits to poor families seeking to finance homes, businesses, or educations. In addition, banks could issue low-rate, low-balance credit cards to working-class Mexicans, thus providing them with a means of financing large-ticket consumer purchases without having to resort to international migration.

Finally, a dramatic reduction in the size of the Border Patrol would permit a shift of resources from the border to the interior of the United States; resources could be targeted instead at regions and economic sectors known to employ large numbers of immigrant workers. Rather than focusing on the identification and apprehension of undocumented migrants, however, inspections would enforce the tax, labor, environmental, health, and safety laws of the United States, reducing the incentives for employers to hire undocumented migrants as a means of circumventing these regulations.

As mentioned earlier in this chapter, social capital formation is a powerful force propelling international migration. Although it will occur no matter what immigration policies a government pursues, the allocation of visas along kinship lines reinforces the process of network formation. Every migrant who receives a green card becomes entitled to sponsor the entry of his or her spouse and minor children, subject to quota limitations. Moreover, every legal resident who goes on to acquire citizenship becomes eligible to sponsor the entry of his or her spouse, parents, and minor children *without numerical limitation,* as well as eligible to petition for the numerically restricted entry of older married children and siblings.

These visa allocations were implemented for humanitarian reasons. It seems clear that states cannot humanely separate husbands from wives or parents from children. Adult siblings, however, are another matter, and if there is one action that could be taken to reduce the reinforcing effect of visa allocation on social capital formation it would be to eliminate the fifth preference category, which makes adult siblings of U.S. citizens eligible for admission under quota limitations. This category is more responsible than any other for reifying the process of "chaining" (see Jasso and Rosenzweig 1988). In contemporary society, most people do not live near their siblings anyway. Most native American citizens see their brothers and sisters only occasionally on holiday visits and at certain formal rites of passage (baptisms, weddings, confirmation ceremonies, and so on). Given modern transportation and communication, being physically separated from one's siblings hardly seems like a major infringement of basic human rights.

Although we do not advocate revoking the right of U.S. citizens to sponsor the legal immigration of their parents, U.S. policies currently *force* many elderly Mexicans of modest means to become permanent resident aliens when they only seek to visit their children and grandchildren in the United States as tourists. In an overzealous attempt to forestall illegal migration, U.S. consular officials routinely deny such tourist visas. These routine denials create a strong incentive for legal immigrants to naturalize so as to be able to sponsor the legal immigration of their parents, when all they really want is for their parents to have periodic access to a tourist visa. Simply being more flexible in granting non-immigrant visas to older Mexicans with children in the United States would do a lot to reduce migratory momentum, with no change in legislation.

Finally, the Mexican government should guarantee the secure, rapid, and efficient passage of migrants wishing to return home, and it should ensure the political rights of those Mexicans choosing to remain in the United States. Current government programs such as Programa Paisano, which seeks to protect the property and civil liberties of returning migrants, and Grupo Beta, a special police force that polices the border and protects the rights of undocumented migrants, should be evaluated by independent agencies and improvements made to offer better services and to extend them more widely. The recent recommendation by a special commission impaneled by Mexico's Federal Elections Institute that procedures be established so that Mexican citizens in the United States can vote in federal elections should also be implemented.

Beyond Smoke and Mirrors

Dan Baum (1997) has referred to the U.S. war on drugs as "smoke and mirrors." We believe the metaphor is equally apt with respect to U.S. immigration policy. Despite a flurry of hand waving, smoke, and fire along the border, immigration continues as before, except on more unfavorable terms. The massive increase in the Border Patrol, the monumental deployment of matériel and equipment, the striking construction of an iron wall along the border—all this has made for great political theater, provided the media with impressive video footage, and allowed reporters to produce vivid copy. These props may have reassured U.S. citizens that the border is under control, but they have not come close to solving the problems associated with Mexico-U.S. migration. Without exception, all of these measures have made them worse.

Rather than running as a smooth piece of machinery within the broader engine of North American economic integration, recent U.S. policies have thrown a series of wrenches into the gears of economic growth and social development in both Mexico and the United States. The policy initiatives we propose here will not eliminate undocumented migration or solve all of the problems associated with it. They will, however, reverse the deleterious consequences of current U.S. policies by eliminating the black market in immigrant labor, minimizing the long-term settlement of Mexican immigrants, encouraging flows of capital and people to Mexico, promoting economic growth within migrant-sending communities, constraining social capital formation, and moving Mexican markets for capital, credit, futures, and insurance more rapidly to fruition. In the short run, the disruptions that follow from the consolidation of the North American economy will continue, but long-term economic growth within Mexico will soon eliminate the incentives for international movement and allow that nation to move quickly over the "migration hump" to become a full partner in the global market economy.

Appendix A:

The Mexican Migration Project Database

Many of the tables and figures presented in this volume are based on official statistics, mostly from the U.S. Immigration and Naturalization Service and the U.S. Bureau of the Census. We also draw upon data from the Mexican National Statistical Institute, the World Bank, the International Monetary Fund, and the United Nations. Many aspects of Mexico-U.S. migration cannot be measured from official sources, however, such as the probability of undocumented migration in a given year, the likelihood of apprehension while attempting a clandestine border crossing, or the social characteristics of undocumented migrants. Whenever our analyses depart from official sources, we rely on data compiled by the Mexican Migration Project (MMP), a binational research project affiliated with the University of Guadalajara and the University of Pennsylvania and directed by Jorge Durand and Douglas S. Massey.

Since 1987 the MMP has been funded by the U.S. National Institute of Child Health and Human Development (grants HD-23415 and HD-35643) and the William and Flora Hewlett Foundation (grants 94–7795 and 99–4106)) to gather reliable, representative data on documented and undocumented migration from Mexico to the United States. The project employs a data collection strategy developed in earlier fieldwork (Massey et al. 1987) that has come to be known as the ethno-survey (Massey 1987c, 2000b). Rather than attempting to sample national populations using standard survey techniques, the ethno-survey targets specific communities for intensive study by a team of anthropological fieldworkers. They spend several months at each site interviewing a representative sample of households and gathering standardized data using a semistructured interview while conducting ancillary in-depth interviews with local officials and informants.

Each year four to eight Mexican communities are selected for study, and a team of trained fieldworkers is sent to each site to conduct a census of dwellings, yielding a list of units that is then used as a sampling frame. The census is generally conducted in November, and the sample is drawn in early December. Interviewing takes place during December, January, and February because seasonal migrants return home in the winter to dwellings they have left unoccupied during the rest of the year. To avoid bias stemming from errors of omission, we include in our census anything that might be used as a dwelling, whether or not it appears to be occupied or occupiable at the time of the enumeration. In most communities we select a random sample of two hundred households, although in smaller places smaller numbers have been chosen, and in a few cases a larger sample has been compiled. Rather than attempting to sample large urban areas in their entirety, we demarcate specific working-class neighborhoods and sample them. If a dwelling proves to be empty at the time of the survey, we simply select a random replacement from the sampling frame. The Mexican community samples are thus representative of dwelling units occupied during the winter months of each survey year.

Communities are *not* selected because they are known or thought to contain large numbers of U.S. migrants. Rather, research sites are chosen so as to build into the sample variation with respect to population size, geographic location, climate, economic base, social structure, and ethnic composition (Indian versus mestizo). Fieldwork has generally proceeded on a state-by-state basis, beginning in the core migrant-sending region of west-central Mexico, which comprises the states of Aguascalientes, Colima, Guanajuato, Jalisco, Michoacán, Nayarit, San Luis Potosí, and Zacatecas. The sample was then broadened to include newer sending regions in the southwestern states of Guerrero, Oaxaca, and Puebla before moving to incorporate northern-tier states such as Baja California Norte and Sinaloa. The database has been expanded annually through the addition of newly sampled communities; at this writing, it includes seventy-one communities in thirteen Mexican states.

The communities are listed by number in table A.1, and their approximate locations are plotted in the map reproduced in figure A.1. (Community names are suppressed to preserve confidentiality.) As can be seen, the sample embraces a rather wide cross-section of communities. Demographically the sample includes everything from tiny rural *ranchos* to dense urban neighborhoods within Mexico's largest metropolitan areas. It includes agrarian villages, industrial towns, commercial cities, fishing villages, tourist cities, and centers of *maquila*

Figure A.1 Geographic Distribution of Communities Sampled by the Mexican Migration Project

Source: Mexican Migration Project.

production, as well as numerous diverse metropolitan areas. Although most of the communities are mestizo (a mixture of European and Indian origins), a few are predominantly Indian (mainly Tarascan and Mixtec).

We have attempted to pair each Mexican survey with a parallel survey of out-migrants from the same community who have settled permanently in the United States. We experimented with different ways of defining populations of permanent out-migrants and gathering representative samples of them, but these approaches proved to be costly and cumbersome, leading us to fall back on snowball sampling as the preferred method of compiling samples of U.S. settlers (Goodman 1961). Under this method, also known as the chain-referral method, we gather names and contact information for friends and relatives living in the United States from respondents and informants located during fieldwork in Mexico. We then go to the United States to locate these people, interview them, and ask them whether they can direct us to other community members living nearby. Using this approach, we have sought to compile a U.S. sample equal to 10 percent of the Mexican community sample, usually around twenty households. Most of the U.S. interviews are conducted during the summer following each winter's survey.

The interviewing is guided by a semistructured schedule that gathers information in successive stages. Interviewers begin by identifying the household head, the spouse, and all living children of the head. Then they determine which of the children are still household members (generally unmarried sons and daughters who have not yet established a home) and whether any other people share the household. Across the 71 communities, the MMP has gathered data on 83,527 subjects located in 12,322 households. For each subject, interviewers compile social, economic, and demographic data and ask whether he or she has ever migrated within Mexico or to the United States. All those with migratory experience are asked to report the location, job, wage, duration, and (in the United States) legal status on their first and most recent trip. Using this procedure, we have identified 17,602 persons who have made at least one trip to the United States, constituting 21 percent of the total sample.

Interviewers then gather basic information about the household itself, including type of construction and tenure in the dwelling, the presence of consumer goods, and the ownership of land, businesses, livestock, cars, and other assets. All household heads are asked for a complete life history that includes, beginning at age fifteen, separate histories of marriage, fertility, property ownership, business ownership, labor, migration, and border crossing. All spouses are asked for an abbreviated labor history. Finally, household heads with prior U.S. experience are asked a series of questions about experiences on their last trip.

The MMP data are organized into five data files that are publicly available from the project website at *www.pop.upenn.edu/mexmig/*. PERSfile contains general social and demographic information on each household member as well as those children of the household head who are no longer at home, including information on first and last trips made by each individual within Mexico and abroad. MIGfile provides detailed information about the experiences reported by 4,881 migrant household heads during their most recent U.S. trip. HOUSEfile contains data on each household's family composition; labor force activity; land, business, property, and livestock holdings; home construction and amenities; and the nature and extent of U.S. migratory experience in the head's family of origin.

Finally, LIFEfile and SPOUSEfile contain detailed life and labor histories compiled from household heads and their spouses. (The spouse histories are only available beginning in 1994.) The unit of observation is the person-year; the household heads contributed a total of 584,694 person-years of information, compared with 221,726 person-years from spouses. The analyses presented in this volume are based on data from one of these five files, but the MMP also offers a range of supplemental data files on economic conditions in Mexico and the United States in different years, as well as characteristics of Mexican and U.S. communities, again by year.

Despite the potentially sensitive nature of the subjects under study (undocumented migration and clandestine border crossing), refusal rates have generally been low, ranging from a minimum of zero to a high of 18.6 percent, but averaging only 5.3 percent overall. Higher refusal rates generally reflect not suspicions about the study per se but the circumstances specific to a time or locality. As can be seen in table A.1, refusal rates are greater in urban than in rural areas, and higher in areas of Indian as opposed to mestizo ethnicity. They also tend to spike during periods of political turmoil, particularly during presidential election years. The highest refusal rate occurred in Guerrero in 1995, when considerable guerrilla activity and public mistrust made fieldwork quite difficult. (Indeed, the MMP had to abandon plans to survey one community after police massacred peasants who lived there.)

Data from the seventy-one Mexican community samples are strictly representative only of those communities, not of Mexico as a whole. Likewise, the samples of out-migrants to the United States are probably not fully representative of U.S. settlers, since they were compiled using nonrandom snowball sampling. Nonetheless, the Mexican and U.S. samples together offer a reasonably accurate snapshot of the population of seventy-one binational communities created through recurrent migration and settlement.

Massey and Zenteno (2000) sought to evaluate the representativeness of the MMP data set by comparing it to comparable information extracted from Mexico's 1992 National Survey of Population Dynamics (known as ENADID), a large and nationally representative sample of 57,916 households and 277,552 individuals that reports a response rate of just over 90 percent. This survey determines whether each household member has ever lived in another country, "even if for a short time," and for respondents age twelve or older, whether they have ever worked or looked for work in the United States, along with the dates of departure and return.

Systematic comparisons between the U.S. migrants identified in the MMP and ENADID found that the former produces a remarkably accurate profile of migrants to the United States with respect to basic social, economic, and demographic characteristics. As table A.2 indicates, the MMP is more successful at capturing older, unmarried sons and daughters who are temporarily working in the United States (a desirable characteristic actively sought by MMP investigators). Aside from this difference, the distributions of migrants with respect to sex, age, household status, marital status, schooling, and trip duration are very similar in the two data sets. After conducting additional comparisons involving multivariate models, Massey and Zenteno (2000) concluded that the MMP offers valid and reliable data for studying patterns and processes of Mexico-U.S. migration (see also Zenteno and Massey 1999).

Table A.1 Community Samples Included in the MMP Data Set, September 2001

Community Number	State	1990 Population[a]	Year of Survey	Size of Mexican Sample	Size of U.S. Sample	Refusal Rate
1	Guanajuato	52,000	1987	200	21	0.034
2	Guanajuato	868,000	1987	200	10	0.119
3	Jalisco	4,000	1988	200	22	0.140
4	Guanajuato	17,000	1988	200	22	0.057
5	Guanajuato	2,000	1988	150	10	0.085
6	Jalisco	5,000	1988	200	20	0.115
7	Jalisco	3,000	1988	200	15	0.010
8	Michoacán	6,000	1989	200	20	0.050
9	Michoacán	32,000	1989	200	20	0.037
10	Michoacán	2,000	1990	150	20	0.152
11	Nayarit	20,000	1990	200	20	0.029
12	Nayarit	12,000	1990	200	20	0.010
13	Guanajuato	21,000	1990	200	20	0.047
14	Michoacán	7,000	1990	200	20	0.057
15	Guanajuato	265,000	1991	200	20	0.057
16	Guanajuato	1,000	1991	100	10	0.029
17	Jalisco	31,000	1991	200	20	0.044
18	Zacatecas	8,000	1991	365	20	0.127
19	Michoacán	428,000	1991	200	20	0.083
20	Jalisco	3,000	1982	106	20	0.038
21	Jalisco	2,000	1982	94	10	0.037
22	Michoacán	7,000	1982	200	20	0.015
23	Jalisco	12,000	1982	200	20	0.038
24	Jalisco	1,650,000	1982	200	16	0.048
25	Jalisco	1,000	1992	100	7	0.029
26	Guanajuato	34,000	1992	200	15	0.095
27	Guanajuato	24,000	1992	200	15	0.127
28	Jalisco	73,000	1992	200	20	0.074

Table A.1 *Continued*

Community Number	State	1990 Population[a]	Year of Survey	Size of Mexican Sample	Size of U.S. Sample	Refusal Rate
29	Michoacán	188,000	1992	200	13	0.083
30	Zacatecas	1,000	1991	187	0	0.025
31	Guerrero	83,000	1993	100	12	0.089
32	San Luis Potosí	489,000	1993	200	25	0.048
33	Colima	7,000	1994	200	20	0.087
34	Zacatecas	2,000	1994	149	10	0.063
35	Zacatecas	100,000	1994	239	10	0.142
36	San Luis Potosí	13,000	1994	201	5	0.024
37	San Luis Potosí	1,000	1994	102	5	0.000
38	San Luis Potosí	42,000	1994	200	15	0.052
39	San Luis Potosí	1,000	1994	100	0	0.000
40	Zacatecas	34,000	1995	201	30	0.107
41	Guerrero	7,000	1995	153	11	0.186
42	Guerrero	1,000	1995	100	0	0.107
43	Guerrero	515,000	1995	200	0	0.074
44	San Luis Potosí	1,000	1995	99	17	0.000
45	San Luis Potosí	1,000	1996	142	11	0.000
46	Zacatecas	1,000	1995	111	0	0.142
47	San Luis Potosí	3,000	1996	197	11	0.032
48	San Luis Potosí	3,000	1996	94	0	0.021
49	Oaxaca	1,000	1996	100	0	0.000
50	Oaxaca	1,000	1996	100	10	0.000
51	Oaxaca	9,000	1997	199	0	0.083
52	Oaxaca	213,000	1996	200	9	0.087
53	Sinaloa	5,000	1998	100	6	0.020
54	Puebla	1,007,000	1997	201	1	0.016
55	Guanajuato	1,000	1997	80	8	0.000
56	Guanajuato	1,000	1998	87	9	0.033
57	Jalisco	4,000	1998	201	20	0.057
58	Jalisco	1,000	1998	100	10	0.029
59	Puebla	2,000	1997	100	0	0.010
60	Puebla	2,000	1997	100	0	0.010
61	Puebla	10,000	1998	199	0	0.050
62	Sinaloa	3,000	1998	150	11	0.020
63	Baja Calif. Norte	699,000	1998	150	8	0.068
64	Baja Calif. Norte	699,000	1998	150	7	0.011
65	Baja Calif. Norte	699,000	1998	150	8	0.085
66	Baja Calif. Norte	699,000	1998	152	7	0.080
67	Colima	3,000	1998	72	10	0.029
68	Colima	1,000	1998	100	10	0.000

(Table continues on p. 172.)

Table A.1 *Continued*

Community Number	State	1990 Population[a]	Year of Survey	Size of Mexican Sample	Size of U.S. Sample	Refusal Rate
69	Aguascalientes	18,000	1998	150	1	0.013
70	Sinaloa	5,000	1998	202	0	0.010
71	Aguascalientes	2,000	1997	100	6	0.010

Source: Mexican Migration Project.
a. Population of the town or city where the survey took place, rounded to the nearest 1,000. For those communities that are barrios in a large city, the population of the city is reported.

Table A.2 Characteristics of Mexican Labor Migrants to the United States Enumerated in the MMP and the ENADID

Characteristic	MMP	ENADID
Sex		
Male	87.5%	87.7%
Age		
Median age	38.0	37.0
Mean age	40.7	40.2
Standard deviation	16.7	15.6
Relation to head		
Household head	65.5%	70.9%
Spouse	6.3%	7.1%
Son/daughter	27.0%	17.0%
Other	1.2%	5.1%
Marital status		
Currently married	72.0%	79.7%
Never married	23.7%	15.0%
Years of schooling		
Under six	52.4%	56.1%
Six to eight years	26.2%	27.4%
Nine to eleven years	13.1%	12.6%
Twelve years or more	8.2%	14.0%
Median	5.0	4.0
Mean	5.0	4.6
Standard deviation	4.0	3.6
Duration of last U.S. trip (months)		
Median	7.0	7.0
Mean	21.2	19.8
Standard deviation	46.5	36.7

Source: Mexican Migration Project.

Appendix B

Table B.1 Logistic Regression of Migrating to a State Other Than California

	Analysis of Maximum Likelihood Estimates			
Parameter	Estimate	SE	Chi-Sq	Pr > ChiSq
Intercept	2.211	0.0670	1089.8	<.0001
Age				
Fifteen to nineteen	—	—	—	—
Twenty to twenty-four	−0.449	0.0400	126.0	<.0001
Twenty-five to twenty-nine	−0.370	0.0516	51.4	<.0001
Thirty to thirty-four	−0.308	0.0666	21.4	<.0001
Thirty-five or older	−0.274	0.0615	19.8	<.0001
Male (dummy)	−0.091	0.0367	6.2	0.0129
Years of education	−0.004	0.0054	0.5	0.4723
State				
Jalisco	—	—	—	—
Guanajuato	0.741	0.0649	130.1	<.0001
Michoacán	0.119	0.0679	3.1	0.0797
Nayarit	0.280	0.0947	8.7	0.0032
Zacatecas	0.475	0.0582	66.4	<.0001
Guerrero	2.115	0.1167	328.1	<.0001
San Luis Potosí	1.166	0.0606	370.2	<.0001
Colima	0.810	0.0870	86.7	<.0001
Oaxaca	0.701	0.0819	73.2	<.0001
Puebla	2.424	0.1472	271.3	<.0001
Baja California Norte	0.446	0.1540	8.4	0.0038
Aguascalientes	1.986	0.1038	365.9	<.0001
Sinaloa	0.944	0.1022	85.2	<.0001
Period				
Pre-IRCA (1980 to 1986)	—	—	—	—
Transition (1987 to 1990)	−0.800	0.0381	441.0	<.0001
Post-IRCA (1991 to 1999)	−1.349	0.0467	833.0	<.0001
Community size				
Rancho	—	—	—	—
Town	−0.202	0.0471	18.4	<.0001
City	−0.055	0.0510	1.2	0.2818
Metropolitan area	0.025	0.0755	0.1	0.7429

Source: Mexican Migration Project.

Table B.2 Logistic Regression of Making First Illegal Crossing Through Tijuana

	Analysis of Maximum Likelihood Estimates			
Parameter	Estimate	SE	Chi-Sq	Pr > ChiSq
Intercept	2.379	0.2295	107.4	<.0001
Age				
Fifteen to nineteen	—	—	—	—
Twenty to twenty-four	−0.382	0.1089	12.3	0.0005
Twenty-five to twenty-nine	−0.209	0.1243	2.8	0.0930
Thirty to thirty-four	−0.428	0.1393	9.4	0.0021
Thirty-five or older	−0.329	0.1295	6.4	0.0112
Male (dummy)	−0.060	0.1787	0.1	0.7390
Years of education	−0.007	0.0122	0.3	0.5921
State				
Jalisco	—	—	—	—
Guanajuato	−0.140	0.1593	0.8	0.3809
Michoacán	−0.363	0.1860	3.8	0.0513
Nayarit	−0.236	0.2244	1.1	0.2928
Zacatecas	−0.345	0.1658	4.3	0.0372
Guerrero	−0.146	0.2321	0.4	0.5291
San Luis Potosí	0.294	0.1588	3.4	0.0639
Colima	0.339	0.1948	3.0	0.0819
Oaxaca	0.449	0.1691	7.1	0.0079
Puebla	0.786	0.1901	17.1	<.0001
Baja California Norte	−0.511	0.2925	3.1	0.0807
Aguascalientes	0.135	0.2014	0.4	0.5041
Sinaloa	0.647	0.2823	5.3	0.0219
Period				
Pre-IRCA (1980 to 1986)	—	—	—	—
Transition (1987 to 1990)	−0.913	0.0885	106.4	<.0001
Post-IRCA (1991 to 1999)	−1.486	0.1232	145.5	<.0001
Community size				
Rancho	—	—	—	—
Town	−0.055	0.1157	0.2	0.6369
City	−0.127	0.1448	0.8	0.3812
Metropolitan area	0.229	0.1655	1.9	0.1672

Source: Mexican Migration Project.

Table B.3 Logistic Regression of Apprehension During Border Crossing

	Analysis of Maximum Likelihood Estimates			
Parameter	Estimate	SE	Chi-Sq	Pr > ChiSq
Intercept	2.650	0.2926	82.0	<.0001
Age				
Fifteen to nineteen	—	—	—	—
Twenty to twenty-four	0.003	0.1362	0.0	0.9843
Twenty-five to twenty-nine	0.256	0.1651	2.4	0.1210
Thirty to thirty-four	0.500	0.2045	6.0	0.0146
Thirty-five or older	0.234	0.1625	2.1	0.1498
Male (dummy)	−0.315	0.2468	1.6	0.2015
Years of education	0.059	0.0158	14.1	0.0002
State				
Jalisco	—	—	—	—
Guanajuato	0.194	0.1890	1.1	0.3049
Michoacán	−0.313	0.2200	2.0	0.1554
Nayarit	0.483	0.3287	2.2	0.1421
Zacatecas	−0.233	0.1839	1.6	0.2044
Guerrero	0.507	0.3375	2.3	0.1333
San Luis Potosí	0.425	0.1828	5.4	0.0202
Colima	1.318	0.3669	12.9	0.0003
Oaxaca	0.095	0.2216	0.2	0.6678
Puebla	1.163	0.2949	15.6	<.0001
Baja California Norte	0.112	0.4924	0.1	0.8204
Aguascalientes	0.160	0.2114	0.6	0.4489
Sinaloa	0.671	0.3412	3.9	0.0493
Period				
Pre-IRCA (1980 to 1986)	—	—	—	—
Transition (1987 to 1990)	−0.112	0.1271	0.8	0.3800
Post-IRCA (1991 to 1999)	−0.779	0.1562	24.9	<.0001
Community size				
Rancho	—	—	—	—
Town	−0.130	0.1299	1.0	0.3171
City	0.243	0.1843	1.7	0.1882
Metropolitan area	0.374	0.2267	2.7	0.0993

Source: Mexican Migration Project.

Table B.4 Logistic Regression of Making First Illegal Trip

	Analysis of Maximum Likelihood Estimates			
Parameter	Estimate	SE	Chi-Sq	Pr > ChiSq
Intercept	−3.598	0.1518	562.0	<.0001
Age				
Fifteen to nineteen	—	—	—	—
Twenty to twenty-four	−0.104	0.0783	1.8	0.1835
Twenty-five to twenty-nine	−0.745	0.0890	69.9	<.0001
Thirty to thirty-four	−1.075	0.0977	120.9	<.0001
Thirty-five or older	−2.259	0.0864	684.0	<.0001
Male (dummy)	0.713	0.1195	35.6	<.0001
Years of education	−0.032	0.0068	22.6	<.0001
State				
Jalisco	—	—	—	—
Guanajuato	0.507	0.1045	23.5	<.0001
Michoacán	0.575	0.1221	22.1	<.0001
Nayarit	0.559	0.1610	12.1	0.0005
Zacatecas	0.467	0.1114	17.6	<.0001
Guerrero	−0.082	0.1579	0.3	0.6027
San Luis Potosí	0.169	0.1029	2.7	0.0997
Colima	0.121	0.1471	0.7	0.4106
Oaxaca	−0.037	0.1349	0.1	0.7858
Puebla	−0.453	0.1444	9.8	0.0017
Baja California Norte	−0.212	0.2031	1.1	0.2967
Aguascalientes	0.727	0.1380	27.8	<.0001
Sinaloa	−0.904	0.1944	21.6	<.0001
Period				
Pre-IRCA (1980 to 1986)	—	—	—	—
Transition (1987 to 1990)	0.272	0.0629	18.7	<.0001
Post-IRCA (1991 to 1999)	0.061	0.0810	0.6	0.4531
Community size				
Rancho	—	—	—	—
Town	−0.247	0.0743	11.0	0.0009
City	−0.564	0.0931	36.7	<.0001
Metropolitan area	−1.150	0.1100	109.3	<.0001

Source: Mexican Migration Project.

Table B.5 Logistic Regression of Making First Illegal Trip: Males

Parameter	Analysis of Maximum Likelihood Estimates			
	Estimate	SE	Chi-Sq	Pr > ChiSq
Intercept	−2.817	0.0498	3198.1	<.0001
Age				
Fifteen to nineteen	—	—	—	—
Twenty to twenty-four	0.074	0.0351	4.4	0.0362
Twenty-five to twenty-nine	−0.558	0.0460	147.0	<.0001
Thirty to thirty-four	−0.922	0.0568	264.0	<.0001
Thirty-five or older	−1.881	0.0532	1249.7	<.0001
Years of education	−0.041	0.0039	113.9	<.0001
State				
Jalisco	—	—	—	—
Guanajuato	0.056	0.0550	1.0	0.3075
Michoacán	0.683	0.0630	117.5	<.0001
Nayarit	0.382	0.0930	16.8	<.0001
Zacatecas	0.530	0.0546	94.3	<.0001
Guerrero	0.086	0.0762	1.3	0.2618
San Luis Potosí	0.140	0.0514	7.4	0.0065
Colima	−0.380	0.0849	20.0	<.0001
Oaxaca	−0.362	0.0816	19.7	<.0001
Puebla	−0.788	0.0853	85.3	<.0001
Baja California Norte	−0.723	0.1650	19.2	<.0001
Aguascalientes	0.434	0.0730	35.3	<.0001
Sinaloa	−1.009	0.1010	99.8	<.0001
Period				
Pre-IRCA (1980 to 1986)	—	—	—	—
Transition (1987 to 1990)	0.309	0.0343	81.1	<.0001
Post-IRCA (1991 to 1999)	0.326	0.0379	74.2	<.0001
Community size				
Rancho	—	—	—	—
Town	−0.341	0.0401	72.4	<.0001
City	−0.519	0.0465	124.5	<.0001
Metropolitan area	−1.556	0.0661	555.0	<.0001

Source: Mexican Migration Project.

Table B.6 Logistic Regression of Making First Illegal Trip: Females

	Analysis of Maximum Likelihood Estimates			
Parameter	Estimate	SE	Chi-Sq	Pr > ChiSq
Intercept	−5.079	0.0977	2704.5	<.0001
Age				
Fifteen to nineteen	—	—	—	—
Twenty to twenty-four	0.220	0.0594	13.8	0.0002
Twenty-five to twenty-nine	−0.370	0.0734	25.5	<.0001
Thirty to thirty-four	−0.837	0.0930	80.9	<.0001
Thirty-five or older	−1.558	0.0832	351.0	<.0001
Years of education	−0.012	0.0068	3.2	0.0753
State				
Jalisco	—	—	—	—
Guanajuato	0.179	0.1081	2.7	0.0986
Michoacán	1.331	0.1059	158.0	<.0001
Nayarit	1.426	0.1428	99.7	<.0001
Zacatecas	0.834	0.0970	74.0	<.0001
Guerrero	1.001	0.1153	75.3	<.0001
San Luis Potosí	0.572	0.0943	36.7	<.0001
Colima	0.696	0.1268	30.2	<.0001
Oaxaca	0.210	0.1416	2.2	0.1374
Puebla	−0.901	0.1910	22.2	<.0001
Baja California Norte	0.220	0.2139	1.1	0.3030
Aguascalientes	0.188	0.1587	1.4	0.2366
Sinaloa	−0.065	0.1485	0.2	0.6630
Period				
Pre-IRCA (1980 to 1986)	—	—	—	—
Transition (1987 to 1990)	0.504	0.0569	78.6	<.0001
Post-IRCA (1991 to 1999)	0.617	0.0623	98.0	<.0001
Community size				
Rancho	—	—	—	—
Town	−0.463	0.0662	48.8	<.0001
City	−0.253	0.0734	11.9	0.0006
Metropolitan area	−1.298	0.1029	159.0	<.0001

Source: Mexican Migration Project.

Table B.7 Logistic Regression of Making First Illegal Trip: Males Fifteen to Thirty-Five

	Analysis of Maximum Likelihood Estimates			
Parameter	Estimate	SE	Chi-Sq	Pr > ChiSq
Intercept	−2.956	0.1114	703.7	<.0001
Age				
Fifteen to nineteen	—	—	—	—
Twenty to twenty-four	−0.093	0.0796	1.4	0.2405
Twenty-five to twenty-nine	−0.751	0.0914	67.6	<.0001
Thirty to thirty-four	−1.072	0.1006	113.5	<.0001
Years of education	−0.040	0.0078	26.6	<.0001
State				
Jalisco	—	—	—	—
Guanajuato	0.644	0.1253	26.4	<.0001
Michoacán	0.728	0.1439	25.6	<.0001
Nayarit	0.567	0.1953	8.4	0.0037
Zacatecas	0.699	0.1301	28.8	<.0001
Guerrero	−0.208	0.2052	1.0	0.3101
San Luis Potosí	0.273	0.1225	5.0	0.0258
Colima	0.311	0.1662	3.5	0.0615
Oaxaca	−0.058	0.1632	0.1	0.7236
Puebla	−0.352	0.1675	4.4	0.0357
Baja California Norte	−0.014	0.2278	0.0	0.9503
Aguascalientes	0.848	0.1594	28.3	<.0001
Sinaloa	−0.679	0.2187	9.6	0.0019
Period				
Pre-IRCA (1980 to 1986)	—	—	—	—
Transition (1987 to 1990)	0.304	0.0740	16.9	<.0001
Post-IRCA (1991 to 1999)	0.197	0.0968	4.1	0.0420
Community size				
Rancho	—	—	—	—
Town	−0.234	0.0866	7.3	0.0069
City	−0.642	0.1121	32.8	<.0001
Metropolitan area	−1.192	0.1309	82.9	<.0001

Source: Mexican Migration Project.

Table B.8 OLS Regression of Logged Real Wages: Undocumented Individuals

Parameter	Estimate	SE	t Value	Pr > t
Intercept	0.936	0.044	21.48	<.0001
Age				
Fifteen to nineteen	—	—	—	—
Twenty to twenty-four	0.050	0.028	1.80	0.0721
Twenty-five to twenty-nine	0.083	0.031	2.69	0.0072
Thirty to thirty-four	0.069	0.035	2.00	0.0452
Thirty-five or older	0.022	0.033	0.68	0.4993
Education on last trip	0.019	0.003	6.20	<.0001
Male	0.274	0.026	10.60	<.0001
State				
Jalisco	—	—	—	—
Guanajuato	−0.109	0.034	−3.24	0.0012
Michoacán	−0.028	0.040	−0.70	0.4834
Nayarit	−0.115	0.057	−2.00	0.0461
Zacatecas	−0.103	0.036	−2.90	0.0038
Guerrero	−0.106	0.056	−1.89	0.0590
San Luis Potosí	−0.218	0.034	−6.42	<.0001
Colima	−0.109	0.050	−2.17	0.0304
Oaxaca	−0.134	0.055	−2.45	0.0144
Puebla	−0.168	0.071	−2.37	0.0178
Baja California Norte	−0.065	0.082	−0.79	0.4287
Aguascalientes	0.088	0.054	1.63	0.1038
Sinaloa	−0.144	0.089	−1.63	0.1040
Period				
1980 to 1986	—	—	—	—
1987 to 1992	−0.041	0.022	−1.85	0.0651
1993 to present	−0.051	0.030	−1.71	0.0878
Community size				
Rancho	—	—	—	—
Town	−0.022	0.027	−0.81	0.4173
City	−0.048	0.030	−1.58	0.1143
Metropolitan area	−0.048	0.043	−1.10	0.2726
Duration of last trip (months)	0.003	0.000	9.35	<.0001
Total prior trips	0.020	0.004	5.54	<.0001

Source: Mexican Migration Project.

Table B.9 OLS Regression of Logged Real Wages: Documented Individuals

Parameter	Estimate	SE	t Value	Pr > t
Intercept	1.137	0.079	14.41	<.0001
Age				
Fifteen to nineteen	—	—	—	—
Twenty to twenty-four	0.127	0.054	2.37	0.0179
Twenty-five to twenty-nine	0.149	0.052	2.85	0.0045
Thirty to thirty-four	0.116	0.056	2.08	0.0377
Thirty-five or older	0.116	0.054	2.14	0.0323
Education on last trip	0.016	0.004	4.29	<.0001
Male	0.206	0.034	6.01	<.0001
State				
Jalisco	—	—	—	—
Guanajuato	−0.130	0.047	−2.79	0.0054
Michoacán	0.099	0.042	2.33	0.0197
Nayarit	−0.026	0.081	−0.31	0.7532
Zacatecas	−0.114	0.047	−2.43	0.0151
Guerrero	0.097	0.147	0.66	0.5104
San Luis Potosí	−0.166	0.059	−2.81	0.0050
Colima	0.046	0.074	0.62	0.5364
Oaxaca	−0.661	0.235	−2.81	0.0051
Puebla	−0.423	0.187	−2.27	0.0236
Baja California Norte	−0.316	0.103	−3.08	0.0021
Aguascalientes	0.157	0.118	1.34	0.1813
Sinaloa	−0.012	0.207	−0.06	0.9536
Period				
1980 to 1986	—	—	—	—
1987 to 1992	−0.063	0.041	−1.54	0.1234
1993 to present	−0.114	0.057	−1.99	0.0467
Community size				
Rancho	—	—	—	—
Town	−0.028	0.034	−0.82	0.4115
City	0.031	0.039	0.79	0.4300
Metropolitan area	0.058	0.062	0.94	0.3485
Duration of last trip (months)	0.004	0.000	8.68	<.0001
Total prior trips	0.003	0.002	1.58	0.1132

Source: Mexican Migration Project.

References

Adelman, Irma, and J. Edward Taylor. 1992. "Is Structural Adjustment with a Human Face Possible? The Case of Mexico." *Journal of Development Studies* 26: 387–407.

Adler-Lomnitz, Larissa A., and Marisol Pérez-Lizaur. 1987. *A Mexican Elite Family: 1820–1980.* Princeton, N.J.: Princeton University Press.

Akerman, June. 1976. "Theories and Methods of Migration Research." In *From Sweden to America: A History of the Migration,* edited by Harold Runblom and Hans Norman. Minneapolis: University of Minnesota Press.

Andreas, Peter. 1998. "The Escalation of U.S. Immigration Control in the Post-NAFTA Era." *Political Science Quarterly* 113: 591–601.

———. 2000. *Border Games: Policing the U.S.-Mexico Divide.* Ithaca, N.Y.: Cornell University Press.

Bansak, Cynthia, and Steven Raphael. 1998. "Immigration Reform and the Earnings of Latino Workers: Do Employer Sanctions Cause Discrimination?" Discussion paper 98–20. San Diego, Calif.: Department of Economics, University of California at San Diego.

Baum, Dan. 1997. *Smoke and Mirrors: The War on Drugs and the Politics of Failure.* Boston: Back Bay Books.

Bean, Frank D., Georges Vernez, and Charles B. Keely. 1989. *Opening and Closing the Doors: Evaluating Immigration Reform and Control.* Washington, D.C.: Urban Institute.

Bewley, Truman F. 1999. *Why Wages Don't Fall During a Recession.* Cambridge, Mass.: Harvard University Press.

Billings, Deborah. 1999. "Meissner Announces New INS Strategy to Combat Smuggling of Illegal Workers." *Daily Labor Report* 61, March 31, 1999.

Böhning, Wolf. R. 1972. *The Migration of Workers in the United Kingdom and the European Community.* Oxford: Oxford University Press.

Borjas, George J. 1989. "Economic Theory and International Migration." *International Migration Review* 23: 457–85.

———. 1990. *Friends or Strangers: The Impact of Immigrants on the U.S. Economy.* New York: Basic Books.

Bourdieu, Pierre. 1986. "The Forms of Capital." In *Handbook of Theory and Research for the Sociology of Education,* edited by John G. Richardson. New York: Greenwood Press.

Bourdieu, Pierre, and Loic Wacquant. 1992. *An Invitation to Reflexive Sociology.* Chicago: University of Chicago Press.

Brettell, Caroline. 1979 "Emigrar para Voltar: A Portuguese Ideology of Return Migration." *Papers in Anthropology* 20: 21–38.

Calavita, Kitty. 1992. *Inside the State: The Bracero Program, Immigration, and the INS.* New York: Routledge.

Camp, Roderic A. 1989. *Entrepreneurs and Politics in Twentieth-Century Mexico.* New York: Oxford University Press.

———. 1996. *Democracy in Latin America: Patterns and Cycles.* Wilmington, Del.: SR Books.

Cardoso, Lawrence. 1980. *Mexican Emigration to the United States 1897–1931.* Tucson: University of Arizona Press.

Castells, Manuel. 1989. *The Informational City: Information Technology, Economic Restructuring, and the Urban-Regional Process.* Oxford: Basil Blackwell.

Ceballos, Manuel. 1999. "Frontera e Identidad: La Versión Nacional y la Versión de los dos Laredos a Finales del Siglo XIX." Paper presented at the tenth reunion of Mexican and North American Historians, Dallas, Texas, November 19–22.

Centeno, Miguel Angel. 1994. *Democracy Within Reason: Technocratic Revolution in Mexico.* University Park, Pa.: Pennsylvania State University Press.

Cerrutti, Marcela, and Douglas S. Massey. 2001. "On the Auspices of Female Migration Between Mexico and the United States." *Demography* 38: 187–200.

Chavez, Leo R. 1992. *Shadowed Lives: Undocumented Immigrants in American Society.* Fort Worth, Tex.: Harcourt Brace Jovanovich.

Christiansen, Drew. 1996. "Movement, Asylum, Borders: Christian Perspectives." *International Migration Review* 30: 7–17.

Clune, Michael S. 1998. "The Fiscal Impacts of Immigrants: A California Case Study." In *The New Americans: Economic, Demographic, and Fiscal Effects of Immigration,* edited by James P. Smith and Barry Edmonston. Washington, D.C.: National Academy Press.

Cobb-Clark, Deborah A., and Clinton R. Shiells, and B. Lindsay Lowell. 1995. "Immigration Reform: The Effects of Employer Sanctions and Legalization on Wages." *Journal of Labor Economics* 13: 472–98.

Coleman, James S. 1990. *Foundations of Social Theory.* Cambridge, Mass.: Harvard University Press.

Cornelius, Wayne A. 1978. *Mexican Migration to the United States: Causes, Consequences, and U.S. Responses.* Cambridge, Mass.: MIT Center for International Studies.

Cornelius, Wayne A., Philip L. Martin, and James F. Hollifield. 1994. "Introduction: The Ambivalent Quest for Immigration Control." In *Controlling Immigration: A Global Perspective,* edited by Wayne A. Cornelius, Philip L. Martin, and James F. Hollifield. Stanford, Calif.: Stanford University Press.

Cortés, Fernando, and Rosa María Rubalcava. 1992. "El Ingreso Familiar: Su Distribución y Desigualdad 1984–1989." *Demos: Carta Demográfica sobre México* 5: 28–30.

Dávila, Alberto, José Pagán, and Montserrat Vladrich Grau. 1998. "The Impact of IRCA on the Job Opportunities and Earnings of Mexican-American and Hispanic-American Workers." *International Migration Review* 32: 79–95.

Donato, Katharin M. 1994. "U.S. Policy and Mexican Migration to the United States, 1942–92." *Social Science Quarterly* 75: 705–29.

———. 1998. "Mexican Migration Project Data." In *Binational Study of Migration Between Mexico and the United States*, vol. 3, *Research Reports and Background Materials.* Washington, D.C., and Mexico City: U.S. Commission on Immigration Reform and the Mexican Ministry of Foreign Affairs.

Dunn, Timothy J. 1996. *The Militarization of the U.S.-Mexico Border, 1978–1992: Low-Intensity Conflict Doctrine Comes Home.* Austin: University of Texas, Center for Mexican American Studies.

Durand, Jorge. 1988. "Los Migradólares: Cien Años de Inversión en el Medio Rural." *Argumentos: Estudios Críticos de la Sociedad* 5: 7–21.

———. 1994. *Más Allá de la Línea: Patrones Migratorios entre México y Estados Unidos.* México, D.F.: Consejo Nacional para la Cultura y las Artes.

———. 1997. "De Enganchadores a Contratistas: La Difusion de un Nuevo Sistema de Contratación de Mano de Obra Mexicana." Paper presented at the meetings of the Latin American Studies Association, Guadalajara(April 17–19, 1997).

Durand, Jorge, and Paricia Arias. 2000. *La Experiencia Migrante: Iconografía de la Migración México-Estados Unidos.* México, D.F.: Altexto.

Durand, Jorge, Douglas S. Massey, and Fernando Charvet. 2000. The Changing Geography of Mexican Immigration to the United States: 1910–1996." *Social Science Quarterly* 81: 1–15.

Durand, Jorge, Emilio Parrado, and Douglas S. Massey. 1996. "Migradollars and Development: A Reconsideration of the Mexican Case." *International Migration Review* 30: 423–44.

Eschbach, Karl, Jacqueline Hagan, and Nestor Rodriguez. 2001. "Causes and Trends in Migrant Deaths Along the Mexico-U.S. Border, 1985–1998." Working Paper. Houston, Tex.: University of Houston, Center for Immigration Research.

Eschbach, Karl, Jacqueline Hagan, Nestor Rodriguez, Ruben Hernandez-Leon, and Stanley Bailey. 1999. "Death at the Border." *International Migration Review* 33: 430–54.

Espenshade, Thomas J. 1990. "Undocumented Migration to the United States: Evidence from a Repeated Trials Model." In *Undocumented Migration to the United States: IRCA and the Experience of the 1980s*, edited by Frank D. Bean, Barry Edmonston, and Jeffrey S. Passel. Washington, D.C.: Urban Institute Press.

———. 1994. "Does the Threat of Apprehension Deter Undocumented U.S. Immigration?" *Population and Development Review* 20: 871–92.

Espenshade, Thomas J., and Dolores Acevedo. 1995. "Migrant Cohort Size, Enforcement Effort, and the Apprehension of Undocumented Aliens." *Population Research and Policy Review* 14: 145–72.

Espenshade, Thomas J., and Charles A. Calhoun. 1993. "An Analysis of Public Opinion Toward Undocumented Immigration." *Population Research and Policy Review* 12: 189–224.

Espenshade, Thomas J. and Katherine Hempstead. 1996. "Contemporary American Attitudes Toward U.S. immigration." *International Migration Review* 30: 535–70.

Espinosa, Kristin, and Douglas S. Massey. 1997. "Undocumented Migration and the Quantity and Quality of Social Capital." *Soziale Welt* 12: 141–62.

Espinosa, Victor M. 1998. *El Dilemma del Retorno: Migración, Género y Pertenencia en un Contexto Transnacional.* Zamora: El Colegio de Michoacán.

Foreman-Peck, James. 1992. "A Political Economy Model of International Migration, 1815–1914," *The Manchester School* 60: 359–76.

Freeman, Gary P. 1994. "Can Liberal States Control Unwanted Immigration?" *Annals of the American Academy of Political and Social Science* 534: 17–30.

———. 1995. "Modes of Immigration Politics in Liberal Democratic States." *International Migration Review* 29: 881–902.

Friedman, John. 1986. "The World City Hypothesis." *Development and Change* 17: 69–83.

Fuchs, Lawrence H. 1990. "The Corpse That Would Not Die: The Immigration Reform and Control Act of 1996." *Revue Européenne des Migrations Internationales* 6: 111–27.

Garvey, Deborah L., and Thomas J. Espenshade. 1998. "Fiscal Impacts of Immigrant and Native Households: A New Jersey Case Study." In *The New Americans: The Economic, Demographic, and Fiscal Effects of Immigration,* edited by James P. Smith and Barry Edmonston. Washington, D.C.: National Academy Press.

Glazer, Nathan. 1980. "Introduction." In *Clamor at the Gates: The New American Immigration,* edited by Nathan Glazer. San Francisco, Calif.: ICS Press.

Goldin, Claudia. 1994. "The Political Economy of Immigration Restriction in the United States, 1890 to 1921." In *The Regulated Economy: A Historical Approach to Political Economy,* edited by Claudia Golden and Gary Libecap. Chicago: University of Chicago Press.

González, Luis. 1981. *Historia de la Revolución Mexicana, 1934–1940.* México, D.F.: El Colegio de México.

Goodis, Tracy Ann. 1986. "A Layman's Guide to the 1986 U.S. Immigration Reform." Discussion Paper on the Impacts of Immigration in California. Washington, D.C.: Urban Institute.

Goodman, Leo. 1961. "Snowball Sampling." *Annals of Mathematical Statistics* 32: 117–51.

Goss, Jon D., and Bruce Lindquist. 1995. "Conceptualizing International Labor Migration: A Structuration Perspective." *International Migration Review* 29: 317–51.

Gregory, Peter. 1986. *The Myth of Market Failure: Employment and the Labor Market in Mexico.* Baltimore, Md.: Johns Hopkins University Press.

Haber, Stephen H. 1989. *Industry and Underdevelopment: The Industrialization of Mexico, 1890–1940.* Stanford, Calif.: Stanford University Press.

Hagan, Jacqueline M., and Susan Gonzalez Baker. 1993. "Implementing the U.S. Legalization Program: The Influence of Immigrant Communities and Local Agencies on Immigration Policy Reform." *International Migration Review* 27: 513–36.

Hansen, Roger D. 1971. *The Politics of Mexican Development.* Baltimore, Md.: Johns Hopkins University Press.

Harker, Richard, Cheleen Mahar, and Chris Wilkes. 1990. *An Introduction to the Work of Pierre Bourdieu: The Practice of Theory.* London: Macmillan.

Hart, John M. 1987. *Revolutionary Mexico: The Coming and Process of the Mexican Revolution.* Berkeley, Calif.: University of California Press.

Hatton, Timothy J., and Jeffrey G. Williamson. 1994. "What Drove the Mass Migrations from Europe in the Late Nineteenth Century?" *Population and Development Review* 20: 533–60.

———. 1998. *The Age of Mass Migration: Causes and Economic Impact.* Oxford: Oxford University Press.

Heyman, Josiah M. 1995. "Putting Power in the Anthropology of Bureaucracy: The Immigration and Naturalization Service at the Mexico-United States Border." *Current Anthropology* 36: 261–87.

———. 1998. *Finding a Moral Heart for U.S. Immigration Policy: An Anthropological Perspective.* Fairfax, Va.: American Anthropological Association.

Higham, John. 1955. *Strangers in the Land: Patterns of American Nativism, 1860–1925.* New Brunswick, N.J.: Rutgers University Press.

Hoffman, Abraham. 1974. *Unwanted Mexican Americans in the Great Depression: Repatriation Pressures, 1929–1939.* Tucson, Ariz.: University of Arizona Press.

Hugo, Graeme J. 1981. "Village-Community Ties, Village Norms, and Ethnic and Social Networks: A Review of Evidence from the Third World." In *Migration Decisionmaking: Multidisciplinary Approaches to Microlevel Studies in Developed and Developing Countries,* edited by Gordon F. DeJong and Robert W. Gardner. New York: Pergamon Press.

Jacobson, David. 1997. *Rights Across Borders: Immigration and the Decline of Citizenship.* Baltimore, Md.: Johns Hopkins University Press.

Jaffe, A. J., Ruth M. Cullen, and Thomas D. Boswell. 1980. *The Changing Demography of Spanish Americans.* New York: Academic Press.

Jasso, Guillermina, and Mark R. Rosenzweig. 1982. "Estimating the Emigration Rates of Legal Immigrants Using Administrative and Survey Data: The 1971 Cohort of Immigrants to the United States." *Demography* 19: 279–90.

———. 1988. "Family Reunification and the Immigration Multiplier: U.S. Immigration Law, Origin-Country Conditions, and the Reproduction of Immigrants." *Demography* 23: 291–311.

———. 1990. *The New Chosen People: Immigrants in the United States.* New York: Russell Sage Foundation.

Joppke, Christian. 1998. "Why Liberal States Accept Unwanted Immigration." *World Politics* 50: 266–93.

Kamen, Al. 1990. "Central America Is No Longer the Central Issue for Americans." *Austin American Statesman,* October 21.

Kanaiaupuni, Shawn M. 2000. "Reframing the Migration Question: An Analysis of Men, Women, and Gender in Mexico." *Social Forces* 78(4): 1311–49.

Kaplan, Robert D. 1996. *The Ends of the Earth: A Journey at the Dawn of the Twenty-first Century.* New York: Random House.

———. 2000. *The Coming Anarchy: Shattering the Dreams of the Post–Cold War.* New York: Random House.

Koussoudji, Sherrie A. 1992. "Playing Cat and Mouse at the U.S.-Mexican Border." *Demography* 29: 159–80.

Lee, Ronald D., and Timothy W. Miller. 1998. "The Current Fiscal Impact of Immigrants and Their Descendants: Beyond the Immigrant Households." In *The New Americans: Economic, Demographic, and Fiscal Effects of Immigration,* edited by James P. Smith and Barry Edmonston. Washington, D.C.: National Academy Press.

Lindstrom, David P. 1996. "Economic Opportunity in Mexico and Return Migration from the United States." *Demography* 33: 357–74.

Lomnitz, Larissa. 1977. *Networks and Marginality: Life in a Mexican Shantytown.* New York: Academic Press.

Lowell, B. Lindsay, and Zhongren Jing. 1994. "Unauthorized Workers and Immigration Reform" What Can We Ascertain from Employers?" *International Migration Review* 28: 427–48.

Lowell, B. Lindsay, Jay Teachman, and Zhongren Jing. 1995. "Unintended Consequences of Immigration Reform: Discrimination and Hispanic Employment." *Demography* 32: 617–28.

Lozano Ascencio, Fernando. 1993. *Bringing It Back Home: Remittances to Mexico from Migrant Workers in the United States.* La Jolla, Calif.: University of California at San Diego, Center for U.S.-Mexican Studies.

———. 1998. "Las Remesas de los Migrantes Mexicanos en Estados Unidos: Estimaciones para 1995." In *Migration Between Mexico and the United States: Binational Study, Vol. 3, Research Reports and Background Materials.* Washington, D.C.: U.S. Commission on Immigration Reform.

MaCurdy, Thomas, Thomas Nechyba, and Jay Bhattacharya. 1998. "An Economic Framework for Assessing the Fiscal Impacts of Immigration." In *The New Americans: Economic, Demographic, and Fiscal Effects of Immigration,* edited by James P. Smith and Barry Edmonston. Washington, D.C.: National Academy Press.

Martin, Philip L. 1996. *Promises to Keep: Collective Bargaining in California Agriculture.* Ames, Iowa: Iowa State University Press.

Martin, Philip L., and J. Edward Taylor. 1991. "Immigration Reform and Farm Labor Contracting in California." In *The Paper Curtain: Employer Sanction, Implementation, Impact, and Reform,* edited by Michael Fix. Washington, D.C.: Urban Institute.

———. 1996. "The Anatomy of a Migration Hump." In *Development Strategy, Employment, and Migration: Insights from Models,* edited by J. Edward Taylor. Paris: Organization for Economic Cooperation and Development.

Martin, Philip L., J. Edward Taylor, and P. Hardiman. 1988. "California Farmworkers and the SAW Legalization Program." *California Agriculture* 42: 4–6.

Massey, Douglas S. 1986. "The Settlement Process Among Mexican Migrants to the United States." *American Sociological Review* 51: 670–85.

———. 1987a. "Do Undocumented Migrants Earn Lower Wages Than Legal Immigrants?: New Evidence from Mexico." *International Migration Review* 21: 236–74.

———. 1987b. "Understanding Mexican Migration to the United States." *American Journal of Sociology* 92: 1372–1403.

———. 1987c. "The Ethno-survey in Theory and Practice." *International Migration Review* 21: 1498–1522.

———. 1988. "International Migration and Economic Development in Comparative Perspective." *Population and Development Review* 14: 383–414.

———. 1990. "Social Structure, Household Strategies, and the Cumulative Causation of Migration." *Population Index* 56: 3–26.

———. 2000a. "Higher Education and Social Mobility in the United States, 1940–1998." In *America's Research Universities: Quality, Innovation, Partnership,* edited by Ann Leigh Speicher. Washington, D.C.: Association of American Universities.

———. 2000b. "When Surveys Fail: An Alternative for Data Collection." In *The Science of Self-Report: Implications for Research and Practice,* edited by Arthur A. Stone et al. Mahwah, N.J.: Lawrence Erlbaum.

Massey, Douglas S., Rafael Alarcón, Jorge Durand, and Humberto González. 1987. *Return to Aztlan: The Social Process of International Migration from Western Mexico.* Berkeley, Calif.: University of California Press.

Massey, Douglas S., Joaquín Arango, Graeme Hugo, Ali Kouaouci, Adela Pellegrino, and J. Edward Taylor. 1998. *Worlds in Motion: International Migration at the End of the Millennium.* Oxford: Oxford University Press.

Massey, Douglas S., and Marcela Cerrutti. 2001. "Trends in Mexican Migration to the United States, 1965–1995." *Population Research and Policy Review,* forthcoming.

Massey, Douglas S., and Kristin E. Espinosa. 1997. "What's Driving Mexico-U.S. Migration?: A Theoretical, Empirical, and Policy Analysis." *American Journal of Sociology* 102: 939–99.

Massey, Douglas S., and Felipe García España. 1987. "The Social Process of International Migration." *Science* 237: 733–38.

Massey, Douglas S., Luin P. Goldring, and Jorge Durand. 1994. "Continuities in Transnational Migration: An Analysis of Nineteen Communities." *American Journal of Sociology* 99: 1492–1532.

Massey, Douglas S., and Zai Liang. 1989. "The Long-term Consequences of a Temporary Worker Program: The U.S. Bracero Experience." *Population Research and Policy Review* 8: 199–226.

Massey, Douglas S., and Emilio A. Parrado. 1994. "Migradollars: The Remittances and Savings of Mexican Migrants to the United States." *Population Research and Policy Review* 13: 3–30.

Massey, Douglas S., and Audrey Singer. 1995. "New Estimates of Undocumented Mexican Migration and the Probability of Apprehension." *Demography* 32: 203–13.

Massey, Douglas S., and René Zenteno. 1999. "The Dynamics of Mass Migration." *Proceedings of the National Academy of Sciences* 96(8): 5328–35.

———. 2000. "A Validation of the Ethnosurvey: The Case of Mexico-U.S. Migration." *International Migration Review* 34: 765–92.

McBride, John. 1963. *The Vanishing Bracero.* San Antonio, Tex.: Naylor.

McCaa, Robert. 2001. "Missing Millions: The Mexican Revolution, a Demographic Catastrophe." Paper presented at the annual meetings of the Population Association of America, Washington, D.C. (March 29–31, 2001).

Morales, Patricia. 1982. *Indocumentados Mexicanos.* México, D.F.: Editorial Grijalbo.

Morawska, Ewa. 1990. "The Sociology and Historiography of Immigration." In *Immigration Reconsidered: History, Sociology, and Politics,* edited by Virginia Yans-McLaughlin. New York: Oxford University Press.

Meyer, Michael C., and William L. Sherman. 1991. *The Course of Mexican History.* New York: Oxford University Press.

Meyers, Eytan. 1995. "The Political Economy of International Migration Policy: A Comparative and Quantitative Study." Ph.D. diss., University of Chicago, Department of Political Science.

Myrdal, Gunnar. 1957. *Rich Lands and Poor.* New York: Harper and Row.

Petras, Elizabeth M. 1981. "The Global Labor Market in the Modern World-Economy." In *Global Trends in Migration: Theory and Research on International Population Movements,* edited by Mary M. Kritz, Charles B. Keely, and Silvano M. Tomasi. New York: Center for Migration Studies.

Phillips, Julie A., and Douglas S. Massey. 1999. "The New Labor Market: Immigrants and Wages After IRCA." *Demography* 36: 233–46.

———. 2000. "Engines of Immigration: Stocks of Human and Social Capital in Mexico." *Social Science Quarterly* 81: 33–48.

Piore, Michael J. 1979. *Birds of Passage: Migrant Labor in Industrial Societies.* New York: Cambridge University Press.

Poniatowska, Elena. 1971. *La Noche de Tlatelolco.* México, D.F.: Era.

Portes, Alejandro, and John Walton. 1981. *Labor, Class, and the International System.* New York: Academic Press.

Prothero, R. Mansell. 1990. "Labor Recruiting Organizations in the Developing World: Introduction." *International Migration Review* 24: 221–28.

Ranis, Gustav, and J. C. H. Fei. 1961. "A Theory of Economic Development." *American Economic Review* 51: 533–65.

Reichert, Joshua S. 1981. "The Migrant Syndrome: Seasonal U.S. Wage Labor and Rural Development in Central Mexico." *Human Organization* 40: 56–66.

Reichert, Joshua S., and Douglas S. Massey. 1979. "Patterns of U.S. Migration from a Mexican Sending Community: A Comparison of Legal and Illegal Migrants." *International Migration Review* 13: 599–623.

Reisler, Mark. 1976. *By the Sweat of Their Brow: Mexican Immigrant Labor in the United States, 1900–1940.* Westport, Conn.: Greenwood Press.

Reyes, Belinda I. 2001. "Immigrant Duration in the United States: The Case Study of Mexicans from Western Mexico." *International Migration Review* 35, forthcoming.

Rivenbark, Leigh. 1997. "Help Wanted." *Federal Times,* July 29.

Rotella, Sebastian. 1998. *Twilight on the Line: Underworlds and Politics at the U.S.-Mexico Border.* New York: Norton.

Sassen, Saskia. 1988. *The Mobility of Labor and Capital: A Study in International Investment and Labor Flow.* Cambridge: Cambridge University Press.

———. 1991. *The Global City: New York, London, Tokyo.* Princeton, N.J.: Princeton University Press.

Sheahan, John. 1991. *Conflict and Change in Mexican Economic Strategy: Implications for Mexico and Latin America.* La Jolla: University of California at San Diego, Center for U.S. Mexican Studies.

Sheehan, Helena. 1985. *Marxism and the Philosophy of Science: A Critical History.* Atlantic Highlands, N.J.: Humanities Press.

Singer, Audrey, and Douglas S. Massey. 1998. "The Social Process of Undocumented Border Crossing." *International Migration Review* 32: 561–92.

Sjaastad, Larry A. 1962. "The Costs and Returns of Human Migration." *Journal of Political Economy* 70: S80–93.

Stark, Oded. 1991. *The Migration of Labor.* Cambridge, U.K.: Basil Blackwell.

Stark, Oded, and David E. Bloom. 1985. "The New Economics of Labor Migration." *American Economic Review* 75: 173–78.

Taylor, J. Edward. 1986. "Differential Migration, Networks, Information, and Risk." In *Migration Theory, Human Capital, and Development,* edited by Oded Stark. Greenwich, Conn.: JAI Press.

———. 1987. "Undocumented Mexico-U.S. Migration and the Returns to Households in Rural Mexico." *American Journal of Agricultural Economics* 69: 626–38.

———. 1996. "IRCA's Effect in California Agriculture." In *Immigration Reform and U.S. Agriculture,* edited by Philip L. Martin, Walter Huffman, Robert Emerson, and J. Edward Taylor. Oakland, Calif.: California Division of Agriculture and Natural Resources.

Taylor, J. Edward, Joaquin Arango, Graeme Hugo, Ali Kouaouci, Douglas S. Massey, and Adela Pellegrino. 1996a. "International Migration and National Development." *Population Index* 62: 181–212.

———. 1996b. "International Migration and Community Development." *Population Index* 63: 397–418.

Taylor, J. Edward, Philip Martin, and Michael Fix. 1997. *Poverty Amid Prosperity: Immigration and the Changing Face of Rural California.* Washington, D.C.: Urban Institute.

Taylor, J. Edward, and Dawn Thilmany. 1993. "Worker Turnover, Farm Labor Contractors, and IRCA's Impact on the California Farm Labor Market." *American Journal of Agricultural Economics* 75: 350–60.

Teitelbaum, Michael S. 1980. "Right Versus Right: Immigration and Refugee Policy—the United States." *Foreign Affairs* 59(1): 21–59.

———. 1986. "Intersections: Immigration and Demographic Change and Their Impact on the United States." In *World Population and U.S. Policy: The Choices Ahead,* edited by Jane A. Menken. New York: Norton.

Timmer, Ashley S., and Jeffrey G. Williamson. 1998. "Immigration Policy Prior to the 1930s: Labor Markets, Policy Interactions, and Globalization Backlash." *Population and Development Review* 24: 739–72.

Todaro, Michael P., and Lydia Maruszko. 1987. "Illegal Migration and U.S. Immigration Reform: A Conceptual Framework." *Population and Development Review* 13: 101–14.

Uchitelle, Louis. 1997. "Raises Arrive at Bottom Rung of Labor Force." *New York Times,* May 23.

U.S. Border Patrol. 1994. *Border Patrol Strategic Plan, 1994 and Beyond: National Strategy.* Washington, D.C.: U.S. Border Patrol.

U.S. Department of Labor. 1991. "Employer Sanctions and U.S. Labor Markets: First Report." *Immigration Policy and Research, No 2.* Washington: Bureau of International Labor Affairs, U.S. Department of Labor.

U.S. General Accounting Office. 1997. *Illegal Immigration: Southwest Border Strategy Results Inconclusive.* Washington: U.S. Government Printing Office.

U.S. Immigration and Naturalization Service. 1987. *1986 Statistical Yearbook of the Immigration and Naturalization Service.* Washington: U.S. Government Printing Office.

———. 1992. *1991 Statistical Yearbook of the Immigration and Naturalization Service.* Washington: U.S. Government Printing Office.

———. 1997. *1996 Statistical Yearbook of the Immigration and Naturalization Service.* Washington: U.S. Government Printing Office.

———. 1998. *1997 Statistical Yearbook of the Immigration and Naturalization Service.* Washington: U.S. Government Printing Office.

———. 2000. *1999 Statistical Yearbook of the Immigration and Naturalization Service.* Washington: U.S. Government Printing Office.

Vélez-Ibañez, Carlos G. 1983. *Rituals of Marginality: Politics, Process, and Culture Change in Central Urban Mexico, 1969–1974.* Berkeley, Calif.: University of California Press.

Wallerstein, Immanuel. 1974. *The Modern World System I: Capitalist Agriculture and the Origins of the European World Economy in the Sixteenth Century.* New York: Academic Press.

Warren, Robert, and Ellen P. Kraly. 1985. "The Elusive Exodus: Emigration from the United States." In *Population Trends and Public Policy* 8. Washington, D.C.: Population Reference Bureau.

Wilkie, James W. 1990. *Society and Economy in Mexico.* Los Angeles, Calif.: UCLA Latin American Center Publications.

Zenteno, René. 1995. "Del Rancho de la Tía Juana a Tijuana: Una Breve Historia de Desarrollo y Población en la Frontera Norte de México." *Estudios Demográficos y Urbanos* 10(1): 105–32.

Zenteno, René, and Douglas S. Massey. 1999. "Especifidad versus Representatividad: Enfoques Metodológicos para el Estudio de la Migración Internacional." *Estudios Demográficos y Urbanos* 40: 75–116.

Zlotnik, Hania. 1998. "International Migration 1965–96: An Overview." *Population and Development Review* 24: 429–68.

Index

Boldface numbers refer to figures and tables.